The Shortest and Most Convenient Route

THE SHORTEST AND MOST CONVENIENT ROUTE

Lewis and Clark in Context

ROBERT S. COX

EDITOR

American Philosophical Society
Philadelphia • 2004

Transactions of the
American Philosophical Society
Held at Philadelphia
For Promoting Useful Knowledge
Volume 94, Part 5

Copyright © 2004 by the American Philosophical Society
for its *Transaction* series.
All rights reserved

ISBN: 0-87169-945-1
US ISSN: 0065-9746

Library of Congress Cataloging-in-Publication Data

Bicentennial Conference for Lewis and Clark (2003 : Philadelphia, Pa.)
    The shortest and most convenient route : Lewis and Clark in context / Robert S. Cox, editor.
       p. cm. — (Transactions of the American Philosophical Society ; v. 94, pt. 5)
    "Based on papers delivered at the Bicentennial Conference for Lewis and Clark, held in Philadelphia in August 2003"—Introd.
    Includes bibliographical references and index.
    ISBN 0-87169-945-1 (pbk.)
       1. Lewis and Clark Expedition (1804–1806)—Congresses. 2. West (U.S.)—Discovery and exploration—Congresses. 3. West (U.S.)—Description and travel—Congresses. 4. Explorers—West (U.S.)—Congresses. I. Cox, Robert S., 1958- II. Title. III. Series.

F592.7.B525 2003
917.804'2—dc22

2004062282

Contents

Preface   vii

1 Introduction
ROBERT S. COX   3

2 Reading the Corps of Discovery Backwards:
The Metropolitan Context of Lewis and Clark's Expedition
DOMENIC VITIELLO   12

3 Philanthropic Enterprise:
The Imperial Contradictions of Republican Political Economy in Philadelphia during the Era of Lewis and Clark
S. D. KIMMEL   52

4 "I Never Yet Parted":
Bernard McMahon and the Seeds of the Corps of Discovery
ROBERT S. COX   102

5 "Mineral Productions of Every Kind":
Geological Observations in the Lewis and Clark Journals and the Role of Thomas Jefferson and the American Philosophical Society in the Geological Mentoring of Meriwether Lewis
JOHN W. JENGO   136

6 Displaying the Expanding Nation to Itself:
The Cultural Work of Public Exhibitions of Western Fauna in Lewis and Clark's Philadelphia
BRETT MIZELLE   215

7   Nineteenth-Century Scientific Opinion of
    Lewis and Clark
    ANDREW J. LEWIS   236

    Color Plates, following page 120

    Contributors   251

    Index   253

Preface

THE BICENTENNIAL of the Corps of Discovery was inaugurated in August 2003 with a conference held in Philadelphia to explore new approaches to understanding "Meriwether Lewis in Philadelphia." During three long days of discussion and debate, participants dissected the various motives and meanings behind the expedition and the particular impact of each of the major figures involved in its planning and execution, touching on topics that ranged from cookery and health care to the scientific legacy of the corps and its larger political and social implications. Most of the essays in this volume began in that invigorating exchange and address, directly or indirectly, the organizers' desires to shed light on how the nation's foremost urban center, Philadelphia, helped to shape this quintessential errand into the wilderness.

The authors are grateful to the other participants in the conference for their free-flowing discussions during and after the sessions and for sharing their insights into Lewis and Clark. Among the organizers of the conference, Tom and Nancy Davis, Frank Muhly, and Joe Musselman were exceptionally generous with their time and support, and without Tom's tireless efforts and good-natured prodding, it is doubtful that this volume would have made its trek into print. The names of Muhly, Musselman, and the Davises will come as no surprise to students of the expedition who have come to rely upon their steady support and their contributions to Lewis and Clark scholarship. We were ably abetted in all phases of the work by the expert assistance of the staff at the American Philosophical Society, particularly Valerie Lutz and Charles Greifenstein, and Richard and Mary Dunn were a continual source of encouragement and support. The exacting editorial eyes of Mary McDonald and Susan Babbitt, as much as their patience and good humor, are warmly appreciated. Special thanks are owed to D. Haven, N. Dashwood, and G. Darcy for reading early drafts of the essays.

The Shortest and Most Convenient Route

1

INTRODUCTION

ROBERT S. COX

FROM THE COMPARATIVE comfort of Saint Louis, Meriwether Lewis and William Clark sat down in September 1806 to transcribe their meticulous journals and to inform President Thomas Jefferson that they had at last returned from their odyssey into the northwestern wilds. With an ear for language usually reserved for politicians and their defense attorneys, Lewis reported that the Corps of Discovery had succeeded in "penitrat[ing] the Continent of North America to the Pacific Ocean" and had explored far and wide enough to "affirm with confidence that we have discovered the most practicable rout which dose exist across the continent by means of the navigable branches of the Missouri and Columbia Rivers." No less measured in his words, Clark announced that he, too, had "no hesitation in declaring that such as nature has permitted it we have discovered the best rout which does exist across the continent of North America in that direction." Coyly, the captains managed to avoid saying what soon would become self-evident—that the route they had discovered was manifestly impracticable. Theirs might be the best route by means of the Missouri, or the best "which dose exist," but it nevertheless failed to rise to the great hope of Jefferson's continental scheme: to establish the geographic means by which the commercial and political nation might be extended to the Pacific shore.[1]

The hint of sly evasion and the uncertainty it implies in how the explorers felt about their achievements has not been lost on historians, for whom a suspicion of failure, in some form, has long been a leitmotif. One of the more insightful historiographers (and historians) of the expedition, James Ronda, has traced the two hundred-year transit of Lewis and Clark and the various interpretive streams that have issued forth as the Corps of Discovery waxed and waned in public consciousness. Stripped of its intellectual content, Ronda argues, by the delays and ultimate failure to publish the scientific results, the Corps was seen for much of the nineteenth century as little more than a comma in the national sentence. As the centennial of the expedition approached in the 1890s, however, the fair winds of Turnerian nostalgia for the "loss" of the frontier buoyed their fortunes. With new editions of the explorers' journals in 1893 and 1904, Elliott Coues and Reuben Gold Thwaites reignited interest in the corps by recasting the members as intrepid frontiersmen engaged in a ripping yarn of an adventure, and as a (fore)shadow of the great scientific expeditions to follow and of the white tide of settlers and traders who would eventually claim the continent. Lewis and Clark were again resurrected in the 1940s, when Bernard De Voto figured them as harbingers of a nascent transcontinental empire, and again in the 1960s and 1980s with the appearance of the masterful editions of the explorers' writings edited by Donald Jackson and Gary Moulton. Recent studies have helped flesh out the intentions and ideas surrounding the expedition and the discursive ends to which it has been put: Paul Cutright's paean to its scientific achievements, John Logan Allen's conceptual geography, Tom Slaughter's cultural critique, and Ronda's own focus on the "shared enterprise" between whites and Indians have all mapped new terrain.[2]

And yet throughout, this sense of failure—or its alter ego, an insistent success—has never quite receded. Whether viewing the expedition as a commercial, diplomatic, geographic, or scientific enterprise, as grand adventure, imperial grab, or cultural mirror, writers have lined up to render their verdict. A more pessimistically inclined and generally scholarly stream has cited the expedition for failing to meet Jefferson's first goal of locating a route for commerce and for failing as well at his second goal of contributing to scientific knowledge. These views are matched, however, page for page by a deeply dissonant popular literature in which the transcendent success of Lewis and Clark has become an article of faith in which writers proclaim that "by any standard" the expedition was "as successful as it was monumental" or remind us that "only one man died." They celebrate the explorers' "undaunted courage" or build a picture of the corps as some prelapsarian community of interracial harmony (as if commerce were not war by other means).[3]

While passing judgment of this sort might seem an exercise in aridity, the insistence of both sides in drawing the line of success suggests how vital the experience of Lewis and Clark remains, or to put it in other words, judgment performs a current cultural function. Although well beyond the scope of this volume, the corps clearly touches on the central nervous system of unresolved issues in America, including violence in the construction of the nation, slavery and race, conquest and imperial subjugation. But the persistence of the impulse to judgment might be seen in other ways, as presenting a unique opportunity for historians. As a concept, failure has meaning only with respect to a specific set of expectations, practices, and products and makes sense only in a specific cultural context. As a result, to engage seriously with failure in the Corps of Discovery is to engage seriously with the fundamental principles and issues animating the expedition, its audience, and its interpreters. Rendering judgment, in effect, may fulfill an important analytic function.

With this in mind, a closer look at the expectations set out for the corps is instructive. The usual narrative makes it all seem so simple: Jefferson is the alpha and omega in conceptualizing, organizing, and funding the expedition and in preparing Lewis (if not Clark) for his role as galloping savant. In his instructions to Lewis, Jefferson outlined a score of seemingly concrete goals, ranging from collecting linguistic data and natural historical specimens to finding the shortest route to the Pacific for the purpose of commerce. Yet as several authors in this volume (and elsewhere) note, these plans drew upon a wide range of sometimes contradictory discourses, steeping in Jefferson's own mind across two turbulent decades in which the nation migrated from revolutionary society to republican empire.

Paul Cutright has suggested that Jefferson's interest in westward exploration quickened when he was serving as governor of Virginia in 1780. In the fall of that year, Jefferson and his fellow revolutionary governors received a letter from the newly appointed French minister, François Barbé Marbois, requesting information on the productions, climate, soil, defenses, and economy of their states. While the others responded to Marbois's queries in perfunctory fashion, Jefferson seized the opportunity to transform this commonplace of ancient regime diplomacy into a rumination on the future of his state (and State), culminating both in one of the greatest works of natural history written in eighteenth-century America and in his first attempts to organize a transcontinental expedition. As *Notes on the State of Virginia* was nearing completion in 1783, Jefferson approached George Rogers Clark to lead an expedition across the continent, and when that panned out he discussed the possibility with the pedestrian John Ledyard in 1786 and with the French botanist André Michaux in 1792. Michaux was very nearly successful—at least in starting. He was recalled after becoming entangled in an effort to destabilize Spanish Louisiana and return it to

France, but the instructions that Jefferson prepared for Michaux served as the basis for his instructions to Lewis and Clark ten years later.[4]

This familiar story of the evolution of Jefferson's plans, however, hardly captures the breadth of the intellectual connections involved or the diversity of the expectations the explorers carried with them. For all his importance to conceptualizing the expedition, Jefferson was not the omega. Just as the expedition connects into a long history of diplomatic and administrative thought through Marbois's queries, and into geopolitical considerations through Michaux, it is tied through other channels into a variety of other discourses. One of the most important of these channels, but by no means the only one, was the American Philosophical Society (APS), with its distinctive scientific and political agenda. Although Jefferson was a dominant figure in the APS during the time of Lewis and Clark, the idea of carrying an expedition to the Pacific was broached at the APS as early as 1769, more than a decade before he became a member. Before Jefferson, and in dialogue with him, members of the APS discussed principles, imagined routes, plotted strategies, and set priorities for a transcontinental expedition, bringing their own motives to the enterprise. The plantsman Humphry Marshall, for example, a passionate advocate for a transcontinental expedition for decades, harbored an unusually diverse set of motives ranging from the opportunity to enhance his scientific credentials to an opportunity to enhance his trade in plants, from a sincere desire to support the expansion of natural historical knowledge to a desire to support his nephew, the aspiring botanist Moses Marshall. Another member, Benjamin Smith Barton, signals other shades of meaning that played more harmoniously with Jefferson. While Jefferson spoke of an "empire of liberty" stretching across the continent, Barton envisioned his nation as an "empire of *rational* liberty" that would become "the theatre on which mankind are to act the part of wisdom & of virtue." If this were a city on hill for Barton, science and an expansive republican government, integrally bound, would be the stage.[5]

Nor was the corps, as too often imagined, an isolated enterprise. It was, of course, only one element in a grander vision of continental exploration conceived by Jefferson that was to include a pair of parallel expeditions to the southwest led by William Dunbar and Thomas Freeman. But there is a broader, transnational context as well. Beyond Jefferson, Lewis and Clark played off against the Scotsman Alexander Mackenzie (often, though not often enough, recognized as a spur to the corps), but also against James Cook (whom Ledyard had accompanied), against the great inoculator Francisco Xavier de Balmis (astutely mentioned in this volume by Shawn Kimmel), the archaeologist Guillermo Dupaix, and perhaps most closely against Martin Sessé y Lacasta and Mariano Moçiño, whose grand survey of Spanish America between 1788 and 1803 resulted in the collection of more than eight thousand botanical specimens, five hundred birds, and three hundred fish gathered from a region stretching from California to Costa Rica. Although the relationships among these expeditions were not always direct, the American West was crawling with explorers, bearing in from all the cardinal points, during the early national period.[6]

Donald Jackson has observed that the Corps of Discovery was "an enterprise of many aims and a product of many minds," not only Jefferson but Barton, Marshall, and Wistar, Albert Gallatin and Benjamin Rush, not only in the United States but in England, Spain, and France. Although commerce may have been the measure of success at one level, when the expedition finally decamped from Saint Louis in 1804, the explorers carried with them the ghosts of other ideas, other agendas, and other priorities, exercising the problems of diplomacy, governance, and nation, of scientific opportunism and the lure of private gain.

BASED ON PAPERS delivered at the Bicentennial Conference for Lewis and Clark held in Philadelphia in August 2003, the essays in this volume grapple in different ways with the complex of motives underlying the Corps of Discovery and the impact they have had on American culture. In one way or another, the question of failure is used by the authors as a means of interrogating the intellectual and cultural context in which the expedition was framed and in which its results were distributed.

In a synoptic overview of the Corp of Discovery, Domenic Vitiello inverts the usual formula in which the Corps of Discovery is seen, turning away from the Turnerian "opening of the frontier" in favor of reading the Corps "backwards" as a carefully contrived effort "to draw western territories and their resources and markets into the orbit of eastern cities." For Vitiello, the focus lies on the rivalries and relationships connecting the urban centers of the East and on their influence in setting the goals, timing, and course of the enterprise, and the shifting center of political and financial gravity was as significant as anything taking place in the West. He provides an important glimpse into the dense social, political, and intellectual networks in Philadelphia, going beyond the familiar pantheon of Jefferson, Barton, and Rush, and the equally familiar halls of the American Philosophical Society, to delineate the mechanics of how individuals such as John and Nathan Sellers and Israel Whelen operated through an array of civic and political organizations to create the intellectual, industrial, and institutional infrastructure for the expedition.

Shawn Kimmel expands upon some of the themes outlined by Vitiello, offering a radical reinterpretation of the origin of the Corps of Discovery by situating it within the culture of philanthropic societies in late eighteenth-century Philadelphia and the political and ideological conflicts they sought to address. The distinctive concerns of organizations such as the Philadelphia Society for the Promotion of Agriculture (PSPA) reflect the fundamental contradictions in republican political economy: the desire for extensive empire set against the desire for democratic self-government. Deeply involved in the planning for the Corps of Discovery, the membership of the PSPA was committed to the principle of educating a virtuous citizenry, and they conceived of the expedition, in Kimmel's words, as "a particular enterprise of republican philanthropy and political economy," as an instrument for instilling national virtue. The inherent conflict in republican political economy, however, and the tensions between public and private interest were not so easily resolved. In an evocative case study, Kimmel turns to the controversy over Patrick Gass, the sergeant who preemptively published his own journal of the expedition before Lewis could go to press, generating a running battle over who "owned" the proceeds of the expedition and who held the right to gain from it.

Curiously, though perhaps not coincidentally, the story of Gass's usurpation of Lewis's "rights" was echoed when it came to publication of the scientific results. Although Lewis (with Barton's assistance) had originally intended to devote two volumes of a planned three to the natural historical results, only the botanical results were properly published. The seedsman Bernard McMahon, who lurks behind much of the botanical work of Lewis and Clark, is the subject of my essay. An elusive figure at best, McMahon was an Irish immigrant with a suitably radical republican shadow who inculcated himself into the heart of Lewis and Clark's scientific enterprise. Unknown to President Jefferson in 1805, McMahon skillfully played nationalist ideology and republican politics to cultivate a close association with the president and by 1806 had largely supplanted his rival horticulturist William Hamilton as primary overseer of the seeds and cuttings. To facilitate publication of the botanical results, already delayed, McMahon was instrumental in hiring the German botanist Frederick Pursh to help illustrate and describe the specimens. Like Gass, Pursh purloined the credit "due" to Lewis and Barton by beating them to press, though with the twist that it was a foreigner, publishing abroad, who reaped credit for describing these most American of plants.[7]

While the botanical results actually made it into print, the natural historical and ethnographic observations mostly lay fallow. John Jengo offers one of the first systematic appraisals of the position of geologic knowledge in the Corps of Discovery and concludes that despite the failure to publish, these observations were not unimportant. Jengo demonstrates that geology (as well as what today would be called mineralogy, geomorphology, and other cognate disciplines) was an important concern during the planning of the expedition and that Lewis remained remarkably diligent in commenting on the geological features of the regions through which he passed. Perhaps more surprisingly, Jengo suggests that Lewis demonstrated a strong grasp of the nomenclature and priorities of a field that was only then emerging as a distinct science and was interested enough to record information on what Jengo calls "ethnogeology." Seen in the context of the geological practice of the day, Lewis's mineralogical and lithological identifications were not perfect, but they offered the first informed descriptions of the geomorphology, stratigraphy, and sedimentology of a broad swath of the American West.

In shifting the focus from the elite producers of knowledge to their relationship with their popular audience, Brett Mizelle recasts several of themes raised in earlier essays, including nationalism and nation, the reach of knowledge, and the relation of public and private. Focusing neither on the scientific observations nor publications but on the popular exhibitions of western nature mounted by "cultural entrepreneurs" such as Charles Willson Peale, Mizelle argues that animal displays were useful sites for thinking about uncertain and shifting identities in postrevolutionary America, with the dialectic between the entrepreneurs' presentation and the audience's interpretation mirroring the relationship between popular culture and public interest. Displays of American productions, Mizelle suggests, were often cast in a nationalist context, presenting themes of regional and national harmony between competing interests, emphasizing the stability of the new political and social order that made national expansion seem "just, orderly, and benevolent." Yet interestingly, Mizelle argues that while these exhibits were intended to "display the expanding nation to itself," the public (as opposed to the elite) showed less interest in the natural productions of their own country, including those collected by Lewis and Clark, than they did in exotic animal displays and performing pigs.

In the final essay in this volume, Andrew Lewis asks anew why Lewis and Clark were so generally ignored during most of the nineteenth century. To address this question, he asserts that it is first necessary to view early national science on its own terms and in the context of the period. Lewis and Clark, he notes, were part of a world in which natural historical knowledge was indeed of broad interest; however, it was knowledge of a particular kind. American natural historians were becoming more, not less, interested in "mysteries and wonders," and they sought not to demystify but to use empirical precision to enhance the individual's sense of awe. "If wonder and awe were what natural history exploration literature aimed at," Lewis suggests, "it is little wonder that Lewis and Clark didn't endure." Even in this context, however, the explorers' observations did not measure up. Situated somewhere on the continuum between travel writing and formal, systematically driven natural historical texts, Lewis suggests that the explorers' observations were considered by at least some contemporaries as superficial and incomplete, as little more than lists of names of plants and animals.

With the privilege of hindsight, we know that the goal of locating a water route to the West was impossible and that the scientific results, so long delayed and ultimately abandoned, had slender impact. But for all that, can it be said that one has failed when attempting the difficult and discovering the impossible? These essays suggest that while failure may be too easy a word, the consideration of failure can serve as a useful means of investigating the context and motives that framed the expedition and the ways in which it has been interpreted ever since that September day in 1806 when the explorers arrived in St. Louis. Although Lewis and Clark can be made to seem like little more than blank slates on which the generations have drawn their preferences, they are far from blank. In its manifold and conflicting origins, the Corps of Discovery has attained a peculiar resilience that has enabled it to be resurrected again and again, to be cast and recast into imperial schemes and adventurous dreams.

Notes

1. Meriwether Lewis to Thomas Jefferson, Sept. 23, 1806, in Donald Jackson, ed., *Letters of the Lewis and Clark Expedition with Related Documents, 1783–1854*, 2d ed., 2 vols. (Urbana: University of Illinois Press, 1978), 1:319–24; William Clark to ?, Sept. 23, 1806, Jackson, *Letters*, 1:326.

2. James Ronda, "'The writingest explorers': The Lewis and Clark Expedition in American Historical Literature," *Pennsylvania Magazine of History and Biography* 112 (1988): 607–30; Bernard De Voto, *Course of Empire* (Boston: Houghton Mifflin, 1952); Paul Cutright, *Lewis and Clark: Pioneering Naturalists* (Urbana: University of Illinois Press, 1969); John Logan Allen, *Passage through the Garden: Lewis and Clark and the Image of the American Northwest* (Urbana: University of Illinois Press, 1975); James P. Ronda, *Lewis and Clark among the Indians* (Lincoln: University of Nebraska Press, 1984); Gary Moulton, ed., *The Journals of the Lewis and Clark Expedition*, 11 vols. (Lincoln: University of Nebraska Press, 1983–97). See also Thomas Slaughter, *Exploring Lewis and Clark: Reflections on Men and Wilderness* (New York: Knopf, 2003); James P. Ronda, *Finding the West: Explorations with Lewis and Clark* (Albuquerque: University of New Mexico Press, 2001); Albert Furtwangler, *Acts of Discovery: Visions of America in the Lewis and Clark Journals* (Urbana: University of Illinois Press, 1993).

3. Herman J. Viola, Review of *Undaunted Courage* by Stephen Ambrose, *William and Mary Quarterly* 54 (1997): 273; Stephen Ambrose, *Undaunted Courage: Meriwether Lewis, Thomas Jefferson, and the Opening of the American West* (New York: Simon and Schuster, 1996).

4. On diplomatic queries similar to Marbois's, see those issued by Henry Strachey, the Earl of Dartmouth, to British governors in North America in 1773, or those issued during the 1760s in the Papers of William Petty, Lord Shelburne. Henry Strachey Papers and the Earl of Shelburne Papers, William L. Clements Library, University of Michigan. Cutright fleshes out the relationship between *Notes* and the instructions to Lewis and Clark, but see also Andrew Lewis's essay in this volume. Cutright, *Lewis and Clark*.

5. Benjamin Smith Barton to Thomas Pennant, April 7, 1793. Benjamin Smith Barton Papers, APS. Emphasis in the original. On the APS, see John C. Greene, *American Science in the Age of Jefferson* (Ames: Iowa State Press, 1984); Brooke Hindle, *The Pursuit of Science in Revolutionary America* (Chapel Hill: University of North Carolina Press, 1956); Whitfield J. Bell, *Patriot-Improvers*, 2 vols. (Philadelphia: American Philosophical Society, 1997–99).

6. Dan L. Flores, *Jefferson and Southwestern Exploration* (Norman: University of Oklahoma Press, 1984).

7. Ronda implies that Attorney General Levi Lincoln may have persuaded Jefferson to emphasize the scientific aims of the expedition, in case the commercial failed, though of course scientific interests were integral to Michaux, Marshall, and other precursors. James P. Ronda, "The writingest exploreres': The Lewis and Clark Expedition and American Historical Literature," *Pennsylvania Magazine of History and Biography* 112 (1988): 607–30.

2

READING THE CORPS OF DISCOVERY BACKWARDS

The Metropolitan Context of Lewis and Clark's Expedition

DOMENIC VITIELLO

IN 1890, THE U.S. Census Bureau announced the "closing" of the western frontier that Lewis and Clark had explored less than a century earlier. Three years later, at the World's Fair in Chicago celebrating the four hundredth anniversary of Christopher Columbus's "discovery," historian Frederick Jackson Turner alerted Americans to what the West had meant for the nation.[1] For Turner, the nineteenth-century West "Americanized" settlers from Europe and the cities of the East Coast. The frontier wilderness forced people to abandon the institutional and class-stratified mores of metropolitan life, creating a culture of democratic individualism. Like Thomas Jefferson, Turner believed that the West acted as a social and political safety valve. "[W]henever social conditions tended to crystallize in the East, whenever capital tended to press upon labor or political restraints to impede the freedom of the mass," he wrote, "there was this gate of escape to the free conditions of the frontier."[2]

Not surprisingly, the Corps of Discovery played a key role in Turner's narrative of opening up the frontier. Although he spent few words on Lewis and Clark themselves, a decade after the Chicago fair the centennial celebration of their expedition employed Turner's vision of the West to elevate them in the pantheon of American history. For the past century, therefore, Lewis and Clark's voyage has loomed large in Americans' imagination of their relationship with the frontier and its role in defining national identity. To the present day, historians continue to cast the Corps of Discovery largely in Turner's terms, as men sent "into the uncharted" wilderness to encounter "another America" with their "undaunted courage" and "open the American West" for Jefferson's empire of would-be agrarian republicans.[3]

Yet at least one historian, William Cronon, has proposed that to understand the American West, Frederick Jackson Turner must be "read backwards." In his history of nineteenth-century Chicago, *Nature's Metropolis,* Cronon demolishes the dichotomy between city and countryside, arguing that the Great Plains and upper Midwest were *metropolitan* frontiers. The grain, livestock, and woods of the country gave the Windy City and its markets and industries a raison d'être. In turn, the city's railroads, grain elevators, Board of Trade, stockyards, and lumber marts structured the material and economic lives of mid- and late nineteenth-century farmers, cattle ranchers, and woodsmen. No matter how rugged they perceived their lives to be, frontier dwellers ultimately furnished their little houses on the prairie or in the woods with manufactured goods from the great department stores whose catalogs integrated the rural West into a national industrialized market.[4]

Following Cronon's lead, this chapter reads America's long-standing Turnerian interpretation of Lewis and Clark's frontier not from the frontier outposts of the West but from the context of Philadelphia, the cultural and commercial metropolis of the early United States. From this perspective, the Corps of Discovery's work was not just a mission to widen the safety valve and open the frontier to diplomatic, military, and trading activities; it was also a carefully planned attempt to draw western territories and their resources and markets into the orbit of eastern cities. In one sense, Lewis and Clark set out from Washington, as Jefferson gave their orders and Congress appropriated the funds to purchase supplies. But the federal capital could not furnish the equipment and merchandise they required, nor could it give the travelers the training they needed to carry out their assignment. Therefore, in the spring of 1803, Jefferson sent Lewis to his colleagues at the American Philosophical Society and Schuylkill Arsenal, where he was educated and outfitted for the trip. In this sense, the voyage to the Pacific was a project conceptualized and launched from the scientific institutions and workshops of Philadelphia.

Lewis and Clark's journey also held different meanings for different cities. Politicians in Washington required a map of transportation routes and Native American habitats with which they could chart the future of military and political expansion. In 1803, Philadelphians were still nursing their wounded egos following the departure three years earlier of both the state and federal capitals. But the city had a chance to remain what Washington would never be—the mercantile, financial, scientific, and manufacturing capital of the United States. New York and Baltimore aspired to the same goals, and the Corps of

Discovery promised a first foray into territories where these economic centers hoped to cultivate and capture future trade. At the turn of the nineteenth century, the Quaker City still clung to its position as the nation's largest center of population and commerce, though it would soon be surpassed by the Empire City. Philadelphia's scientific institutions and industrial production, however, remained unrivaled in North America.

For Thomas Jefferson and Meriwether Lewis, Philadelphia provided the knowledge, skills, technologies, and provisions necessary for their expedition. For Philadelphia, the Corps of Discovery promised something much greater—an opportunity to reap new information that could give its scientists, merchants, and manufacturers competitive advantages in the race to extend their influence across the continent. Of course, Lewis and Clark were by no means the only explorers who set out from the city to expand scientific knowledge for the benefit of trade and production. Their expedition represents one part of a much longer history of metropolitan ambitions and economic development.[5] The scientific community, institutions, and early industrial base that made their voyage a logistical success grew out of explicit attempts to make Philadelphia a commercial, cultural, and manufacturing capital—first of Britain's North American colonies and later the United States. And the patterns of scientific inquiry, institutional development, and industrialization that benefited Lewis and Clark continued long after they left the city. Beyond this temporal context, the Corps of Discovery's geographic context was also much larger than the Great Plains, the Rockies, and the Pacific coast. For the urban East, the resources and markets of these frontiers were just the left side of a map whose right side was dense with Atlantic networks of scientists, technology transfer, and trade. Thus the story of Lewis and Clark's relationship with—and meanings for—Philadelphia begins like so many other accounts of the city's development, with William Penn and the colonization of Britain's western Atlantic frontier.

Little more than a century before Lewis arrived in the city, Philadelphia was founded on the periphery of an empire in which London was the metropolis—the administrative, economic, and cultural capital. But it quickly gained a more central place in the Atlantic world. In planning his province, Penn sought to make his capital city the metropolis of British North America. Like other colonial ports, it would supply agricultural produce, furs, and timber to merchants whose ships connected market centers in Europe, Africa, and the Americas. Unlike New York, Boston, or other North American cities, however, Penn's city would be built without a military garrison or defensive walls to restrict entry or delimit its growth. In the hinterland, he hoped to avoid "Wilderness vacancies" through a network of townships and villages, connected by "distinct and beaten roads," that would foster "Society, Assistance, Busy Commerce, Instruction of Youth, Government of Peoples Manners, Conveniency of Religious Assembly, [and] Encouragement of Mechanics."[6]

Penn's early attempts to develop a diverse economy met with mixed success. But the colony's agricultural, milling, and mercantile sectors took off in the eighteenth century, as poor harvests and food shortages in Europe initiated a wave of inflation that would continue for nearly a century. The first signs of this "price revolution" came in 1739, as the wholesale price of grain in the colony witnessed a sharp rise.[7] With heightened demand for wheat and flour in countries from Ireland to the Mediterranean, settlers flocked from Germany and Britain to clear land for family farms that extended the region's farming hinterland into the Pennsylvania backcountry and the northern Chesapeake.[8] The trees they felled helped shipbuilders expand local merchants' fleets. Transporting vast quantities of wheat and flour to the Portuguese capital of Lisbon, Marseille in southern France, and the Spanish port of Cadiz at the Straits of Gibraltar, Philadelphia ships returned carrying salt, Madeira wine, and European manufactures. The Delaware Valley soon became the breadbasket of the Atlantic.

In the words of historical geographer Carville Earle, "tobacco stunted the growth of towns" because it was shipped directly overseas, whereas "wheat built them into . . . cities" by encouraging the development of processing and packaging industries as well as wagon transport, warehousing, and shipping.[9] Wheat spurred urban and industrial expansion that made Philadelphia the metropolis in North America, with the largest and most diverse economy. The flour and saw mills built by early settlers added value in the Atlantic economy. This processing sector formed the foundations of the region's industrialization, and the development of more efficient milling equipment initiated a process of continual technological experimentation and improvement.

The Delaware Valley thus became home to a diverse crafts and processing economy, fed in large part by agriculture and supplying both regional markets for tools and consumer goods and Atlantic markets for staple foods. The region's most important commodity, flour, generated wealth for the farmers growing wheat, millwrights grinding it, blacksmiths and wire weavers furnishing farmers and millers with equipment, coopers and wagon makers supplying equipment for packaging and land transportation, wholesalers assembling and dispensing bulk orders, shipping merchants arranging for their passage, dockhands carrying the orders between warehouses and ships, shipbuilders and sail makers fitting up vessels to carry the flour, sailors transporting it to other markets, bakers making bread for local consumption, retailers catering to individual households, and tavern keepers serving meals to their customers. Makers of clothing, hats, shoes, trunks, and all sorts of other manufactured products, in turn, relied in part on the demand of a growing population and the wealth generated by flour and other exports to sustain their business. As the city and its economy grew, Philadelphians launched institutions to cultivate specialized knowledge and enhance metropolitan transportation and communication systems that would further expand and diversify the region's agriculture, industries, and trade.

By the mid-eighteenth century, North America and the Caribbean were an important part of an industrializing empire. New England timber built Liverpool ships; cotton from the Carolinas supplied the burgeoning mills of Manchester; Barbados sugar and molasses fueled the growth of English and North American refining and distilling; and the colonies provided a large market for British manufactures.[10] In the specialized trading and processing centers of New England and Mid-Atlantic seaports, merchants, manufacturers, and a growing professional class sought to shape the economic, social, and material life of their communities through systems of provincial and municipal government, civic institutions, and transportation and communications infrastructure. While all towns and provinces used public and private institutions to foster and regulate economic growth, Philadelphia was the leading colonial center of Enlightenment science and institution building.[11]

The principal scientific association of the American Enlightenment was the American Philosophical Society (APS), founded in 1743 at the urging of Benjamin Franklin. The APS formed part of a larger complex of institutions established by Franklin in the mid-eighteenth century that made Philadelphia a cultural metropolis and a city capable of addressing major issues of urban public health, safety, and education.[12]

FIGURE 2.1. William Birch, South 5th Street showing the Library Company and Surgeon's Hall, ca. 1800. Courtesy American Philosophical Society. (See Color Plate 1.)

Pennsylvania Hospital, the first teaching hospital in the Americas, enabled the city to cope with the disease vectors that arrived at its port on ships from all parts of the world. The Philadelphia Contributionship for the Insurance of Houses from Loss by Fire, along with fire fighting companies founded by Franklin and his contemporaries, combated one of the most common threats to a city made largely of wood houses. Franklin's Library Company, the Academy and College of Philadelphia (later the University of Pennsylvania), and the APS cultivated the specialized knowledge necessary to further grow the region's diverse economy and enhance its material life.[13] With the first medical school in the Americas, the college attracted aspiring professionals from throughout the English and Spanish colonies, helping make the city *the* center of professional training and research in the Western Hemisphere.

College of Philadelphia professors and other learned citizens gathered at the APS, elaborating their Enlightenment worldview by applying scientific study of their natural surroundings to the improvement of the region's material life in order to advance the human condition.[14]

Meeting in the State House, the Academy and College of Philadelphia, and in 1771 in its own Philosophical Hall adjacent to City Hall, the APS's early members included botanist John Bartram, college provost William Smith, mathematician Thomas Godfrey, "mechanician" Samuel Rhoads, natural philosopher Dr. Phineas Bond, miller John Sellers, surveyor John Lukens, as well as merchants, judges, architects, physicians, and printers. Connections to the scientific communities of other regions proved critical for the dissemination of knowledge, and the APS's early corresponding members hailed from nearly all the thirteen colonies as well as Antigua, Barbados, England, Stockholm, Heidelberg, Edinburgh, and Paris.[15]

In 1769 the APS engaged in its first large-scale research, recording the transit of Venus, the passing of the planet between the earth and the sun that occurs approximately once every hundred years. In practical terms, this astronomical event represented an opportunity to calculate the distances between the planets and improve navigation on both land and sea. The APS lobbied the Pennsylvania Assembly "to purchase a reflecting Telescope with its proper apparatus," and in thanking the assembly for its appropriation, the members stressed that their efforts were "calculated to promote the public good":

> It would be needless . . . to point out to you, how many and various benefits may accrue to any country, and especially to young colonies, from a society instituted on so extensive a plan as that of the American Society held at Philadelphia for promoting useful knowledge. The experience of ages shews, that by such institutions, arts and sciences in general are advanced; useful discoveries made and communicated; many ingenious artists, who might otherwise remain in obscurity, drawn forth, patronized and placed in public usefulness; and (what is of great consequence to these young countries, especially in their present situation) every domestic improvement, that may help either to save or acquire wealth, may, by such means, be more effectually carried on.[16]

A Transit of Venus Committee of fourteen members was appointed, including John Lukens, John Sellers, Delaware miller William Poole, astronomer David Rittenhouse, Provost Smith, and merchant Owen Biddle. Four men were responsible for the erection and operation of an observatory in the State House yard. Biddle and an assistant traveled south to Cape Henlopen in Delaware, taking a telescope on loan from the Library Company. Poole watched from Wilmington and sent his "Observation of the Contacts of the Limbs of Venus and the Sun,

June 3, 1769," on to Biddle, who conveyed it to the APS.[17] Sellers, Rittenhouse, Lukens, and Smith observed the transit at Norrington, about twenty miles to the northwest of Philadelphia. And other members of the committee were charged with recording the event from points as far west as Fort Pitt (modern-day Pittsburgh) deep in the interior of the province. The APS's journal published the results of their research and disseminated them among institutions of Enlightenment science in the principal commercial and cultural centers of Europe and America. The observation of this astronomical event both literally and figuratively put Philadelphia and its scientific community on the map of the Atlantic world.

Collaborative research such as the transit of Venus recording would prove vital to the region's industrialization and economic development. The APS established committees to track and pursue a range of issues. Some were organized around specific professions and branches of science, such as Natural History, Merchants, Mechanics and Architecture, and a Medical Committee that concerned itself with the purity of the city's drinking water. More specific proposals resulted in the formation of groups such as the Committee on Silk Culture, which examined European practices and promoted the development of that industry in North America. In the same year they observed the transit of Venus, John Sellers, John Lukens, and two others formed a Canal Committee "appointed to go & examine which will be the most proper place for cutting" a passage between the Delaware River and the Chesapeake Bay, "to take the proper levels, to compare the respective times of high water on both bays & see whether a direct communication can be opened by a canal, or whether locks and dams are necessary, & if so, what head of waters to supply those dams, to make an estimate of the probable expense . . . & report" back to the APS.[18]

This work of economic and infrastructure improvement through science was not limited to civic forums such as the APS. Sellers and Lukens simultaneously served in the Pennsylvania Assembly, where they leveraged public support for networks of transportation to grow Philadelphia's influence in the interior. In the 1760s, they served on assembly committees to survey a road from Philadelphia to the market town of Lancaster, gauge the potential for port and ferry improvements along the Schuylkill River, and explore the branches of the Schuylkill, Lehigh, and Susquehanna Rivers to assess "whether the opening [of] a Communication between them for the Purposes of Navigation or

FIGURE 2.2. William Scull's 1770 "map of Pennsylvania exhibiting not only the improved parts . . . but also its extensive frontiers." From a survey commissioned by the APS in 1769; APS #649: 1770: Scu 47pn; Large—see *Realms of Gold* entry 904. Courtesy American Philosophical Society. (See Color Plate 2.)

Land-Carriage be practicable at a reasonable Expence."[19] Sellers also engaged in private practice surveying roads, creeks, and property boundaries in his district of Darby, in the farming and milling hinterland outside Philadelphia. By fixing boundaries and determining routes of transportation and communication, these surveys replaced Indian trails and hunting grounds with a regulated landscape of private property holdings and physically integrated Philadelphia with networks of towns in its hinterland.[20] Franklin and his contemporaries thus used government together with other organized forums to create a civic institutional infrastructure that, by the time the thirteen colonies gained political independence, made Philadelphia the model for urban and industrial development in the early United States.

It was therefore no accident that the Continental Congress chose the city as the thirteen colonies' Revolutionary capital. Writing to the president of Congress, John Hancock, in 1777, Philadelphian Robert Morris—the wealthiest man in North America and soon Financier of the Revolution—declared, "You will consider Philadelphia from its centrical situation, the extent of its commerce, the number of its artificers, manufacturers and other circumstances, to be to the United States what the heart is to the human body in circulating the blood."[21] While Morris procured muskets from Martinique, Delaware Valley mills provided food, wood, and gunpowder to the army. John Sellers and his son Nathan fashioned tent poles for the Continental army at their sawmill and furnished saltpeter to neighboring gunpowder mills on the outskirts of the city.[22] Adapting their wire-weaving skills to wartime production, they made brushes and priming wires that rebel troops used to pierce paper packets of gunpowder before firing their muskets.[23] Nathan's service in a reserve militia unit ended abruptly when "a petition from sundry paper makers" convinced Congress to order his "return home, to make and prepare suitable moulds, washers & utensils for carrying on the paper manufactory," so that Morris could continue issuing paper money to pay for the war.[24]

Following the conflict, East Coast cities pursued internal improvements with newfound zeal. In 1784, the State Assembly engaged David Rittenhouse and Nathan Sellers to revisit the possibility of a canal to link the Schuylkill and Susquehanna Rivers. The main impetus for the project's revival lay in Philadelphia's increasing competition from Baltimore for access to the produce and markets of central and western Pennsylvania.[25] In 1791, Morris, Rittenhouse, and Tench Coxe, founder of the Society to Establish Useful Manufactures and assistant secretary of the Treasury under

Alexander Hamilton, launched the Pennsylvania Society for the Improvement of Roads and Inland Navigation. This was just one of several promotional associations that pushed a wave of transportation investments in the 1790s.[26] Like their counterparts in other legislatures, John Sellers and his colleagues in the Pennsylvania Senate supported this agenda. In a 1791 address to the governor, they congratulated the state "on the prosperous Situation of her Finances and Resources . . . on the Prospect of being speedily delivered from the Incursions and Ravages of the hostile Indians,—and of a more easy and speedy Communication between its remotest Parts, by the Improvement of its Roads and navigable Waters."[27] This vision for improving the frontier imbued the rhetoric and actions of boosters, investors, and explorers throughout the early republic.

Taking advantage of the Pennsylvania legislature's support, Robert Morris gained a charter for his Schuylkill & Susquehanna Navigation Company to build a canal along the route that the APS and the Pennsylvania Assembly had earlier surveyed. "To combine the interests of all parts of the State, and to cement them in a perpetual commercial and political union, by the improvement of . . . natural advantages," was, he asserted, "one of the greatest works" that Americans could submit "to Legislative wisdom."[28] The Susquehanna, Morris claimed, "we may properly call our own," and if "duly improved," it could open "such numerous sources and channels of inland trade, all leading to the port of Philadelphia, as perhaps no other nation or sea-port on the whole globe can boast of."[29] The city, in short, should serve as the outlet for the riches of the North American interior.

Although "internal improvements" would become synonymous with transportation by the 1820s, in the late eighteenth century the term referred to a broad range of institutions and infrastructure established to expand, diversify, and integrate the new nation's economy and society. The city enjoyed early advantages in the financial sector as home to the Treasury Department; the Bank of the United States; the Philadelphia Board of Brokers, the first stock exchange in the Americas; and a complement of state-chartered banks and insurance companies.[30] David Rittenhouse directed the locally based U.S. Mint, which fast became the most important center of metallurgical science in the Americas. The city's Federalist elite also continued to expand their complex of scientific, promotional, and charitable institutions such as the Pennsylvania Society for Encouragement of Manufactures and the Useful Arts and the Philadelphia Society for Promoting Agriculture (PSPA).

As its name suggests, the PSPA focused primarily on supporting the region's farming sector. To this end, Nathan Sellers's brother, John Jr., experimented with gypsum, or plaster of Paris, that he ground at one of his mills, attempting to rejuvenate the soils of his century-old farm. His research proved of particular interest to farmers and scientists seeking new fertilizers and was published in PSPA president Richard Peters's *Agricultural Inquiries on Plaister of Paris* in 1810.[31] As farms in the Susquehanna Valley and western Pennsylvania increasingly supplied staple grains for eastern markets, this and other agricultural improvements tracked and tested by the PSPA and displayed at its fairs aided the increasing specialization of farms in Philadelphia's more immediate hinterland. Many farmers on the outskirts of the city turned to such higher-priced produce as dairy, eggs, and vegetables, which in turn enabled the region's agriculturalists to increase their demand for manufactures. The PSPA's efforts also led to the University of Pennsylvania's establishment of a Faculty of Natural Sciences and Rural Economy in 1816, though its plans for a veterinary school, pattern farm, and botanical garden saw only partial implementation.[32]

The APS, too, continued to support the diffusion of knowledge and the transfer of technology for the "improvement" of the region and its position in the national and Atlantic economies. Delaware powder miller and corresponding member Eleuthère Irénée du Pont provided a link to French science, importing the journals of the École Polytechnique and École des Mines. When British engineers William Weston and Benjamin Henry Latrobe arrived in the United States in the 1790s, the APS became their intellectual home. Its members put Weston and Latrobe's expertise in mechanical drawing and waterway engineering to use in canal projects and development of the city's waterworks.[33] Prompted by devastating outbreaks of yellow fever and cholera, the waterworks reduced city dwellers' dependence on wells and streams contaminated by slaughterhouses, tanneries, and other processing industries. Providing fresh water for drinking, bathing, and street cleaning, the works helped prevent future epidemics and proved a critical foundation for future urban growth. Its elegant neoclassical edifices on the Schuylkill River, with their steam engines and pumps, became a major tourist attraction, and the fountains supplied by the works lent the city an air of refinement reminiscent of European capitals.[34] Other early steam engines built by John Fitch, Oliver Evans, and John Stevens powered steamboats that promised to integrate the continent's interior lakes and river valleys into the trading hinterlands of Philadelphia and New York. These inventors likewise found their way to the APS to present and debate their technologies.

In 1794, APS member Charles Willson Peale introduced a new sort of institution to the city—a museum of natural history. Cultural historian David Brigham asserts that this "was more than a static repository of . . . specimens and artifacts. It was a dynamic social site through which Peale helped to define" and increase public participation in education and edifying entertainment—or as Peale put it, the "improvement" of the mind.[35] To promote the "diffusion of knowledge" through "rational amusement," he organized entertaining lectures and demonstrations as well as displays of his permanent collection. The museum originally resided in Philosophical Hall and later expanded to the upper floors of the adjacent State House after the state and federal governments abandoned the city in 1800.[36]

The institutional infrastructure of early national Philadelphia gave the city an unparalleled capacity to launch exploration of the American interior. Thomas Jefferson's interests in botany, natural history, and ethnology made him a welcome guest among the region's natural philosophers, who elected him to membership in the APS in 1780. For a variety of scientific and metropolitan economic motives, other members shared Jefferson's desire to explore the Rocky Mountain and Pacific regions. When the Treaty of Paris formally ended hostilities with Britain in 1783, they approached Indian fighter George Rogers Clark in an attempt to launch such an expedition, though he declined the offer. A decade later, as president of the APS, Jefferson drafted instructions for a voyage up the Missouri River and to the Pacific to be led by French botanist André Michaux. Although they aborted this mission, these plans would serve as the basis for the president's directives to Lewis and Clark ten years afterward. Moreover, as Edward Carter II has argued, the "process of reviewing 'instruction' by qualified members of the society was begun and an intellectual and organizational framework was created for future exploration."[37]

In April 1803, Jefferson sent Meriwether Lewis to meet with his colleagues in Philadelphia, who made him a member of the APS. Jefferson advised him to turn over "the rough draufht of the instructions I have prepared for you" to Robert Patterson, Caspar Wistar, Benjamin Rush, and Benjamin Smith Barton "for their perusal so that they may suggest any additions that they think useful. . . . A considerable portion of [the instructions] being within the field of the Philosophical society, which once undertook the same mission, I think it my duty to consult some of its members."[38] More than a collegial duty, Lewis's trip to Philadelphia presented an opportunity to acquire the surveying and medical skills, botanical books and knowledge, and specialized equipment necessary for his transcontinental expedition.[39]

Before arriving in Philadelphia, he spent close to three weeks in the new state capital of Lancaster. APS member Andrew Ellicott had recently moved there to serve as secretary of Pennsylvania's Land Office, overseeing settlement and road building in the western part of the commonwealth. An astronomer, mathematician, and official surveyor of the United States, Ellicott had laid out the streets of Washington, D.C.; extended the Mason-Dixon line to the western ends of Pennsylvania and Virginia; and charted the boundary between the United States and Spanish Florida. He tutored Lewis in celestial measurement with the sextant, octant, and chronometer, navigational instruments he would use to record his route to the Pacific. Ellicott and fellow mathematician and natural philosopher Robert Patterson rejected Jefferson's choice of the theodolite, which they concluded was too sensitive and complex an instrument for a novice surveyor to carry across the continent.[40]

In Philadelphia, Patterson furthered Lewis's understanding of latitude, longitude, and navigation, subjects he taught at the University of Pennsylvania and other local schools. His colleague, professor of botany and natural history Benjamin Smith Barton, instructed him in the systematic gathering, recording, and preservation of flora and fauna, imparting the Linnaean system of classification by Latin names. Barton lent Lewis books for his trip, including Antoine Simon Le Page DuPratz's *The History of Louisiana* and his own textbook, *Elements of Botany*, the first volume on the subject in the United States. Another physician and natural philosopher, Caspar Wistar, prepared Lewis to identify fossils. Jefferson himself had learned paleontology from Wistar, who held the chair of anatomy at the university and was vice president of the APS. Both Wistar and the president hoped that the Corps of Discovery might find remains of mammoths, mastodons, and other prehistoric beasts.

Barton, Wistar, and Benjamin Rush had all studied medicine in Edinburgh, Scotland, the foremost center of medical education in Europe, and all three held positions at Pennsylvania Hospital. But the job of instructing Lewis in this area fell to Rush, whom his contemporaries viewed as the foremost physician in the United States. As a professor of chemistry at the university, he, too, published the first American textbook in his field. After the Revolution, he joined the medical faculty, where he ultimately trained more than three thousand students from throughout the Americas. Rush spent hours with Lewis, educating him on matters of health, diet, and emergency medicine, while also alerting him to the importance of chronicling diseases among the Indians in the West.[41]

Through Patterson, Barton, Wistar, and Rush, Lewis became well acquainted with Philadelphia's institutional core. Next to the university medical school on Fifth Street stood Franklin's old Library Company. Philosophical Hall was just across the street, nestled next to City Hall and the State House, and Peale's Philadelphia Museum was spitting distance away. These institutions and their members prepared Lewis's mind, eye, and hands for his trip. He found the material necessities for the voyage along Market Street, a block north of the State House, and on the streets to the east that clustered by the Delaware River port. Here, the city's wholesalers, retailers, workshops, printers, coffeehouses, banks, insurance offices, and merchant countinghouses made up the greatest concentration of market activity in the Western Hemisphere.

Even before Lewis's arrival in Philadelphia, Jefferson's secretary of the Treasury, Pennsylvanian Albert Gallatin, forwarded $1,000 to Israel Whelen, purveyor of public supplies for the federal government. The Schuylkill Arsenal on the edge of the city provided tents, clothing, and a Conestoga wagon to transport the supplies that Whelen and Lewis procured downtown. On Front Street by the Delaware River, they bought $102 worth of knives, hatchets, saws, and other tools from merchants Harvey & Worth; 500 brooches and 72 rings to use as gifts for Indians from gold and silversmith Samuel Williamson; and vermillion and red lead—also for use as Indian gifts—from apothecary and paint maker Samuel Wetherill. On Second Street, Whelen and Lewis obtained lead canisters for gunpowder from plumber George Ludlam, and they spent $137 on medical supplies from druggists Gillaspy and Strong. Purchases on Third Street included 30 gallons of "Strong Sp[iri]t Wine" from druggist David Jackson; $151 worth of looking glasses, ribbon, beads, and bells—presumably more Indian gifts—from merchant Christian Denckla; and a $250 gold chronometer from clockmaker Thomas Parker. Excepting the 193 pounds of dried soup bought for $289.50 from a cook named François Baillet, the chronometer was their most expensive acquisition. To make sure it would keep accurate time, Benjamin Barton took it to Andrew Ellicott in Lancaster for tinkering. Together with the $90 sextant, $22 quadrant, and several compasses obtained

FIGURE 2.3. William Birch, Corner of 3rd and Market Streets, ca. 1800. Courtesy American Philosophical Society. (See Color Plate 3.)

from instrument maker Thomas Whitney, the chronometer would allow Lewis and his Corps to locate themselves in time and space.

Lewis and Whelen did most of their shopping on Market Street. They paid $40 to hardware merchant Edward Shoemaker & Co. for scissors, scales, and other small tools. Tobacconist Thomas Leiper Jr. sold them 130 rolls of pigtail tobacco, while merchants John and Charles Wister supplied cloth and beads—all of which was presumably destined for Native Americans whom Lewis and Clark would meet along their trip. For their cooking needs, coppersmith Benjamin Harbeson & Sons furnished brass kettles and a saucepan. Harbeson's neighbor on Market Street, noted machine maker Isaiah Lukens, presented Lewis with a compressed air rifle of his own invention, while saddler Robert Martin provided fifteen rifle pouches for this and other guns. In all, Whelen and Lewis spent more than $2,000 on some 3,500 pounds of equipment and provisions.[42] Decades before the proliferation of railroads and steam-powered manufacturing, their purchases revealed an already robust industrial base, including scientific instrument and hardware manufacturers, chemical and pharmaceutical makers, tanners and leather goods producers, textile weavers, and metalworkers and machine builders.

Benjamin Rush helped package many of the fragile and perishable items, including medical apparatus and drugs.[43] For Rush and his colleagues at the university, the APS, and other local institutions, the Corps of Discovery was an opportunity to expand their scientific horizons. For the city's manufacturers and merchants, including Israel Whelen, it raised the prospect that their markets might someday soon extend beyond the Mississippi and as far as the Pacific. In addition to his position as the federal purveyor, he was president of the Philadelphia Board of Brokers, a founding director of the Bank of the United States, the regional agent for London's Phoenix Insurance Company, and one of the city's largest shipping merchants.[44] Like Robert Morris before him, Whelen sought the greatest possible access to tradable resources in the interior of North America, which would only help grow his financial and transatlantic interests.

Whelen's concern for economic expansion aligned with that of other prominent public servants, including Andrew Ellicott, who in early 1803 published his maps of the mouths of the Mississippi and Missouri Rivers. These maps offered material support in Ellicott's advocacy for purchasing Louisiana, and they helped cartographer Nicholas King produce a map of North America expressly for Lewis and Clark's expedition. Albert Gallatin, too, drew up a map of the West for Lewis. As secretary of the Treasury, he fervently hoped that sales of public land in the West would help pay off the nation's $80 million debt, and the information collected by the Corps of Discovery promised to raise the value of and public interest in that land. Gallatin was born in Geneva, Switzerland, but migrated to the United States in 1780 and soon embarked on land speculation in western Pennsylvania. In 1790, the citizens of Fayette County elected him to serve in the state legislature in Philadelphia. There, he joined Morris's Pennsylvania Society for the Improvement of Roads and Inland Navigation and became a prominent spokesman for the power of transportation networks and trade to integrate urban and frontier America.

When he retired from public life in 1827, Gallatin realized that New York was the best place in America to restart his career in business, so he accepted John Jacob Astor's invitation to head the new National Bank (a private institution). However, when Lewis and Clark completed their voyage twenty years earlier, Philadelphia remained home to the Bank of the United States, and the city's hopes of remaining the nation's commercial capital had not yet been dashed. Robert Morris's old partner, Thomas Willing, was still the bank's president, although a stroke in 1807 would force him to resign in a move that much diminished Philadelphians' control over the federal finances, and Congress would allow the bank's charter to expire four years later. While Astor was building a fortune in fur trading and New York real estate, Stephen Girard's Philadelphia trading fleet made him the nation's first millionaire by 1807. On the manufacturing front, Robert Patterson became director of the U.S. Mint in 1805, strengthening its ties to local scientific societies and making it an engine of growth in the region's machine building and metalworking sectors. These manufacturers would, in turn, spur mechanization and product diversification in other sectors of the local economy, aiding Philadelphians in applying new steam power technologies to expand production and trade.

A local mechanic named Oliver Evans led the way in applying steam power to metropolitan infrastructure. In 1804, he constructed what he called the Oruktor Amphibolos, a dredger commissioned by the Philadelphia Board of Health for cleaning docks and removing sandbars. By his own account, its launching was a major public spectacle:

> To show that both steam carriages and steamboats were practicable (with my steam engine) I first put wheels to it and propelled it by the engine a mile and a half up Market street, and around Center Square to the river Schuylkill. I then fixed a paddlewheel at the stern and propelled it by the engine down the Schuylkill and up the Delaware 16 miles, leaving all the vessels that were under sail full half way behind me (the wind being ahead) ... all of which was performed in the presence of thousands.[45]

Seeking more customers and uses for his high-pressure steam engine, Evans pitched a plan for a steam-powered wagon to the directors of the Lancaster Turnpike. Though this proposal was turned down, his innovations and publications pointed the way for continental transportation systems of the future. In his *Young Steam Engineer's Guide* of 1805, Evans promoted the application of steam engines to a wide range of factories and vehicles, noting in particular that "the navigation of the river Mississippi, by steam engines ... has for many years been a favorite subject of the author, and among the fondest wishes of his heart."[46]

FIGURE 2.4. Evans's "Oruktor Amphibolos," 1804, from Joseph Jackson, *America's Most Historic Highway: Market Street, Philadelphia* (Philadelphia: John Wanamaker, 1926), 242. Author's collection.

In this context of financial, commercial, and especially industrial competition and expansion, Philadelphians welcomed the return of Lewis and Clark and the things they collected. Already in 1805, the Corps of Discovery had shipped plant and animal specimens and Indian objects back to Jefferson, who sent them to the APS for further study. When he arrived in the city in April 1807, Lewis brought more seeds to be planted, stuffed birds and mammals and Indian artifacts for display in Peale's museum, dried plants that would ultimately find a home in the Academy of Natural Sciences (founded five years later), and his journals and maps to be archived at the APS and published by local printers. For Lewis and Jefferson, these institutions were the logical repositories of such scientific records.[47]

In Philadelphia, Lewis sat for a portrait by Charles Willson Peale, with whom he spent considerable time unpacking and sorting the zoological and ethnological collection from the West. APS member Alexander Wilson, the nation's foremost ornithologist, hired an artist to paint newly discovered species such as Lewis's woodpecker (*Melanerpes lewisi*), Clark's nutcracker (*Nucifraga columbiana*), and other birds accumulated by the Corps of Discovery for his soon to be published *American*

Ornithology. Jefferson's friend, botanist William Hamilton, entertained Lewis at his Woodlands estate on the outskirts of the city, where his gardens and hothouses contained one of the largest collections of exotic plants in the nation. There, Hamilton propagated some of the seeds brought back from the West.

Meriwether Lewis left Philadelphia in late July 1807, headed for what should have been a prosperous career as governor of the Louisiana Territory. His friends in Philadelphia presumably hoped to benefit—scientifically and economically—from their close connections to the chief political authority west of the Mississippi. Sadly for both Lewis and the city's economic future, these prospects would not pan out. In October 1809, in an inn outside of Nashville, Lewis shot himself in the head and chest. He was bankrupt, recently spurned in several romances, and plagued by alcoholism and opium addiction. Ironically, Philadelphia commerce may have played a small role in Lewis's death, as Stephen Girard was one of North America's largest importers of Chinese opium.

William Clark took up the task of publishing Lewis's expedition journals. In January 1810 he traveled to Philadelphia, visiting with APS members and looking for a suitable editor. Back in his home state of Virginia in March, he met with Philadelphia lawyer and scholar Nicholas Biddle, to whom he entrusted the job of turning the journals into readable prose.[48] Biddle took another four years to produce *The History of the Expedition under the Command of Captains Lewis and Clark to the Sources of the Missouri, Thence Across the Rocky Mountains and Down the River Columbia to the Pacific Ocean*. In the meantime, however, Philadelphia-based publisher and political economist Mathew Carey beat Biddle to press, putting out Corps of Discovery member Patrick Gass's journal in 1810. With its six full-page engravings, the Gass volume gave American readers the first written and illustrated account of the expedition.[49]

Their personal accomplishments notwithstanding, the careers of Mathew Carey and Nicholas Biddle marked Philadelphia's early nineteenth-century commercial and financial decline relative to New York. Carey spearheaded Pennsylvania's disastrous attempt to compete with the Erie Canal, while Biddle fought President Andrew Jackson in the "Bank War" of the 1830s that removed the Second Bank of the United States from the city—this time for good. These events helped make the Empire City the metropolis of trade and finance in North America. Philadelphia capitalists, however, fought to maintain their competitive position, continuing to develop infrastructure, technologies, and institutions that made their city the nation's industrial capital. Although the Corps of Discovery brought no great boost for their scientific or economic aspirations, they continued to invest in the things that had brought Lewis and Clark—as well as the Continental Congress, the Bank of the United States, and the U.S. Mint—to the Quaker City.

On the infrastructure front, Philadelphians fought a losing battle for commerce, but the residual benefits of this battle spurred the region's industrialization. Sometime in the early national period, Israel Whelen's colleagues in the Board of Brokers tried to limit the damage incurred by New York's superior port by building an optical telegraph between the two cities. Their system consisted of a series of towers across New Jersey that sent coded messages using fires at night and mirror flashes during the day. It reportedly took just ten minutes to transmit news of ships, prices, and exchange rates, effectively ending the practice of New York brokers taking stagecoaches south to manipulate the information-poor Philadelphia market.[50] When construction began on the Erie Canal in 1817, Pennsylvanians initiated a new wave of boosterism and transportation improvements. After careful examination of the canal's engineering, in early 1822 an aging Nathan Sellers penned a frantic warning to the state legislature's Committee on Roads and Inland Navigation:

> [I]t is indeed a sweeping improvement in itself; but taken in connection & with reference to the further views of that state, is Monstrous! or rather Stupendous* and, as a Pennsylvanian, I am alarm'd with the magnitude of its consequences to our own State, and my mind has been hurried thro' the State to discover, if possible, any means of averting those consequences, and at the same time participating in the advantages the State and City of New York will most certainly reap, to an incalculable extent if drawn to that state and city alone.[51]

On the margin of the page, he added that New Yorkers' "view and prospects extend thro the Ohio, Indiana, and Illinois and [then] unto Missurie, the produce of all which States would rather go to N. York than anywhere else—not excepting New Orleans."[52] Citing his own experience in surveying canals, Sellers proposed several routes to connect Philadelphia with Lake Erie and the Ohio River. He corresponded with Carey and Biddle, who together founded the Pennsylvania Society for the Promotion of Internal Improvement in 1824. This society sent architect and engineer William Strickland and his assistant Samuel

Kneass to study marine engineering in Liverpool and Manchester as well as early railroads and ironworks in Glasgow and the coal mining regions of northeastern England. Lobbying the state legislature, they won appropriations for a combined canal and portage railroad system from Philadelphia to Pittsburgh, the first major city across the northern Appalachian Mountains that was effectively connected to the Ohio and Mississippi Valleys.[53]

These investments enjoyed limited commercial and financial success, though they helped catalyze the expansive energies of Philadelphia capitalists. Historian John Lauritz Larson has argued that "Pennsylvania's plunge into internal improvements [in the 1820s] was guided by a remnant of the old commercial gentry hoping to preserve their sovereign state and fend off the chaos of unguided competition in either the political or economic marketplace."[54] But even if the region's trade did not keep up with that of New York, its commercial infrastructure supported industrialization. The city's manufacturers required a robust network of transportation and communications to connect them to settlements and resource-rich regions outside of their immediate hinterland, most importantly in the coal mining districts of the Lehigh and Schuylkill Valleys. Despite their inefficiencies and immense costs that virtually bankrupted the state treasury, turnpikes and canals facilitated the growth and integration of the industrial metropolis.[55] The trading relationships of Delaware River shipping merchants with ports in the South, the West Indies, and Europe proved vital to expanding and maintaining manufacturers' networks of supply and distribution. And, as market exchange remained the principal force shaping demand for manufactures, the region's wholesalers, retailers, and banks remained critical to the livelihood of industrial firms and sectors.[56]

When the federal government took the first national census of manufacturers in 1809, it was the only city that warranted reporting separately, tallying an output valued at $10 million. Two years later, physician James Mease, a subscriber to Peale's museum and member of the Society for Promoting Agriculture, published a promotional *Picture of Philadelphia*. He observed that manufactures "have much increased in variety and extent, since the late interruption to our foreign commerce" resulting from the Embargo Act of 1808 and Non-Intercourse Law of 1809.[57] The War of 1812 further stimulated production, as it cut off most trade with Europe and encouraged the growth of an already robust military-industrial complex that included the Naval Shipyard on the Delaware, the federal arsenals on the Schuylkill and at the industrial village of Frankford, and the powder mills, gun makers, and iron founders that supplied them.

Mease revealed the great diversity of Philadelphia's early industrial base in his enumeration of its products and factories: coarse and fine metals; chemicals, drugs, and "Paints of twenty-two different colours"; "Tobacco in every form"; "Excellent japanned and pewter ware"; textiles and textile making equipment; "innumerable articles into which leather enters," including boots and shoes with a large market in the South; 102 hatters; 15 rope walks; 10 sugar refineries; superior carriage makers; marble quarries and carvers; type founders and paper manufacturers; and cabinet and furniture makers.[58] The region's mechanical arts ranged from the highly skilled crafts of smiths and clockmakers to the less skilled trades of sail makers, brick makers, and bakers. And their output varied from the light consumer goods of tailors and cane makers to the more complex and highly capitalized products of brewers, machine builders, and shipbuilders.[59]

Complementing the region's well-developed mercantile and agricultural sectors, manufacturing drove urban expansion. Philadelphia County was home to 110,000 inhabitants by 1810 and 190,000 just two decades later.[60] Most of this increase resulted from migration from the city's rural hinterlands, while economic growth derived principally from demand for raw materials and manufactured goods within the Middle Atlantic states (overseas migration and trade accounted for a small proportion of overall growth). As agriculture expanded in Ohio and western Pennsylvania, entrepreneurs in rural southeastern Pennsylvania, southern New Jersey, and Delaware shifted capital and labor out of farming and into intensive forestry, mining, and manufacturing. By 1833, protectionists calculated that each ton of iron produced in Pennsylvania resulted in $27.35 of agricultural produce consumed, for a total of $3,415,850 in that year alone. Early market towns such as Norristown, Phoenixville, and Pottstown on the Schuylkill River, Columbia on the Susquehanna, and Easton at the confluence of the Lehigh and Delaware Rivers became not only major transshipment centers but also sites of small-time banking, iron forging, and machine works.[61] With the expansion of the Pennsylvania Railroad in subsequent decades, Philadelphia would become the capital of America's industrial heartland, the densely settled region of mill towns, mining communities, and manufacturing cities between New Jersey and St. Louis.

Although New York capital dominated the American South and West, these regions, too, remained important suppliers and consumers for Philadelphia manufacturers. If Empire City banks and shipping fleets reaped the main financial and mercantile benefits of Jefferson and Gallatin's Louisiana Purchase, the new territories were equally significant for the Quaker City's industrialization. With the rapid adoption of Eli Whitney's cotton gin and high federal tariffs on imports of British cloth, swelling cotton production in the Deep South fueled a burgeoning textile industry in New England and the Mid-Atlantic.[62] Although Lowell and Lawrence, Massachusetts, gained fame as mighty centers of textile manufacture, Philadelphia's woolen and cotton mills out-produced these one-industry towns, earning it the moniker the "Manchester of America." In the neighborhoods of Manayunk, Germantown, and Kensington—and along the mill creeks that flowed into the Delaware—millers and craftspeople shifted production from flour grinding and small-scale weaving to serve the market for American-made cloth and garments.

Skilled mechanics and machine builders played key roles in mediating economic growth, extending industrial Philadelphia's influence in the South and West. One establishment to which James Mease paid detailed attention was Oliver Evans's Mars Works, probably the city's largest employer among manufacturing firms, that produced steam engines, millstones, and cast and wrought iron in all forms. These works built engines for several Delaware River boats and the U.S. Mint, and in 1812 Evans organized the Pittsburgh Steam Engine Company to serve western markets for steamboats and steam-powered flour milling machinery.[63] Other manufacturers soon replicated his efforts to mechanize the infrastructure of western trade and processing.

In 1817, Nathan Sellers's son formed a partnership to build fire engines with banknote engraver Jacob Perkins. On a friendly wager of an oyster dinner with Commodore Murray of the Philadelphia Navy Yard, Perkins invented a pump that, as Nathan's grandson George Escol Sellers wrote in the 1890s, proved vital to keeping thousands of American riverboats and barges above water. "Among the onlookers" at the trial where Perkins demonstrated his pump were "Josiah White and Erskine Hazard, who at that time were engaged in their effort to float anthracite coal down the Lehigh and Delaware in small barges. Mr. White was so well pleased with the plan of these box pumps with leather buckets, that he adopted them for their barges." Nathan Sellers loaned White

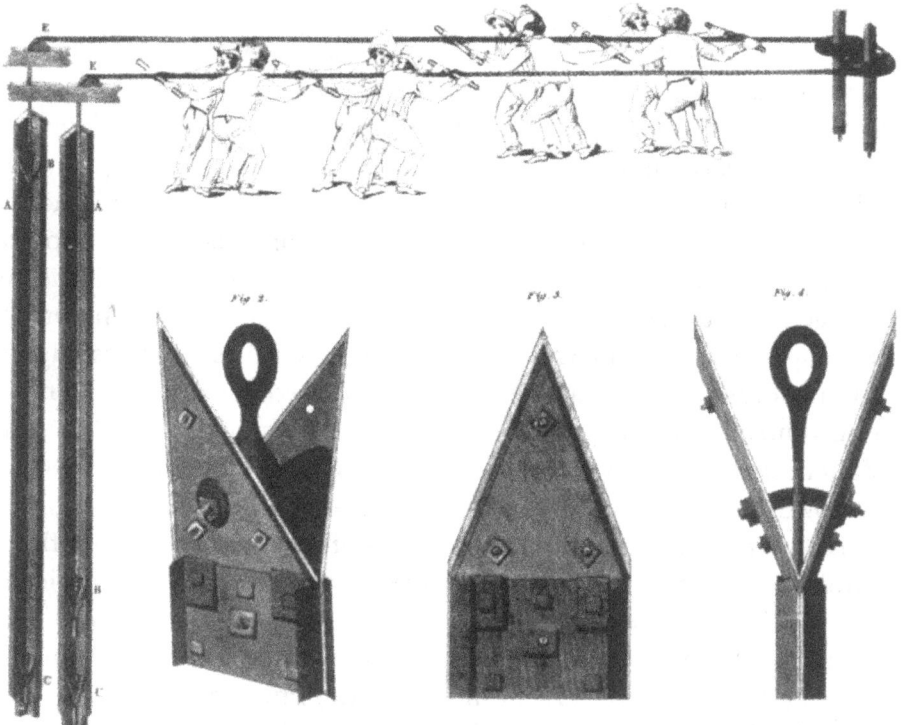

FIGURE 2.5. Perkins's pump, "Hydraulics" plate from Abraham Rees, ed., *The Cycolpaedia*, American edition (Philadelphia, 1822), plates vol. 3. Reprinted from Eugene S. Ferguson, ed., *Early Engineering Reminiscences of George Escol Sellers* (Washington, D.C.: Smithsonian, 1965), 25.

and Hazard the money to start their Lehigh and Schuylkill navigation companies, which gave Philadelphia unparalleled access to the nineteenth century's most important source of energy. From there, Perkins's pumps "found their way to the flat boats of the Susquehanna, and finally to the Ohio river, and the Mississippi and its tributaries." By the end of the century, Escol declared that

> there is not a single coal barge or shell that descends the Ohio with its millions of tons of coal, or a flat boat carrying millions worth of produce from all the tributaries of the mighty "Father of Waters" [the Mississippi] that has not two or more of these simple box pumps, worked by spring poles and man power, and on which the safety of its cargo depends, and the leather buckets, or suckers as they are technically called in the West, are to be found ready made for sale in all the supply stores on the rivers.[64]

Although the Sellers's firm sold few of these pumps itself, other products made in its Market Street workshops served metropolitan and continental markets. It produced riveted leather hose for fire companies throughout the East and mailbags for the U.S. Postal Service (the firm's patented process of riveting leather was developed with the aid of Escol's uncle, Charles Willson Peale). The firm sold large versions of its patent fire engine, the Hydraulion, to the cities and fire companies of Philadelphia; Providence, Rhode Island; Washington, D.C.; and Alexandria, Virginia; smaller towns and the University of Virginia ordered smaller versions. Since these engines were new and complicated machines, members of the firm delivered and set up the finished product personally, training firefighters in its use and thus spreading mechanical skills throughout the East.[65] The firm would later make some of the region's earliest locomotives for railroads linking Philadelphia with Pittsburgh, Baltimore, and northern New Jersey. Its engines served the energy revolution through such customers as the Phoenix Coal Company, and it helped spread metalworking technologies through orders for the branch U.S. Mints established by President Andrew Jackson in North Carolina and Georgia.[66]

One reason Nathan Sellers located his workshop at Sixth and Market Streets had to do with its oldest product line—papermaking equipment and machines. Downtown Philadelphia was the region's principal concentration of printers, bookstores and newspapers, government and corporate offices, mercantile houses, literary societies, and the University of Pennsylvania and its medical school, the main consumers of paper and printing services in the metropolis. This was also the center of shipping merchants who helped link the firm to customers and correspondents who hailed from throughout the United States and Europe, from London and Paris to Cleveland, Boston, and South Carolina.[67] Escol later claimed, "There was not a Paper Mill south of Mason and Dixon's line that we had not something to do with in the way of machinery," as the South lacked sophisticated machine makers.[68]

When a German coppersmith named Henri Mogeme arrived seeking employment at Sellers's engine shop on Market Street around 1820, Escol's father inquired about his past experience. After learning to use tools at the Heidelberg Polytechnic, the visitor replied, he had worked in various shops in London, Manchester, Liverpool, and the famous West Point and Allaire shops in New York. Escol remembered that "Father made some remark about his wandering habits," to which Mogeme replied, "Yes, but the more move the more learn and the better work do."[69] This pattern of migration, learning, and technical improvement characterized the community of scientists and manufacturers in northern Europe and the northeastern United States.[70] The ties that bound them together included business relationships among firms that supplied one another with equipment, technical societies such as the APS and corresponding institutions in other cities, a highly transient population of workers traveling from one city to another in search of employment, and extended families of manufacturers such as the Sellers who sent their children to acquire knowledge and skills in machine shops from England to New England to Cincinnati.[71] While Lewis and Clark's expedition to the West set out to be a landmark in scientific and territorial exploration, these less publicized voyages and migrations served to disseminate the skills and knowledge of an increasingly integrated industrializing world.

Located just two blocks from the APS and even closer to the Mint on Seventh Street, the Sellers's shop became a magnet for scientists and mechanics who came to work, observe, and experiment. Although the Sellers lived amidst the homes and offices of the city's social elite, Escol recalled that neither his father "nor mother [Sophonisba Peale Sellers] made any [pretensions] to the St. Peter's set or the Codfish aristocracy," shunning their "High wine, sugar, rum and molasses with a spice of African blood." Avoiding the slave-owning mercantile elite, his "Father's circle of acquaintances was large but it was among *producers* and *scientific* men he had some intimate and warm friends."[72] Among those who gathered in the front office on High Street were engine maker Patrick Lyon; jeweler and later locomotive builder Matthias Baldwin; Meriwether Lewis's old gun supplier Isaiah Lukens; Dr. James Mease; Robert Patterson and his employee at the Mint, Franklin Peale; and Dr. Thomas Jones, who would serve as superintendent of the federal patent office in the late 1820s.[73]

Two decades after the APS helped launch the Corps of Discovery, this community of university professors and mechanics remained ever more committed to applying science to regional economic growth. Their institutional infrastructure of the colonial and early national periods had fostered scientific and technological improvements, but it was ill-equipped to accommodate the rapid growth of the nineteenth century. The exhibits and demonstrations of Peale's museum provided scientific entertainments for the upper and middle classes, and the APS, the Library Company, and the Academy of Natural Sciences offered access to recent research and publications. While these institutions largely served the interests of the elite, Philadelphians formed another set of institutions to educate a growing industrial workforce.

The expansion of manufacturing required the development and transmission of a wide range of knowledge and skills, from literacy to manual expertise to mathematics and science. An equally broad array of institutions, including schools, libraries, technical societies, and colleges, were established or transformed in the 1820s and 1830s to address these needs. One such institution was the Apprentice's Library of Philadelphia, founded in 1820 by a large group of civic leaders and manufacturers. Unlike the older Library Company, which had become an exclusive organization with a closed membership, the Apprentice's Library had free circulation and was open to all elements of the literate workforce. By 1830, it housed some six thousand volumes.[74]

Popular libraries were complemented by a much larger movement centered in the Northeast to found primary schools that responded to the growth of population and the economy as well as the decline of the apprenticeship system among craftspeople. Historian of education Michael Katz points out that this "drive toward institutional innovation *preceded*"—and indeed served as a prerequisite for—the boom in industrial employment in the mid-nineteenth-century North.[75] While many private schools saw their origins in the second quarter of the century, this movement ultimately culminated in the formation of state-supervised public school bureaucracies. Even just the basic reading, writing, and mathematical skills taught to students who attended only a few years would serve manufacturers' need for workers who could read written orders and make simple measurements and calculations. In 1818, Philadelphian Roberts Vaux and his Society for the Promotion of Public Economy pushed through the Pennsylvania legislature an "Act to provide for the education of children at public expense within the city and county of Philadelphia." This provided for the erection of schoolhouses, hiring of teachers, and formation of a board of controllers.[76]

In higher education, the University of Pennsylvania was already home to the foremost medical school in the Americas, and throughout the first half of the nineteenth century it increased its scientific faculty, courses, and laboratories. This growth culminated in 1852 with the establishment of a Department of Mines, Arts and Manufactures, which two years later offered a bachelor of science degree.[77] While the region's leading civil and mechanical engineers studied at the university, industrialists and professionals in the chemical sciences attended the Philadelphia College of Pharmacy, founded in 1821. The college provided skilled labor, cutting-edge research published in its *American Journal of Pharmacy*, and the first (and regularly updated) American encyclopedia of pharmacy, or *Pharmacopoeia*, for the region's pharmacists and chemical manufacturers.

At the top of industrial Philadelphia's institutional hierarchy, however, the most important forum for coordinating education, communication, and innovation was the Franklin Institute for the Promotion of the Mechanic Arts, the leading mechanics' institute in nineteenth-century America. Founded by merchant Samuel Vaughan Merrick, who was catapulted into manufacturing when he took over Jacob Perkins's bankrupt fire engine shop, and by University of Pennsylvania chemistry professor William H. Keating, the institute created an open forum for the interaction of scientists, mechanics, merchants, and businessmen of all sorts.[78] After reading their plan for the institute, Nicholas Biddle responded enthusiastically, noting that the proposed "union of intellectual and physical labor is an object of peculiar interest here. There are countries where it is deemed rather desirable than dangerous," he advised, "that all power and all knowledge should be engrossed by the few, and the routine of mere manual labor devolved on what are fastidiously termed the lower orders of society."[79]

In February 1824, the Pennsylvania legislature unanimously approved a charter for the Franklin Institute. The founders' memorial to the legislature cited the need for an educated workforce to support Philadelphia's competition with other industrial cities in the national and global economy. "The rapid improvement now going on in every department of Industry," they declared, "must be attributed to the steady progress which knowledge is every where making." Mechanics institutes were vital to these efforts, and the Franklin Institute's promoters made sure to point out that "particularly in Great Britain and recently in New York, Societies have been formed and Lectureships established and endowed by them ... which have been attended with the happiest and most gratifying effects." A "similar Institution in Pennsylvania," they told the legislature, would "give a greater development to the resources, powers, and skill of her Manufacturers and Mechanics ... thus leading to important discoveries and Improvements, augment[ing] the wealth and prosperity of the State."[80]

Nicholas Biddle recommended the APS as a model for structuring the Franklin Institute, but there were important differences between the two organizations. Beyond its observation of the transit of Venus in 1769, the APS had sponsored little research, and by the 1820s it had become something of a gentlemen's club. Foreign scientists of note were elected corresponding members, but "the Philadelphia element in the Society was becoming, apparently, a coterie of physicians, lawyers, and clergy-men" who made up what historian of science Thomas Carroll has called a "bastion of provincial establishment status" that "seemingly ignored the professionalization of science and spent its money instead on the collection of the Franklin papers" and "concluded their desultory regular meetings with ribald humor."[81] This contrasted sharply with the socially open structure of the Franklin Institute, which required that "two-thirds of the managers shall be manufacturers or mechanics."[82] Most importantly, as Biddle suggested, the institute was organized as a forum wherein academic science and education, manufacturing business, and initiatives of public import intersected.

The Franklin Institute's first officers and Board of Managers reflected a diverse set of skills and interests at the table.[83] Type founder James Ronaldson was elected its first president, Isaiah Lukens and Mathew Carey its vice presidents, and architect William Strickland recording secretary. Other board members included a shot manufacturer, silver plater, coppersmith, gunsmith, U.S. Mint refiner, acid manufacturer, tanner, brewer, printing press maker, paper miller, bookbinder, bricklayer, carpenter, potter, stockbroker Clement Biddle, and Professor William Keating. Lukens, Carey, Robert Patterson, tobacco manufacturer Thomas Leiper, and paint manufacturer John Price Wetherill made up a considerable cohort of institute managers with direct ties to the Corps of Discovery.[84] While they and their city had profited only modestly from Lewis and Clark's expedition, they continued to pursue scientific exploration that promised to grow their region's pool of knowledge, skilled labor, and innovative industrial concerns.

In its hall just down Seventh Street from the Mint, the Franklin Institute devised systems to coordinate communication, education, publication, and technological oversight. Its Committee on Instruction organized lecture series on chemistry, mechanics, and other branches of applied science, and it offered evening classes in technical drawing to upgrade factory workers' skills. Another committee maintained the library, and the Committees on Models and Minerals & Geological Specimens assembled displays that complemented its printed materials. The Committee on Publications administered the *Journal of the*

FIGURE 2.6. Lithograph of Franklin Institute hall on Seventh Street. From Bruce Sinclair, *Philadelphia's Philosopher Mechanics: A History of the Franklin Institute, 1824–1865* (Baltimore: Johns Hopkins University Press, 1974), 21.

Franklin Institute, which became one of the foremost periodicals in the applied sciences. The Committee on Exhibitions organized fairs where all manner of manufactured goods was displayed, providing forums for the spread and marketing of new information, technologies, and products. Finally, the Committee on Science and the Arts acted as a professional review board and as the institute's research engine, examining and evaluating inventions submitted by all sorts of "mechanic artists" and inquiring into and reporting on "the state of the Arts generally, or of any branch thereof, . . . in order to disseminate useful practical information, or historical facts in relation thereto."[85]

In the 1830s, the Committee on Science and the Arts sponsored research on questions of interest not only to private manufacturers but also on issues of broad public import. Perpetuating the pattern of traveling to collect information valuable to the region and its scientists, the City of Philadelphia and the Franklin Institute sent Samuel Merrick to Britain, France, and Belgium to study municipal gas systems. His findings subsequently shaped the design and development of the city's gas works.[86] In its efforts to regulate trade, the Pennsylvania legislature called on the institute to investigate and report on weights and measures and to make recommendations as to the advantages and liabilities of various systems.[87] At the national level, it was the chief forum for a series of federally sponsored experiments and inquiries into the causes of steam boiler explosions, one of the principal—and often lethal—risks associated with the mechanization of factories, urban infrastructure, and the proliferation of railroads and steamboats across the continent.[88]

The Franklin Institute served as a gathering place and coordinating mechanism for regional and international networks of engineers and industrialists. Its corresponding members hailed from across the United States and Europe. Its visitors' register recorded a steady stream of guests from around the globe—from Maine to St. Louis, and from Edinburgh to Marseilles to Havana. Like the institute's members, these visitors' occupations ranged from farming to journalism, merchant banking to academic chemistry, medicine to military engineering.[89] As a forum for communication, learning, and technology transfer, the Franklin Institute helped reinforce Philadelphia's position as an industrial metropolis in an increasingly interconnected world.

In the early nineteenth century, Philadelphians thus transformed the role of their city within the economy of the nation and the globe. Scientists and mechanics—and even bankers such as Nicholas Biddle and

FIGURE 2.7. Map of the Pennsylvania Railroad and the cities and communities it served by 1946. From *One Hundred Years: Ninety-Ninth Annual Report for Year Ended Dec. 31, 1945, the Pennsylvania Railroad Company.* (See Color Plate 4.)

political economists such as Mathew Carey—tied the city's growth to mechanical systems of production, transportation, and urban infrastructure. Through their firms and institutions, mechanics coordinated networks of production, education, and technology transfer that turned the breadbasket of the Atlantic into the "workshop of the world," the nation's leading center of industry and applied science.[90] While the Corps of Discovery needed Philadelphia, the city did not truly need Lewis and Clark—even if their provisioning purchases, plant and animal specimens, and the prospect of access to the Great Plains and Pacific were more than welcome. The continuous process of exploring the frontiers of science and trade, of which the Corps of Discovery was a small but not insignificant part, remained critical to the city's long-term economic growth.

Like Lewis and Clark, Philadelphians did not always find the shortest or most convenient route to realizing their commercial and industrial ambitions. But those ambitions shaped repeated waves of investment in extending the power and influence of their metropolis. Long after the Corps of Discovery launched its Conestoga wagon from the Schuylkill Arsenal and its flatboat from Pittsburgh, local boosters and institutions continued to act upon the aspirations of Benjamin Smith Barton, Benjamin Rush, Robert Patterson, and Caspar Wistar—as well as William Penn, Robert Morris, Nathan Sellers, and Mathew Carey. At the close of the Franklin Institute's twenty-second Exhibition of American Manufactures in October 1852, state senator William D. Kelley exhorted the assembled capitalists, mechanics, and scientists to continue these investments. The state "ought to be the manufacturer for the increasing millions of luxurious citizens of her sister sovereignties in the South and West, and compete with England in the markets of the world," proclaimed the man later dubbed "Pig Iron Kelley." With an expanded railroad and mining infrastructure, he assured his audience, Pennsylvania "will dispute the manufacturing supremacy of England, and exhibit such a development of natural resources and human power as the world has not yet seen. . . . Then, too," he declared, "will Philadelphia assume her civic supremacy. Then will she speedily become what nature has decreed she must ultimately be—the great city of America—the London of the Western world."[91]

NOTES

1. Frederick Jackson Turner, "The Significance of the Frontier in American History," *Annual Report of the American Historical Association* (1893), 199–227.

2. Frederick Jackson Turner, *The Frontier in American History* (New York: Holt, 1920), 259. For discussions of Turner and his effects on American historiography, see Ray Allen Billington, *America's Frontier Heritage* (New York: Holt, Rinehart and Winston, 1966); William Cronon, "Revisiting the Vanishing Frontier: The Legacy of Frederick Jackson Turner," *Western Historical Quarterly* 18 (1987): 157–76.

3. For a sample of recent scholarship on Lewis and Clark and the American West, see Laurie M. Carlson, *Seduced by the West: Jefferson's America and the Lure of the Land beyond the Mississippi* (Chicago: Dee, 2003); Alan Taylor, ed., *Lewis & Clark: Journey to Another America* (St. Louis: Missouri Historical Society, 2003); James P. Ronda, *Finding the West: Explorations with Lewis and Clark* (Albuquerque: University of New Mexico Press, 2001); Mary Lawlor, *Recalling the Wild: Naturalism and the Closing of the American West* (New Brunswick: Rutgers University Press, 2000); Thomas Schmidt, *The Saga of Lewis & Clark: Into the Uncharted West* (New York: Doring Kindersley, 1999); Stephen Ambrose, *Undaunted Courage: Meriwether Lewis, Thomas Jefferson, and the Opening of the American West* (New York: Simon & Schuster, 1996); Albert Furtwangler, *Acts of Discovery: Visions of America in the Lewis and Clark Journals* (Chicago: University of Illinois Press, 1993).

4. William Cronon, *Nature's Metropolis: Chicago and the Great West* (New York: Norton, 1991), especially 46–54.

5. The long-term origins, growth, and decline of Philadelphia as an industrial city are surveyed in Domenic Vitiello, *Engineering the Metropolis: The Sellers Family and Industrial Philadelphia* (PhD diss., University of Pennsylvania, 2004). This essay is based on chapters 1 and 2 of that study.

6. William Penn, "A Further Account of the Province of Pennsylvania, 1685," in *Narratives of Early Pennsylvania, West New Jersey, and Delaware, 1630–1707*, ed. Albert Cook Meyers, 263 (New York, 1912). See also Sylvia Doughty Fries, *The Urban Idea in Colonial America* (Philadelphia: Temple University Press, 1977).

7. Anne Bezanson, Robert D. Gray, and Miriam Hussey, *Prices in Colonial Pennsylvania* (Philadelphia: University of Pennsylvania Press, 1935); David Hackett Fischer, *The Great Wave: Price Revolutions and the Rhythm of History* (New York: Oxford University Press, 1996), 117–56.

8. Barry Levy, *Quakers and the American Family: British Settlement in the Delaware Valley* (New York: Oxford University Press, 1988).

9. Carville Earle, "Why Tobacco Stunted the Growth of Towns and Wheat Built Them into Small Cities: Urbanization South of the Mason-Dixon Line, 1650–1790," in *Geographical Inquiry and American Historical Problems*, ed. Carville Earle, 88–152 (Stanford: Stanford University Press, 1992).

10. For an account of the imperial context of early British industrialization, see Eric Hobsbawm, *Industry and Empire: The Birth of the Industrial Revolution* (New York: Weinfeld & Nicholson, 1968), especially chapters 1–5.

11. For a discussion of the cultural and material dimensions of the Enlightenment in Philadelphia, see Laura Rigal, *The American Manufactory: Art, Labor, and the World of Things in the Early Republic* (Princeton: Princeton University Press, 1998).

12. For a recent intellectual history of Franklin's Enlightenment, see Douglas Anderson, *The Radical Enlightenments of Benjamin Franklin* (Baltimore: Johns Hopkins University Press, 1997).

13. General histories of the American Philosophical Society in the eighteenth century include Murphy D. Smith, *Oak from an Acorn: A History of the American Philosophical Society Library, 1770–1804* (Wilmington: Scholarly Resources, 1976); Peter Stephen Du Ponceau, *An Historical Account of the Origin and Formation of the American Philosophical Society Held at Philadelphia for Promoting Useful Knowledge* (Philadelphia: APS, 1914). The University of Pennsylvania's history is recounted in George E. Thomas and David B. Brownlee, *Building America's First University: An Historical and Architectural Guide to the University of Pennsylvania* (Philadelphia: University of Pennsylvania Press, 2000).

14. Engineering historian Ken Alder has termed this a "technological life," "a coherent social and ideological world which gives purpose and meaning to a set of material objects." Ken Alder, *Engineering the Revolution: Arms and Enlightenment in France, 1763–1815* (Princeton: Princeton University Press, 1997), xii.

15. *Early Proceedings of the American Philosophical Society for the Promotion of Useful Knowledge . . . 1744 to 1838* (Philadelphia: McCalla & Stavely, 1884), 1–6, American Philosophical Society archives (hereafter APS).

16. Ibid., 30.

17. Whitfield J. Bell Jr., *Patriot-Improvers: Biographical Sketches of Members of the American Philosophical Society*, vol. 2, *1768* (Philadelphia: APS, 1999), 220.

18. *Early Proceedings of the American Philosophical Society*, 36.

19. Quoted in Whitfield J. Bell Jr., *Patriot-Improvers: Biographical Sketches of Members of the American Philosophical Society*, vol. 1, *1743–1768* (Philadelphia: APS, 1997), 502. See also John Sellers et al. to Richard Penn (June 5, 1773), Historical Society of

Pennsylvania (hereafter HSP), Penn Manuscripts, Warrants & Surveys, large folio, 75.

20. For discussion of the importance of fixed boundaries in English colonization, see William Cronon, *Changes in the Land: Indians, Colonists, and the Ecology of New England* (New York: Hill & Wang, 1983); Patricia Seed, *Ceremonies of Possession in Europe's Conquest of the New World, 1492–1640* (New York: Cambridge University Press, 1995).

21. Quoted in Anne Bezanson, *Prices and Inflation During the American Revolution: Pennsylvania, 1770–1790* (Philadelphia: University of Pennsylvania Press, 1951), 18.

22. S. F. Hotchkin, *Rural Pennsylvania: In the Vicinity of Philadelphia* (Philadelphia: Jacobs, 1897), 328.

23. Samuel Breck, "Historical sketch of the continental bills of Credit, from the year 1775 to 1781, with specimens thereof," (1856), APS, Peale-Sellers Papers.

24. Quoted in John W. Maxson Jr., "Nathan Sellers: America's First Large-Scale Maker of Paper Moulds," *Paper Maker* 29(1) (1960): 5; see also Nathan & David Sellers, Account Book (1774–1801), APS, Peale-Sellers Papers.

25. David Rittenhouse, Thomas Hutchins, and Nathan Sellers, *Essay or Report to the Genl. Assembly of Pennsylvania on the Union of the Waters of Susquehanna & Schuylkill by the Tulpehocken & Swatara Creeks* (1784), APS, Sellers Family Papers.

26. Journal of the Society for the Improvement of Roads and Inland Navigation (1791–1793), HSP.

27. Address of the Senate to Gov. Thomas Mifflin (August 26, 1791), Library Company of Philadelphia (hereafter LCP).

28. *American State Papers*, Class X, *Miscellaneous* I:834–38 (quotation from 834).

29. Ibid., 837.

30. For a recent interpretation of the role of financial institutions and state-chartered corporations in the Federalist elite's attempt to retain control of the city and its economy, see Andrew M. Schocket, *Consolidating Power: Technology, Ideology, and Philadelphia's Growth in the Early Republic* (PhD diss., College of William and Mary, 2001).

31. Bell, *Patriot-Improvers*, 1:503; John Sellers, "Answers to Queries on Plaister of Paris," in *Agricultural Inquiries on Plaister of Paris*, ed. Richard Peters (Philadelphia, 1810), 46–52.

32. Simon Baatz, *"Venerate the Plough": A History of the Philadelphia Society for Promoting Agriculture, 1785–1985* (Philadelphia: PSPA, 1985), 21–26.

33. Darwin H. Stapleton, "The Transfer of Early Industrial Technologies to America, With Especial Reference to the Role of the American Philosophical Society," *Proceedings of the American Philosophical Society* 135(2) (June 1991): 286–98.

34. For discussion of early waterworks' engineering, see Martin Melosi, *The Sanitary City: Urban Infrastructure in America from Colonial Times to the Present* (Baltimore: Johns Hopkins University Press, 2000), 31–34. On early government attempts to regulate industrial pollution in Philadelphia, see Michal McMahon, "'Publick Service' versus 'Mans Properties': Dock Creek and the Origins of Urban Technology in Eighteenth-Century Philadelphia," in *Early American Technology: Making and Doing Things from the Colonial Era to 1850*, ed. Judith A. McGaw, 114–47 (Chapel Hill: University of North Carolina Press, 1994).

35. David R. Brigham, *Public Culture in the Early Republic: Peale's Museum and Its Audience* (Washington: Smithsonian, 1995), 1–2.

36. Charles Coleman Sellers, *Mr. Peale's Museum: Charles Willson Peale and the First Popular Museum of Natural Science and Art* (New York: Norton, 1980), 1, 82, 239. See also Edgar P. Richardson et al., *Charles Willson Peale and His World* (New York: Abrams, 1982).

37. Edward C. Carter II, "Living with Lewis & Clark: The American Philosophical Society's Continuing Relationship with the Corps of Discovery from the Michaux

Expedition to the Present," in *Lewis & Clark: Legacies, Memories, and New Perspectives*, ed. Kris Fresonke and Mark Spence, 22–23 (Berkeley: University of California Press, 2004).

38. Thomas Jefferson to Meriwether Lewis (April 27, 1803), Donald Jackson, ed., *Letters of the Lewis and Clark Expedition*, 2d ed., vol. 1 (Chicago: University of Illinois Press, 1978), 44.

39. Lewis's 1803 trip to Philadelphia is detailed in Frank Muhly, "Firm Foundations in Philadelphia: The Lewis and Clark Expedition's Ties to Pennsylvania," *Pennsylvania Heritage* (Summer 2001).

40. Meriwether Lewis to Thomas Jefferson (May 29, 1803), in *Letters of the Lewis and Clark Expedition*, 52; Carter, "Living with Lewis & Clark," 25.

41. Studies of Rush include Wyndham D. Miles, *Benjamin Rush, Chemist* (Philadelphia: University of Pennsylvania Press, 1953); Alvn Brodsky, *Benjamin Rush: Patriot and Physician* (New York: Truman Talley, 2004); Sarah Regal Riedman, *Benjamin Rush: Physician, Patriot, Founding Father* (New York: Abelard-Schuman, 1964); E. G. Chuinard, *Only One Man Died: The Medical Aspects of the Lewis and Clark Expedition* (Glendale, Calif.: Arthur H. Clark, 1980), especially chapter 6.

42. Jackson, *Letters of the Lewis and Clark Expedition*, 78–99.

43. Carter, "Living with Lewis & Clark," 25.

44. J. Thomas Scharf and Thompson Westcott, *History of Philadelphia, 1609–1884* (Philadelphia: Everts, 1884), 2086–87; Lawrence Lewis Jr., *A History of the Bank of North America, the First Bank Chartered in the United States* (Philadelphia: Lippincott, 1882), 138; *Souvenir History: Philadelphia Stock Exchange* (Philadelphia, 1903).

45. Quoted in Joseph Jackson, *America's Most Historic Highway: Market Street, Philadelphia* (Philadelphia: Wanamaker, 1926), 243.

46. Oliver Evans, *Abortion of the Young Steam Engineer's Guide* (Philadelphia, 1805), vi.

47. Paul Russell Cutright, *A History of the Lewis and Clark Journals* (Norman: University of Oklahoma Press, 1976), 44.

48. Kris Fresonke, "Introduction," in *Lewis & Clark: Legacies, Memories, and New Perspectives*, 2.

49. Cutright, *A History of the Lewis and Clark Journals*, 31.

50. Elkins Wetherill, *The Story of the Philadelphia Stock Exchange* (Downingtown, Pa.: Newcomen Society, 1976), 11.

51. Nathan Sellers to Lehman (January 23, 1822), APS, Sellers Family Papers.

52. Ibid. See also Nathan Sellers, Notes on the Erie Canal and Notes on the Route and Mileage for a Canal from Philadelphia to Erie (both ca. 1821), both APS, Sellers Family Papers.

53. Nathan Sellers to Mathew Carey, Nicholas Biddle, et al. (October 23, 1824), LCP, M. Carey, Correspondence on Internal Improvements; Mathew Carey to Nathan Sellers (December 6, 1824), APS, Sellers Family Papers; William Strickland, *Reports on Canals, Railways and Other Subjects* (Philadelphia, 1826).

54. John Lauritz Larson, *Internal Improvement: National Public Works and the Promise of Popular Government in the Early United States* (Chapel Hill: University of North Carolina Press, 2001), 87.

55. While canals typically froze over during winter, wagons traveling stone-paved turnpikes provided year-round transportation. David Meyer, *The Roots of American Industrialization* (Baltimore: Johns Hopkins University Press, 2003), especially chapters 2 and 5; Donald C. Jackson, "Roads Most Traveled: Turnpikes in Southeastern Pennsylvania in the Early Republic," in *Early American Technology*, 197–239.

56. For an interpretation of urban-industrial growth that stresses the role of

exchange, see David Meyer, "The Rise of the Industrial Metropolis: The Myth and the Reality," *Social Forces* 68 (March 1990): 731–52; see also Meyer, *The Roots of American Industrialization*.

57. James Mease, *The Picture of Philadelphia* (Philadelphia: Kite, 1811), 74; see also John J. MacFarlane, *Manufacturing in Philadelphia, 1683–1912* (Philadelphia: Commercial Museum, 1912), 6.

58. Mease, *The Picture of Philadelphia*, 74–76.

59. For discussion of the range of early industrial crafts, see Bruce Laurie, *Working People of Philadelphia, 1800–1850* (Philadelphia: Temple University Press, 1980); Rigal, *The American Manufactory*, especially 13. For an overview of early Delaware Valley shipbuilding, see Thomas Heinrich, *Ships for the Seven Seas: Philadelphia Shipbuilding in the Age of Industrial Capitalism* (Baltimore: Johns Hopkins University Press, 1997), chapter 1.

60. Philip Scranton, *Proprietary Capitalism: The Textile Manufacture at Philadelphia, 1800–1885* (New York: Cambridge University Press, 1983), 75.

61. The principal articulation of this intraregional demand model for Philadelphia is Diane Lindstrom, *Economic Development in the Philadelphia Region, 1810–1850* (New York: Columbia University Press, 1978). This model is expanded for the North and East in the early republic in Meyer, *The Roots of American Industrialization*. See also Laurie, *Working People of Philadelphia*, 9–10; Burton W. Folsom Jr., *Urban Capitalists: Entrepreneurs and City Growth in Pennsylvania's Lackawanna and Lehigh Regions, 1800–1920*, 2d ed. (Scranton: University of Scranton Press, 2000); Donna J. Rilling, *Making Houses, Crafting Capitalism: Builders in Philadelphia, 1790–1850* (Philadelphia: University of Pennsylvania Press, 2001).

62. "Tariff rates rose from about 40 percent around 1820 to a peak near 60 percent around 1830 and then declined to about 20 percent in 1860." Meyer, *The Roots of American Industrialization*, 126.

63. Eugene S. Ferguson, *Oliver Evans: Inventive Genius of the American Industrial Revolution* (Greenville, Del.: Hagley, 1980).

64. Eugene Ferguson, ed., *Early Engineering Reminiscences of George Escol Sellers* (Washington: Smithsonian, 1965), 20. For energy-centered interpretations of the industrial revolution, see Richard G. Wilkinson, "The English Industrial Revolution," in *The Ends of the Earth: Perspectives on Modern Environmental History*, ed. Donald Worster, 80–99 (New York: Cambridge University Press, 1988); E. A. Wrigley, *Continuity, Chance and Change: The Character of the Industrial Revolution in England* (New York: Cambridge University Press, 1988), especially chapter 3.

65. Hotchkin, *Rural Pennsylvania*, 332–34; Ferguson, *Early Engineering Reminiscences of George Escol Sellers*, 6, 43–44; John W. Maxson Jr., "Coleman Sellers: Machine Maker to America's First Mechanized Paper Mills," *Paper Maker* 30(1) (1961): 13–27; James Sellers & Abraham Pennock, Letters Patent (July 6, 1818), HSP; Coleman Sellers to Samuel Sellers (January 15, 1822), and John J. Peabody to William Sellers & Co. (August 16, 1897), both APS, Peale-Sellers Papers.

66. Coleman Sellers & Sons, Order Book (1834–1836), APS, Peale-Sellers Papers; Coleman and George Escol Sellers business/legal papers (1834–1845), HSP, Cadwalader Collection, Series VI, box 103, folder 4; Ferguson, *Engineering Reminiscences of George Escol Sellers*, 62; John H. White, *Cincinnati Locomotive Builders, 1845–1868* (Washington: Smithsonian, 1965), 50.

67. Sellers, Brandt & Co., Letter Book (1828–1834), APS, Peale-Sellers Papers.

68. Quoted in John W. Maxon Jr., "George Escol Sellers: Inventor, Historian, and Papermaker," *Paper Maker* 38(1) (1969): 42.

69. Ferguson, *Engineering Reminiscences of George Escol Sellers*, 46.

70. This process of changing jobs to learn mechanical skills is traced among railroad employees in Walter Licht, *Working for the Railroad: The Organization of Work in the Nineteenth Century* (Princeton: Princeton University Press, 1983).

71. For a discussion of transience in nineteenth-century North America and its effects on both individual cities and the broader integration of systems of cities, see Michael B. Katz, Michael J. Doucet, and Mark J. Stern, *The Social Organization of Early Industrial Capitalism* (Cambridge: Harvard University Press, 1982), chapter 3.

72. George Escol Sellers, "Recollections of Coleman Sellers by his Son George Escol Sellers," 48–49, APS, Peale-Sellers Papers.

73. Anthony F. C. Wallace, *Rockdale: The Growth of an American Village in the Early Industrial Revolution* (New York: Knopf, 1978), 213.

74. Job R. Tyson, *An Address Delivered at the Request of the Board of Managers of the Apprentices' Library Company of Philadelphia* (Philadelphia: Young, 1830).

75. Michael B. Katz, *Reconstructing American Education* (Cambridge: Harvard University Press, 1987), 13.

76. The Pennsylvania Society for the Promotion of Public Economy was founded in 1817 to promote the reform of poor relief by "ascertaining and pointing out" the "most profitable direction" for labor, inculcating in the poor the "prudent and judicious expenditure of money," "instructing the great mass of the community in the modes of economizing in their fuel and diet," and educating "the ignorant and the poor" in order "to strike at the root of poverty and vice." Viewing intemperance and unemployment as the primary sources of these societal ills, the society "sought to redraw the relationship between the state, the economy, and the poor." *Henry Troth, Sept. 4, 1794–May 22, 1842* (Philadelphia, 1903); Pennsylvania Society for the Promotion of Public Economy, *Report of the Library Committee of the Pennsylvania Society for the Promotion of Public Economy* (Philadelphia, 1817); Michael Meranze, *Laboratories of Virtue: Punishment, Revolution, and Authority in Philadelphia, 1760–1835* (Chapel Hill: University of North Carolina Press, 1996), 237.

77. Thomas and Brownlee, *Building America's First University*, 48.

78. The principal modern study of the Franklin Institute's founding and history through the Civil War is Bruce Sinclair, *Philadelphia's Philosopher Mechanics: A History of the Franklin Institute, 1824–1865* (Baltimore: Johns Hopkins University Press, 1974). See also Sydney L. Wright, *The Story of the Franklin Institute* (Philadelphia: Franklin Institute, 1838); Dr. Persifor Frazer, "The Franklin Institute: Its Services and Deserts," *Journal of the Franklin Institute* 165 (April 1900): 245–98.

79. Nicholas Biddle to William Strickland (February 5, 1824), in Franklin Institute, Minutes of the Board of Managers (1823–1831), Franklin Institute archives (hereafter FI).

80. Memorial (February 26, 1824), Franklin Institute, Minutes of the Board of Managers (1823–1831), FI.

81. P. Thomas Carroll, "The Decline of the American Philosophical Society, 1820–1855: A Prosopographical First Look at Some Changes in American Science during the First Half of the Nineteenth Century" (University of Pennsylvania, Department of History and Sociology of Science, paper, February 1974), 14, 18, APS. See also J. Peter Lesley, "The Spirit of a Philosophical Society," *Proceedings of the American Philosophical Society* 18 (1878–1880), 586–87; Whitfield J. Bell Jr., "As Others Saw Us: Notes on the Reputation of the American Philosophical Society," *Proceedings of the American Philosophical Society* 116 (1972), 269–78; Walter Elliot Gross, *The American Philosophical*

Society and the Growth of Science in the United States, 1835–1850 (PhD diss., University of Pennsylvania, 1970).

82. *Constitution and By-Laws of the Franklin Institute* (Philadelphia: Barnard & Jones, 1854), 6.

83. Wallace, *Rockdale*, 229.

84. Election of Board of Managers (February 16, 1824), Franklin Institute, Minutes of the Board of Managers, FI.

85. *Constitution and By-Laws of the Franklin Institute*, 24. See also Percy A. Bivins, *Index to the Reports of the Committee on Science and the Arts* (Philadelphia: Franklin Institute, 1890); A. Michal McMahon and Stephanie A. Morris, *Technology in Industrial America: The Committee on Science and the Arts of the Franklin Institute, 1824–1900* (Wilmington: Scholarly Resources, 1977).

86. Samuel V. Merrick, *Report upon an Examination of Some of the Gas Manufactories in Great Britain, France, and Belgium, under a Resolution Passed by the Select and Common Councils of the City of Philadelphia* (Pittsburgh: Hogan, 1835).

87. *Report of the Managers of the Franklin Institute . . . in Relation to Weights and Measures* (Philadelphia: Harding, 1834).

88. Bruce Sinclair, *Early Research at the Franklin Institute: The Investigation into the Causes of Steam Boiler Explosions, 1830–1837* (Philadelphia: Franklin Institute, 1966).

89. Franklin Institute, Minutes of the Board of Managers and Visitors Register (1830–1853), FI.

90. By "applied science," I do not mean the sort of applied science developed in industrial research and development laboratories of the late nineteenth and twentieth centuries, but rather the application of scientific inquiry and knowledge to manufacturing, infrastructure, resource extraction, and other engineering works.

91. *Report of the Twenty-Second Exhibition of American Manufactures Held in the City of Philadelphia, from the 19th to the 30th of October, Inclusive, 1852 by the Franklin Institute* (Philadelphia, 1852), 14.

3

PHILANTHROPIC ENTERPRISE

The Imperial Contradictions of Republican Political Economy in Philadelphia during the Era of Lewis and Clark

S. D. KIMMEL

Upon the Citizens of Pennsylvania is turned the attention of Europe, observing, whether we know how to use, as well as how to acquire, Empire; whether we are to be admired, or despised; in fine, whether, left as we are to ourselves, upon this fair and solemn trial, before the Nations of the Earth, the cause of Republican Liberty shall be justified by its effects, or shall be condemned as the introducer of more Calamities than it removes.
GEORGE LOGAN, Lancaster, March 14, 1800

I am persuaded no constitution was ever before as well calculated as ours for extensive empire and self-government.
JEFFERSON TO JAMES MADISON, April 27, 1809

FIFTY YEARS AGO Bernard DeVoto's *Course of Empire* called attention to the dual significance of the Lewis and Clark expedition as a marker of the emergence of the United States onto the global stages of both major scientific discovery and empire-building. Since DeVoto's work, the many important scientific accomplishments of the expedition have been detailed and clarified by scholars such as Paul Cutright and those who, under the leadership of Donald Jackson and Gary Moulton, completed the new thirteen-volume edition of the Lewis and Clark journals. Scholarship is only now beginning to address, however, critical aspects of the cultural history of the expedition as part of the imperial development of the United States, most notably in the work of James Ronda and in Thomas Slaughter's recent book *Exploring Lewis and Clark*. As Ronda has eloquently stated at the conclusion of *Finding the West: Explorations with Lewis and Clark*, "the Lewis and Clark homecoming was not the end of the journey" but instead marked "the beginning of a headlong rush to empire that remade (and continues to remake) the landscape we see every day. . . . Coming to terms with Lewis, Clark, and all those touched by their journey compels us to face our own troubled past and our uncertain present. When we describe the Corps of Discovery we are considering our own history and our own moment in time."[1]

In *Empire*, Antonio Negri and Michael Hardt have provocatively argued that the imperial constitution of the early American republic, which matured "throughout the history of the United States," has now emerged "on a global scale in its fully realized form."[2] Whether or not we accept this interpretation of the history of the present, recent developments and the essays gathered together here demonstrate how vital analysis of the Lewis and Clark enterprise remains as an index of critical historical work on the emergence of the United States onto the global stage of scientific discovery and empire-building.

As Ronda noted on the eve of our contemporary bicentennial celebrations of the Lewis and Clark expedition, "unlike us, Jefferson, his captains, and their contemporaries were not so certain about the expedition and what it had accomplished." The supporters of Lewis and Clark were instead burdened by a sense of the failure of the expedition because it had not achieved either one of its two major objectives. The expedition did not discover Jefferson's projected "direct and practicable water communication across the continent for the purposes of commerce." Nor were its leaders and supporters able to achieve timely publication of its scientific accomplishments for the benefit of other natural scientists of the era. Proper understanding of the historical fate of the Lewis and Clark enterprise after 1806 therefore requires that even as we commemorate the bicentennial significance of its achievements, we also examine the specific contexts of its failures.[3]

Early national projects of republican enterprise such as that of Lewis and Clark were often riven by disagreements over how conflicts between private and public interest should be mediated. In order to understand the historical contexts of failures of republican enterprise, we need a deeper understanding of the ways particular enterprises were undermined by the inability of their agents to openly acknowledge, and equitably reconcile, competing public and private interests. Such incapacity was a chief source of the failures that haunted a republican political economy tied to imperial ambition. Closer examination of particular failures to resolve such conflicts may help us to better understand the limitations and contradictions that pervaded republican political economy during the era of Lewis and Clark.[4]

Toward such work, I will examine here two fragments of a larger history of the imperial contradictions of the early nation's political economy. First I will survey how the work of improvement societies such as the Philadelphia Society for Promoting Agriculture (PSPA) helped to shape the broader context of philanthropic and governmental support that made possible, and helped determine the limitations of, the Lewis and Clark expedition as an imperial enterprise of political economy and science. As one improvement society among others, the PSPA, founded in 1785 and incorporated by the Legislature of Pennsylvania in 1809, sought to educate farmers throughout Pennsylvania, and citizens generally, about new technologies and methods of crop rotation that would promote more economical use of the land. The PSPA also advertised premiums and incentives to promote experimentation in the reform of agricultural methods and, by the 1790s, sought to foster the proliferation of county agricultural societies as forums for popular education that would simultaneously improve both "the political economy and the individual happiness of the people." By promoting the formation of small libraries connected to county agricultural societies, the PSPA sought to draw citizens throughout the state "into a spirit of enquiry" that "would not only promote the interests of agriculture, but would diffuse knowledge among the people and assist good government, which," the PSPA suggested, "is never in danger while a free people are well informed."[5]

This statement of purpose distills the broadly encompassing vision at the core of the civic and philanthropic enterprise of republican improvement societies during the era of Lewis and Clark. Because their expedition developed out of the enterprise of republican improvement societies that provided foundation for the Jeffersonian vision of political economy, we may derive deeper insight into both the material and cultural contexts of the expedition by examining the self-understanding and practices of improvement societies such as the PSPA. The comparison of any institution's self-understanding with its actual practices serves well to reveal the limits and contradictions of its historical enterprise. By thus examining how the actual practices of the agricultural society reveal the contradictions of its republican vision, we may gain critical insight into the larger enterprise of Jeffersonian political economy that shaped both the conception and execution of the Lewis and Clark expedition.[6]

Second, by examining some new archival information I have found concerning the Pittsburgh publication of Patrick Gass's journal of the expedition during the term of Lewis's residence in Philadelphia between April 10 and July 21, 1807, I suggest some of the ways the larger contradictions of political economy could shape the personal histories of men such as Lewis involved in the work of republican enterprise. By thus exploring relationships among the political, economic, and more intimate cultural contexts of philanthropic enterprise in the early nation, I seek to clarify the nature of the imperial contradictions at the core of the Jeffersonian vision of republican political economy—a vision that sought simultaneously to embody extensive empire and democratic self-government. Clearer insight into these contradictions should help us to reflect more critically on how some of the winners and losers of the Lewis and Clark enterprise—and of the larger enterprise of Jeffersonian and later U.S. empire-building—were determined.[7]

Because historical understanding requires specification of the meaning of key terms of analysis, the terms *philanthropy* and *political economy* here require explicit definition. During the era of the early republic, and especially after 1789 when philanthropy became associated with the radicalism of democratic groups in England and the United States called "friends of the people"—who advocated the rights of men and women in support of the democratic objectives of the French Revolution—the term was used broadly to apply not merely to charitable or benevolent activities intended to benefit the poor but to any activity organized to further the objectives of democracy and human well-being. Republican citizens of this era thus took the term literally to mean behavior inspired by the "love of humanity." Philanthropy was thus a vital touchstone for the wide transatlantic movement that sought to provide an alternate framework for addressing the challenges of political, economic, and social reform that could not be addressed by traditional means but required broad new forms of citizen participation and mobilization. Far from being merely an expression of a liberalizing civil society, philanthropy was crucial to the work of both redefining and remaking civil society during the revolutionary era of the last quarter of the eighteenth century.[8]

I therefore use the term throughout this essay in the broad sense it had for the people of the era of Lewis and Clark in order to emphasize an essential difference too often missed in discussions of the historical past. In the late eighteenth and early nineteenth centuries, *philanthropy* referenced the potential of radical democratic reform, which challenged not only more traditionally hierarchical eighteenth-century social and political divisions but also the more liberal understandings of "separate spheres" of political and economic, "private" and "public," governmental and nongovernmental activity, which were then being given shape by agents or "projectors" of a liberal civil society. During this era, in other words, *philanthropy* referenced diverse political, economic, and charitable agendas and programs of activity within an inevitably politicized frame of reference, which perpetually haunted any attempt to confine associational activity within a "private sphere" of civil society detached from political struggles to reshape the nature of governmental power. Indeed, given the term's applicability to associational activity intended to further the well-being of humanity, it can be said that challenging the boundaries of political, economic, and charitable realms of activity was the most fundamental objective of any radical "philanthropic" enterprise. Such enterprise, for this reason, was at the epicenter of struggles to create or reform civil society along democratic lines in the early republic.[9]

Recognition of the challenges involved in the philanthropic enterprise of reforming or re-creating civil society during this era runs us directly into issues of political economy. Until the 1790s, *political economy* was largely a scientific term, the meaning of which had been elaborated during the second half of the eighteenth century by British thinkers such as James Steuart and Adam Smith to refer to tasks of governmental administration that had formerly been understood as part of the broad administrative science of *police*. Before the middle of the nineteenth century, when the development of professional urban forces of uniformed men directed toward the tasks of controlling crime considerably narrowed the term's meaning, *police* was understood more positively to encompass all that contributed to a well-ordered polity and its effective administration. Thus for the mid-eighteenth-century British legal commentator William Blackstone, the phrase "public police and economy" defined an ordered polity in which "the individuals of the state, like members of a well-governed family, are bound to conform their behavior to the rules of propriety, good neighborhood, and good manners; and to be decent, industrious, and inoffensive in their respective stations."[10]

Within the framework of mid-eighteenth century British policy science, *political economy* referred to the fundamental tasks of providing a plentiful subsistence or prosperity for the people of a nation and supplying the state with sufficient revenue to fulfill its duties, while recognizing that human activity was governed primarily by self-interest. On this fundamental definition of political economy, which in summary referred to the work of increasing the wealth and power of a country, both the mercantilist Steuart and Adam Smith, the critic of mercantilism, agreed. The pivotal significance of Smith's work was his transformation of political economy from a science of centralized governmental administration into a project that, by recognizing the agency of all members of civil society in producing the "wealth of nations," engaged the concern and capacity of all members of civil society interested in reforming the way government worked to promote political economy.[11]

I am in this essay primarily interested, however, not in the conceptual development of the science of political economy but in understanding some aspects of how the actually existing political economy of the early United States functioned as a system for fostering (with greater or lesser success) the prosperity and well-being of its citizens. First, I am interested in the ways republican civic and philanthropic associations in the United States by the 1790s began to make sense of and incorporate references to political economy into their work: What, for example, did the members of the PSPA mean when they proposed to create a state agricultural society that would improve both "the political economy and the individual happiness of the people"? But this essay also seeks to clarify the primary intersection between philanthropic enterprise and the problems of republican political economy by examining how republican philanthropic enterprise came to include improvement of the system of political economy—upon which the well-being of the people depended—as a necessary part of the work of reforming civil society and government. This essay also suggests how different visions of political economy could be embodied within different types of civic organizations and associations and could thus become the agents of competing programs for shaping both governmental policy and the character of civil society. Far from being singular and monolithic, we need to pay more attention to the plurality of political economies that developed within the contradictions that fissured the early republic.

I am especially interested in exploring how a focus on the work of philanthropic enterprise creates an avenue into understanding the fundamental problems of political economy as it was redirected toward the goal of providing a more democratic provision of prosperity to the nation. While I am primarily engaged with concerns related to internal improvement, parallel problems and concerns were raised by debates during this era over other core aspects of the economy related to banking, tariffs, the protection of manufactures, import substitution, and the need to balance policies for promoting the often competing interests of internal and foreign commerce. How may the study of the problems and contradictions that arose in any of these areas during early struggles to democratize the political economy of the nation help us to better understand the context of the successes and failures of particular republican enterprises such as that of Lewis and Clark? By focusing here on the analysis of the relationship between philanthropic enterprise and political economy, I hope to suggest some approaches to addressing this much larger question.

The Rise of Philanthropic Enterprise in the Early United States Out of the Needs of Republican Political Economy and its Police

Near the end of 1806, John Redman Coxe's *Philadelphia Medical Museum* published an article on the recently completed expedition "for the benefit of the human race ... without example in history," which "omitted no means to render [itself] useful to science and to agriculture" by collecting plants and recording important geological, ethnographic, and other details of the regions through which it traveled. This expedition would be, according to the article, "as famous in the annals of agriculture as in those of medicine and humanity." The expedition being described was not, however, that of Lewis and Clark, but the "philanthropic mission" headed by Dr. Francisco Xavier de Balmis, honorary Surgeon of the Royal Chamber of Spain, which distributed cowpox vaccine throughout the Spanish colonies of New Spain, South America, and the Philippines and to the Portuguese and British colonies in Asia and the Chinese empire. Launched from Spain on November 20, 1803, this expedition completed its transglobal journey two weeks before Lewis and Clark returned to St. Louis on September 23, 1806. As a global enterprise conducted in conspicuous simultaneity with that of Lewis and Clark, the Balmis expedition suggests the broader international contexts of conjoined philanthropic, scientific, and political competition out of which the Lewis and Clark expedition arose. Recognition of such contexts forces us to examine more carefully the distinct cultural and political characteristics of particular national enterprises of exploration, lest we unwittingly continue to interpret them as the expression of some politically innocent and sublimely universalized ideal of enlightenment scientific exploration. By focusing attention on the work of improvement associations such as the PSPA, this section speci-

FIGURE 3.1. Emblem of the Philadelphia Society for Promoting Agriculture, from a membership certificate. Courtesy Library of the American Philosophical Society.

fies the character of the intersections of philanthropic enterprise and early republican political economy in the United States, intersections that gave the Lewis and Clark expedition its particular character.[12]

While Congress's appropriation of twenty-five hundred dollars on February 28, 1803—in response to President Jefferson's formal request for congressional support—provided financing for the Lewis and Clark expedition, this enterprise would have been impossible without the additional scientific and philanthropic support provided by members of the American Philosophical Society (APS) and the PSPA. The APS had acted as both intellectual project manager and fund-raiser for the ill-fated 1793 Michaux expedition, raising its required financing through voluntary subscription. For both the 1793 expedition and the 1803 Lewis and Clark enterprise, Jefferson, who served as APS president from 1797 to 1815, developed his program of instructions in consultation with fellow APS members. And when Lewis arrived in Philadelphia on May 10, 1803, to prepare for the expedition, three of the four APS scientists with whom he consulted at the recommendation of Jefferson were also long-term members of the PSPA. Benjamin Rush had been one of the agricultural society's founding members in 1785; Dr. Caspar Wistar had been a member since 1789; and Benjamin Smith Barton—the main naturalist with whom Lewis studied, and from whom Lewis received detailed instructions on how to collect and preserve specimens—had been a member of the PSPA since 1790.[13]

The two Philadelphia horticulturists who advised the expedition were also members of the PSPA. During his time in Philadelphia between May 10 and June 15, 1803, Lewis probably visited the Woodlands estate of Jefferson's friend William Hamilton, who had been a member of the PSPA since 1786. Hamilton had been a frequent Philadelphia host to Jefferson and was a "wealthy, dedicated votary of landscape gardening" who had surrounded his Woodlands mansion west of the Schuylkill with gardens and greenhouses containing the "largest and most elaborate collection of native and exotic plants then known to the US." While during the course of the expedition Lewis sent seeds, roots, and cuttings to a handful of individuals including Jefferson, Benjamin Smith Barton, Charles Wilson Peale, and various relatives and friends, most were delivered to William Hamilton.[14] In 1807, however, after the conclusion of the expedition and at the recommendation of Jefferson, Lewis began to send much of the remaining botanical bounty from the expedition to the prominent Philadelphia florist, seed merchant, and horticulturist Bernard McMahon. When failing health kept both Benjamin Smith Barton and William Hamilton from fulfilling their commitments to processing and documenting the botanical discoveries of the expedition, the younger McMahon, who was elected to membership in the PSPA in 1811, replaced Hamilton as the key horticultural benefactor to the expedition. McMahon not only helped to connect Lewis to Frederick Pursh, who would become the first to publish detailed scientific information about the botanical discoveries of the expedition, but was also the Philadelphia resident most successful at cultivating plants from the expedition, which he began selling in his 1815 *American Gardener's Calendar*.[15]

Most of the major supporters of the expedition from Philadelphia were thus also members of the PSPA. Even Nicholas Biddle, who prepared the official narrative of the expedition published in 1814, became an important member of the PSPA in 1816 and eventually served as its president from 1831 to 1844. If such memberships were merely an interesting historical detail, however, with no larger relevance to our understanding of the Lewis and Clark enterprise, they would deserve no more than a brief notice here. But because the Lewis and Clark expedition was in many ways an extension of the work of republican improvement societies such as the PSPA, our notice of these intersecting memberships should be extended. The expedition should in fact be understood as an innovative endeavor to carry forward on a national scale both the scientific-educational and political-economic enterprise of these associational memberships, in ways that would forge the Jeffersonian vision of republican empire into reality. And because agriculture was understood to be the primary foundation of the republican system of political economy and was a core interest of republican improvement societies, the significance of these agricultural society memberships to the development of the Lewis and Clark enterprise deserves more sustained examination.[16]

While of primary importance, agriculture was by the 1790s only one element of a larger democratic republican vision of political economy focused on the project of harmonizing the interests of commerce, agriculture, and early manufacturing by promoting internal improvements that would benefit all the people of the nation. As Peter Onuf has written in *Jefferson's Empire*,

> Jefferson's vision reflected his faith in the beneficent, harmonizing, and civilizing effects of commerce that was widely shared by enlightened political economists of the day. The notion of reciprocally beneficial exchange was particularly attractive to colonists who chafed under a mercantilist regime [that enriched the British metropole at the expense of the American provinces]. . . . Jefferson celebrated the prospective operation of a liberal regime of free trade within the framework of a more perfect republican empire . . . an empire without a center, or dominant metropolis . . . or peripheries [since] . . . it would spread, diffuse and equalize benefits through the vast system of inland waterways, improved and extended by the art of man, to its farthest reaches.[17]

In place of dominant metropolitan cities and ports, Jefferson substituted the role of a great system of inland commerce, fostered by improvements in agriculture, manufacturing, and transportation, especially by water, that would serve to distribute the benefits of economic enterprise equally throughout the expanding body of the continental nation-state. Only such equitable distribution of economic benefits, along with a shared commitment of individual citizens to liberty, principles of justice, and the republican virtue needed to sustain empire, would hold such an expanding national system together.[18]

Jefferson's vision of republican empire thus embodied "a regime of equal rights, reciprocal benefit, and progressive improvement" within the embrace of the imperial idea. Far from throwing off their attachment to the idea of empire, as Onuf has clarified, republican leaders of the early United States thought that "by vindicating their independence, [they would also] . . . vindicate the imperial idea." For these leaders, empire was not a bad word but signified the idealism of the aspirations of the nation-builders to constitute a nation that would redeem the world from wars caused by corrupt and unenlightened political and economic policy. Within this Jeffersonian vision, empire "provided the conceptual framework for [an] enlightened, cosmopolitan republicanism."[19]

Building a new kind of empire in accordance with this enlightened republicanism would require the constitution of a new politics and economy—a virtuous political economy of empire- and nation-building within which there could be no clear distinction between the projects of domestic and foreign policy-making. The intimacy of this intersection is in few places clearer than in the complex interaction of the imperial and domestic interests that shaped the enterprise of Lewis and Clark. Unlike the defective imperial power they had overthrown—with what they viewed as its corrupt, grasping, and centralized tyranny—the reformed empire Jeffersonians hoped to construct was to be purified by the republican enterprise of all white men working together in a national association of virtuous citizens. Free of the need for centralized government, such virtuous citizens through their association would project prosperity, freedom, and reciprocal development to all of the politically equal states that would make up the republican empire of the United States.[20]

Of course, the divergence between this ideal vision of harmonious political economy and the realities of competing economic and political interests both within and between the states was often glaring. The extreme difficulties of uniting and constituting a nation through such a vision of harmonious political economy are evident not only to historians looking back on these early years of the nation but also to the men and women of the early republic who were struggling to keep competing economic and political interests from pulling the nation apart. It was, after all, largely the inability of the postrevolutionary confederation of states to deal with their conflicting economic interests that prompted many of the nation's leaders to unite in crafting the federal Constitution as an instrument that would provide new governmental tools for holding the interests of the nation together.[21]

Almost as soon as the new Constitution was approved, however, these new governmental powers to determine the shape of economic and political activity in the states became an ever-renewable source of political contestation. The wisest democrats among the early leaders of the nation, such as Jefferson in his better moments, realized that such conflict was the lifeblood of democracy and that the key to maintaining a republican nation was to find institutional forms for guiding this conflict to positive ends. The most important role of wise republican government was to provide those institutional forms that, rather than repressing conflict, would guide conflict toward resolutions that would strengthen the public sense of the common interests of all. Unless the nation could find ways of creating virtuous citizens—people who would have the best interests of all in mind as they pursued their own interests—republican governmental theorists and political economists realized that the goal of creating a harmony of interests would remain elusive and the nation would fracture.

This struggle to nurture institutional forms that would cultivate virtuous common interests is at the core of the intimate history of republican political economy. As George Logan argued in an address to Pennsylvania's citizens "on the necessity of promoting agriculture, manufactures, and the useful arts,"

> In a state of civil society, man must be considered as a member of a great political family. He is connected with his fellow citizens, by ties of interest and benevolent attachment; and his social affections must extend to the whole community of which he is a member. He should feel the safety, and the common welfare, intimately connected with his own; and he should think nothing unimportant to himself, which concerns the welfare of his country.[22]

Likewise, the medical doctor James Mease, while serving as secretary of the PSPA, wrote in the 1811 preface to his *Archives of Useful Knowledge, Devoted to Commerce, Manufactures, Rural and Domestic Economy, and Agriculture*, that these subjects

> are all intimately connected, and mutually dependent upon each other for their extension, prosperity, and perfection. It is by Commerce that the farmer finds a sale for his produce; by Agriculture, and the introduction and multiplication of Arts and Manufactures, the merchant procures materials for his distant expeditions; while all classes—those who contend with the waves, who plough the earth, or the artists who decompose the raw materials of nature, and contribute so largely to the luxury, or to the real wants of mankind—are all greatly benefited by the extended knowledge of DOMESTIC ECONOMY.[23]

It was these sentiments of mutual interdependency that defined republican political economy from the intimate underside of empire.[24]

The main problem for such a republican political economy, however, rested in finding the institutional means within both government and civil society to support and nurture an intimate interdependency that would function harmoniously rather than descend into unequal dependencies. Since the modern science of political economy recognized that human social life and production were rooted in self-interest, the fundamental challenge of a specifically *republican* political economy would be to harness the self-interested activities of social and economic life to a larger sense of common interest that could function as the common good. But if administrative government was not going to be allowed to play a central role in managing and regulating economic relationships, as in the mercantilism of imperial Britain, then some other instrumentality would need to be found to fill this policing role.

Jefferson recognized that the key strength of the new republic's government would derive from a situation "where every man, at the call of the law, would fly to the standard of the law, and would meet invasions of the public order as his own personal concern." But the republicans of the new United States recognized that such unified sentiment and personal identification with "the call of the law" could not itself be enforced by the law. Such an intimate sense of the mutual obligations of policing could only be cultivated by the work of self-governing republican philanthropic and improvement associations, which would nurture in citizens the sense of mutual obligation and responsibility adumbrated by Logan, and thus draw citizens together into a "great political family." This is what Jeffersonians understood as the core meaning of educating citizens to virtuous self-government, and this form of education to self-disciplining virtue thus became a primary object of the whole range of early republican philanthropic associations.[25]

This civil project of improving citizens and the nation through philanthropic association became the main hope of Jeffersonians for resolving the contradictions of republican political economy. And it was out of the practical need created by the ambitions for republican empire that the work of republican philanthropic enterprise arose. All of the major philanthropic institutions founded immediately after the Revolutionary War were inspired by this vision of improving enterprise needed to build a virtuously self-governing nation.

As just one among many republican philanthropic institutions created during the 1780s and 1790s, the PSPA incorporated the goal of citizen education into the core of its proposal for a state agricultural society in 1794. Its leaders John Bordley, Richard Peters, and Timothy Pickering hoped that by promoting the formation of county agricultural societies, citizens throughout the state could be drawn "into a spirit of enquiry" that "would not only promote the interests of agriculture, but would *diffuse knowledge among the people and assist good government.*" They believed that promoting knowledge of agricultural improvements could and should be combined with "the Education which is practicable and most useful for the great body of citizens."[26]

As an organization founded in the mid-1780s after the conclusion of the Revolutionary War, the PSPA originated at the same time as other major republican philanthropic associations that would assume leading roles in the reform of society and government in the decades ahead, including the Philadelphia Prison Society, the Pennsylvania Society for the Abolition of Slavery, the Pennsylvania Society for the Encouragement of Manufactures, and a reinvigorated American Philosophical Society. These philanthropic associations were composed of the city's leading lawyers, doctors, merchants, and officeholders and, as David Brion Davis states, served as the primary "municipal meeting grounds for men of wealth, influence, and political power." Since, however, most of these elite philanthropic societies contained few members with agricultural interests, agricultural societies filled a significant gap in the city's "interlocking network of public and private organizations designed to give order and direction to municipal life." This governmental network or system of police came to include societies promoting savings banks, libraries, hospitals, Sunday school societies, chambers of commerce, and the internal improvement of canals and roads, as well as those individuals serving as commissioners and directors of almshouses, poorhouses, and prisons.[27]

Guided by what David Brion Davis has termed the Quaker philanthropic ethic, the other major concern of the leaders of these interlocking municipal directorates in Philadelphia was to protect the population from disease and disorder and thus ensure the ordered functioning of the social system. Preserving such order was the primary foundation for establishing the network of economic and social improvements these philanthropic associations wanted to institute. This philanthropic ethic—which saw no contradiction between individually interested business enterprise and the spirit of civic enterprise for what these men understood as the public good—served as the foundation of the vision of municipal improvement and police that guided republican philanthropic societies throughout the first decades of the early republic.[28]

As was generally true during this era, there was much overlap in the leadership of these philanthropic associations, which helped give them a shared perspective on their role in the new nation. This role is nicely summarized by the PSPA proposal for a state agricultural society, as quoted above, which sought to foster forums of education that would simultaneously improve "the political economy and the individual happiness of the people." The PSPA shared this goal of educating citizens for informed participation in the new nation, which included setting up institutional frameworks that would direct and contain the particular forms such participation would assume. It was this same thinking that guided the framing of the new federal Constitution, which was shaped by men across the nation who played leading roles in both their local philanthropic and political associations—roles that were intimately related throughout the early decades of the Republic.

After its founding in February 1785 by an association of twenty-three of Philadelphia's elite men interested in promoting the improvement of agriculture—a group that included, besides its convener John Bordley, Dr. Benjamin Rush, the lawyers Richard Peters and James Wilson, and prominent Philadelphia businessmen such as Robert Morris, Thomas Willing, Philadelphia mayor Samuel Powel, and George Clymer—the PSPA was quite active for several years under the patronage of members of the APS and of President George Washington, who became one of its leading supporters. This active phase soon came to an end, however, as party divisions between Federalists and Democratic Republicans over the meaning of republican government drove the membership of the PSPA apart during the early 1790s. The PSPA had thus already ceased to function effectively before the yellow fever epidemic of 1793 brought an end to its regularly recorded meetings.[29]

The PSPA maintained little more than a nominal existence under the continuing leadership of its vice president John Bordley after the death of its president Samuel Powel in 1793. Not until 1798, when Richard Peters began to work with other members of the PSPA to build the first permanent covered bridge over the Schuylkill River at High Street (now Market Street), did the PSPA begin to move toward revival. This bridge project was based on a plan first developed by the architect John Sellers for the PSPA in 1786, with the bridge superstructure designed and constructed by the Massachusetts architect Timothy Palmer.

In 1798, Peters was successful at winning state legislative approval for incorporation of the Schuylkill Permanent Bridge Company, of which

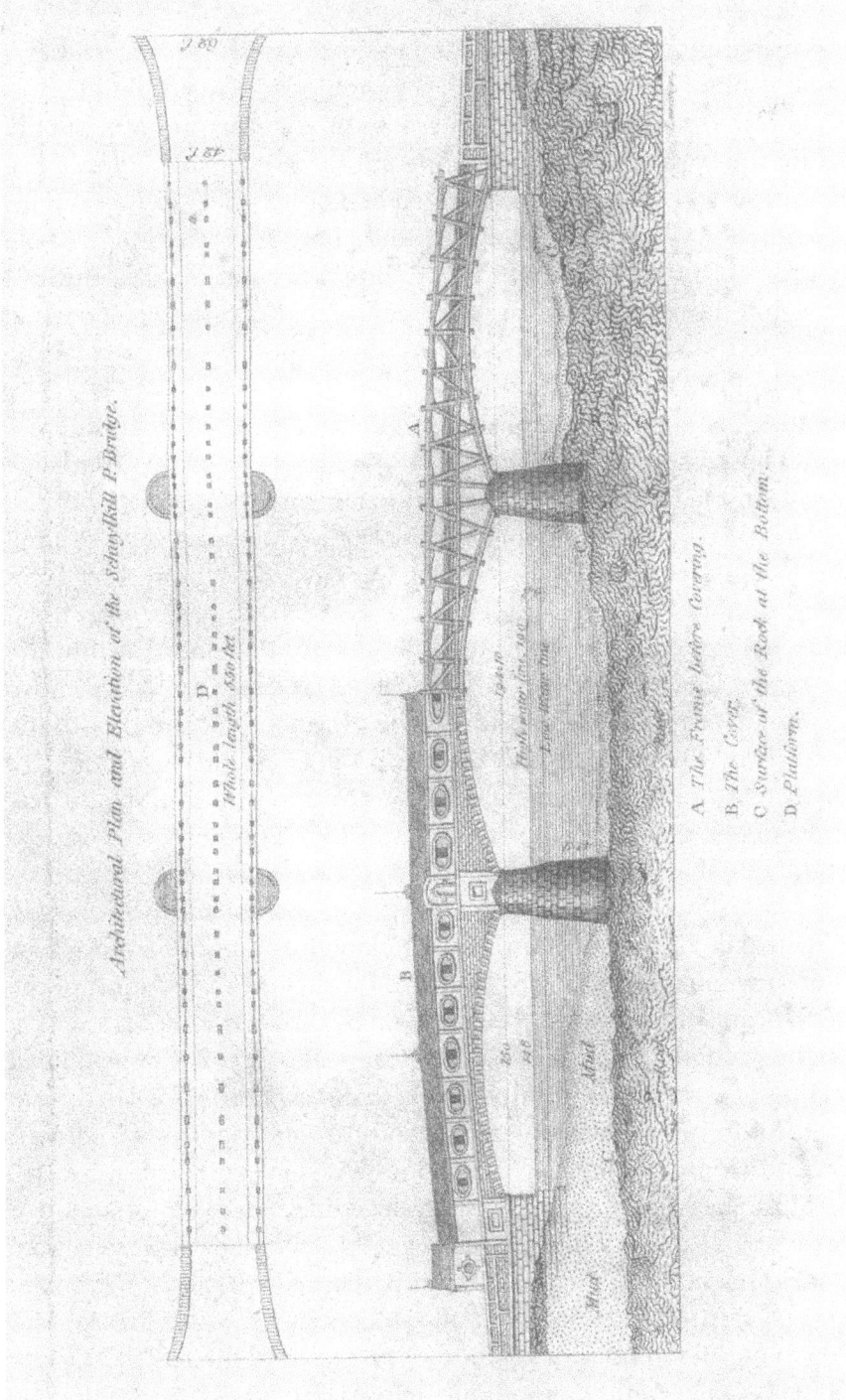

FIGURE 3.2. "Architectural Plan" of the Schuylkill Bridge, engraved by Alexander Lawson. From Richard Peters, *Statistical Account of the Schuylkill Permanent Bridge* (Philadelphia: Jane Aitken, 1807). Courtesy Library of the American Philosophical Society. (See Color Plate 5.)

he was president, and then proceeded to raise three hundred thousand dollars in subscription stock. The bridge took five years to build, most of which time was consumed in the difficult architectural task of constructing the stone piers, and was opened for use at the beginning of 1805 without its cover, which was added during 1805. Thus Lewis in his 1802 and 1803 visits to Philadelphia would have seen the bridge in the early stages of the construction of its stone piers and on his return in 1807 would have passed through the completed covered bridge while traveling to the west side of the Schuylkill to visit the gardened Woodlands estate of William Hamilton.[30]

Because the Schuylkill covered bridge was a great engineering and financial success, and the first such bridge project in the country, it drew considerable prestige to Richard Peters and the members of the PSPA who had been projecting it for over twenty years. By the time of the bridge's completion, the PSPA was thus ripe for revival. John Bordley, the old Federalist leader of the PSPA, had just recently died, and the political split between Republicans and Federalists within the PSPA was itself in the midst of being bridged, as the more conservative Jeffersonian leaders of Philadelphia were driven into coalition with the Federalists by their common interests in opposing the insurgency of Pennsylvania's radical democrats, who were trying to implement major reforms of the state constitution in 1805. The Schuylkill Bridge project had demonstrated the dramatic efficacy of a voluntary association for coordinating and implementing major public improvements. The Schuylkill Permanent Bridge Company thus became a model for what improvement associations could do for the public economy of the country, if only others would be educated by their example.

On the strength of his demonstrated leadership, Richard Peters called a meeting of a renovated group of PSPA members on April 9, 1805, at which the only two surviving members of the original group of founders, Peters and George Clymer, were elected president and vice president. Some of the new members present or elected at that meeting included William Rush, Charles Biddle, prominent APS member John Vaughan, Dr. James Mease, Robert Waln, Richard Wistar, Judge William Tilghman, Stephen Girard, Thomas Lieper, and William Rawle. James Mease, who had served in the important position of physician of the city's Lazaretto and Health Office of the port of Philadelphia, established after the great yellow fever epidemic of 1793, was elected secretary at the next meeting in May and thereafter would be, next to Peters, the prime mover behind

FIGURE 3.3. View of the Schuylkill Permanent Bridge, as Lewis would have seen it in 1807, by an unknown artist. Courtesy Library of the American Philosophical Society. (See Color Plate 6.)

much of the work of the PSPA. In October 1806, the reconstituted PSPA began working for its own act of incorporation, which was finally enacted by a resistant state legislature in February 1809.[31]

Philanthropic leaders of the era of Lewis and Clark hoped that through practices of self-governing association, as modeled by the work of localized and mission-focused philanthropic associations such as the PSPA, major differences of culture, sentiment, and interest could be bridged to forge the common bonds of union upon which Jefferson and his Republican followers placed their redemptive aspirations for the nation. This middle or mediating ground of association would be the intimate space upon which the destiny of the republican nation would be built as citizens learned through their interactions in this space to be virtuously self-governing. Thus it was that intimate relationships of civil association were transformed into governing matters of state as this self-governing virtue was made responsible for obviating the necessity of a coercive centralized governmental administration.

The spirit and practice of republican civic association was thus supposed to provide the governing core to the conduct of the enterprise of republican empire-building. Civic association would provide the opportunity for Americans to discover and work out among themselves the "master principle of equality" that was the key for promoting the kind of harmonious unity in diversity that would allow an extended American empire to fulfill its destiny. We now need to explore how the particular character of the enterprise of these associations was constituted by the contradictions embodied in the bridge built between their visionary imperial aspirations and their actual practices. For it is in the fractures between aspiration and practice that we can read the history of the larger enterprise of the United States as it was then written and is still being written today.[32]

The Political Contradictions of Imperial Enterprises of Republican Improvement

In early 1810 Judge Richard Peters, as president of the PSPA, wrote, "Our association is voluntary, our pursuits neither interested nor selfish, and our efforts zealous, but, from necessity, limited and inadequate." The last two decades of the history of the PSPA had abundantly revealed, however, not only how limited its accomplishments had been in achieving its stated goals of agricultural reform and the education of common farmers, but also that its failures had much to do with public perceptions—rooted in the views of common farmers—that the members of the PSPA pursued goals that were both selfish and interested. Peters's statement thus underlines by the force of its denial a core problem of the PSPA's relationship, and that of other elite improvement societies, to its fellow citizens. Such societies were riven by a fundamental contradiction between the economic and political interests of their elite membership and their goals of educating common people for republican citizenship.[33]

This contradiction between what a previous historian of the PSPA has called its membership interest and its audience was clearly evident in the struggles of the PSPA to accomplish its objectives during the 1790s and early 1800s. On a suggestion from Timothy Pickering, who had received a copy of the Constitution of the Massachusetts State Agricultural Society (MSAS) with a notice of his election as an honorary member to that organization in 1793, Richard Peters used the MSAS's constitution as a model for writing a "Plan for Establishing a State Society of Agriculture in Pennsylvania." Together with Bordley and George Clymer, Peters and Pickering sent to the state legislature this plan along with a memorial that requested an act of incorporation for the proposed state society in early 1794. By this time both New York and Massachusetts had already granted charters to their state agricultural societies, so when the Pennsylvania legislature turned down the PSPA's request both Peters and Bordley gave voice to their negative attitudes toward the rural yeomen of Pennsylvania who had rejected their plan. While Bordley noted merely that the plan was rejected by the very "husbandmen who were principally to be benefited," Peters commented more acerbically that he was defeated in his long-standing attempts to win its approval "by the sottishness of some country members (for whose peculiar interests, I had been labouring)."[34]

The remarks of both leaders of the PSPA, together with many indications in the published Memoirs and Addresses of the Society during the first decades of the nineteenth century, leave little doubt about the great chasm that existed between the membership of the PSPA and the common farmers. While the members of the PSPA viewed themselves as the enlightened, unselfish educators of the common farmers in methods of agricultural reform and improvement, the working farmers viewed the members of the PSPA as self-interested rich men who showed little understanding or true interest in improving the economic or political condition of the common farmer. If we are to understand the contradictions of republican political economy, we must examine more carefully the significance of such divergent perceptions of the meaning of public improvement in the early republic.

The political and economic sources of such divergent perceptions may be clarified by examining the split that occurred within the ranks of the PSPA between 1788 and the state legislature's rejection of the proposed plan for a state agricultural society in 1794. At the center of the politics of this split was one of the leading men of both the PSPA and of Philadelphia society generally. Dr. George Logan was the son of the wealthy and long-established Quaker family that owned the Stenton estate along the Germantown Road in northern Philadelphia. Even before the foundation of the PSPA, George Logan had founded in the neighborhood of Stenton the Germantown Society for Promoting Domestic Manufactures. Of all the founding members of the PSPA, Logan was the only one other than Bordley who pursued no major occupation besides gentleman farming during the 1780s and 1790s.[35]

While many of the leading members of the PSPA including Logan were staunch advocates of the federal Constitution in 1787, Logan grew increasingly antifederalist after that year as he observed the ways in which Federalists were presuming to take advantage of the new powers of the Constitution to pursue their private interests in the name of the public interest. While himself a member of the elite landowning class, debates over the Constitution that began in 1787, in combination with his great admiration for the democratic republicanism of Benjamin Franklin, caused Logan to reconsider the foundations of his political beliefs. Logan grew suspicious of the self-aggrandizing interests of men such as George Clymer and Robert Morris, with whom he came into close contact during the regular monthly meetings of the PSPA.[36]

As Logan observed how Federalists such as Morris and Clymer deployed their skepticism about the people's ability to govern themselves to justify the implementation of laws and policies that seemed to betray the democratic republican faith of the Revolution, Logan began to formulate the political and economic principles that would guide his struggle against what he viewed as a counterrevolution that was being institutionalized through the policies of Hamilton's Federalist "financial revolution." From the moral economy of the French Physiocrats, the doctrine of benevolence taught by the English moralists, and his own Quaker tradition, Logan began to forge a new republican understanding of political economy into a weapon of opposition. Out of this work of synthesis developed the basic principle that became the guide to his thought on public policy: "the only true source" of individual happiness and of the enduring prosperity of both individuals and states was "to promote the happiness of our neighbors." Logan understood that such an intimate bonding of self-interest to a sense of common interest could be achieved only through strict conformity with principles of justice. Only a cultivated sense of the reciprocal relationship of rights and duties would work to bind self-interested individuals together as members of a virtuous republican community. On the basis of this principle of "sound policy," Logan began in 1788 to publicize under the name of Cato his opposition to what he saw as the aristocratic and self-serving policies being championed by the commercial elite of Philadelphia. It was this outspoken opposition to the policies and politics of many of the leading mercantile members of the PSPA that divided its ranks and rendered it ineffective as an improvement association by the early 1790s.[37]

Logan was the only leading man of the early PSPA who had direct contact with the difficult economic plight of the common farmers of rural

Pennsylvania during the 1780s and who attempted to speak for their interests within the PSPA. While his elite social position made it difficult for him to comprehend fully the working conditions and problems of common farmers, the remarkable aspect of Logan's intellectual journey during the 1790s was the long way his sympathy took him toward a position open to alliances with men whom the Federalist elite continued to think were beneath their contempt. As Logan came to doubt that the members of the PSPA had any real interest in promoting the well-being of the common farmer, he invited local farmers to his house in the summer of 1788 and founded the Philadelphia County Society for Promoting Agriculture (PCSPA) as a more democratic form of improvement association dedicated to serving the interests of common farmers. The constitution for the PCSPA restricted membership to actual working farmers.[38]

Logan understood that while local county agricultural societies were one means of promoting the republican education of farmers, no system of agricultural reforms—however progressive and scientific—could make farmers prosperous members of society without a government guided by just and enlightened principles. While warning common farmers not to be deceived "by the pompous, but empty declarations of the Philadelphia Agricultural Society," Logan came to realize by the early 1790s that promoting the real interests of farmers meant encouraging them to take up more direct political action to protect their rights. Especially as he observed how the federal Constitution and, after 1790, the new Pennsylvania Constitution were being exploited as a class charter by merchants and wealthy men to authorize policies that were reducing farmers to poverty and political powerlessness, Logan began to envision county agricultural societies as a base for creating a national network of democratic societies that linked yeomen together for the defense of their rights as men and citizens.[39]

In response to the excise taxes and other policies being imposed on farmers as part of Hamilton's financial revolution, Logan published in three series, between 1790 and 1793, his *Letters to the Yeomanry of Pennsylvania*. These *Letters* attacked almost every component of the Hamiltonian system that PSPA vice president Bordley supported, from excise taxes to protective duties, public finance, and the banking system, for the ways in which these instruments tended to enrich the merchants at the expense of the farmers and small craftsmen. The *Letters* embody his fundamental opposition to the political economy of the Hamiltonian Federalists on the principle that the powers of government should never be used in ways that aggravate economic inequalities by establishing special privileges and accumulating power and wealth in the hands of the few.[40]

Having come to see the Hamiltonian system as a counterrevolution in the nation's political economy that was working to reverse many of the achievements of the revolutionary era, Logan became an avid supporter of developing local democratic societies into a national movement of opposition to the Federalist reforms, and especially to the excise taxes being placed on farmers. Within the elite circle of Philadelphia society, Logan was not alone in his democratic republican sympathies, since Jefferson, along with the astronomer and APS president David Rittenhouse, Franklin's grandson Benjamin Franklin Bache, and Alexander Dallas—the keen legal mind, Republican power broker, and chief administrative advisor to Pennsylvania governors Mifflin and McKean—were frequent visitors to Logan's Stenton estate in the early 1790s.[41]

By the end of the 1790s, Logan had consolidated his principles into an overall philosophy that guided his work in civil association with others to implement his views on "sound policy." In 1800, while serving in his post as state senator in Lancaster, Logan befriended Henry Muhlenberg and together they founded the Lancaster County Society for the Promotion of Agriculture, Manufactures, and the Useful Arts. This society's constitution dramatically embodied Logan's understanding of the principles of a democratic republican vision of political economy and improvement. In a preface to the constitution of this society, from which I quoted above, Logan explained the conception of civil society and social affection that provided a foundation for the work of democratic republican improvement associations. Immediately after the passage cited above, Logan continued:

> In a State of civil society . . . [a citizen] should think nothing unimportant to himself, which concerns the welfare of his country. This it is that constitutes what is called Patriotism, a principle that excites and cherishes every generous sentiment we possess. . . . The public good and our own, are, with respect to their ultimate effects, closely united. . . . Solid advantages can never be attained in a Commonwealth, unless the members of the community are impressed with an affectionate regard for each other. Every individual should constantly remember that he is *a Citizen* . . . [and] that he ought to love his companions, and be as anxious and active for their combined happiness and honor, as for his own welfare; and he should firmly believe that this is his true Interest, as well as his inviolable Duty.

This commentary on the intimate bonds of republican civil society and the integral connection between the individual and common interests of citizens within a republican commonwealth goes to the heart of Logan's conception of the purposes of civil association in a republican government. "Men would never have associated together, if they had not expected that, in consequence of such Association, they would mutually conduce to the advantage and happiness of each other." According to Logan, this is the "real purpose" and "genuine foundation" of civil society.[42]

Logan believed that one of the best ways to foster such sentiments and behavior and thus constitute a virtuous republican civil society was to encourage the development of small patriotic societies where men would be "encouraged to communicate their sentiments freely," in recognition that every man's participation will on some occasion be valuable. The constitution of the Lancaster County Agricultural Society provided his model for the way such societies should be organized. While emphasizing the reciprocal responsibilities of citizens to each other within republican civil society, Logan also emphasized that the prosperity and power of democratic civil society "arises from the independence and prosperity of its members . . . as every citizen affords his aid to support its municipal regulations, by which the property of all is protected."[43]

On the basis of such propertied principles of civil order, however, the democratic republicanism of wealthy men such as Logan had clear limits, which would be demonstrated in the political struggles of the era of Lewis and Clark. By 1805, a common commitment to the judicial protection of property interests had drawn republicans of Pennsylvania such as Logan and Alexander Dallas—who had once been associated with the staunchly antifederalist Democratic societies of the 1790s—into a conservative coalition with Federalists. Logan and Dallas gave leadership to the organization of a third party of "Constitutional Republicans" to oppose the radical insurgency of those Jeffersonians in the state, headed by *Aurora* editor William Duane, who were trying to institute the democratic reform of Pennsylvania's constitution. By seeking to democratize both the politics and economy of the republic, as one recent historian of this movement has written, the radicals "planned to force questions of traditional law, including disputes over property use, title, and contract, into popular political realms where those making decisions would be immediately and frequently accountable to a majority of the people." It was this "Quid" coalition of conservative Republicans and Federalists that narrowly kept the radicals from winning the 1805 Pennsylvania gubernatorial election and reforming the state constitution.[44]

This fundamental political contest between so-called constitutional republicans and radical democrats played itself out in Philadelphia during the years of the Lewis and Clark expedition and emphasized how divided were the followers of Jefferson in Pennsylvania over both the meaning and practice of republican democracy. More significantly for our overarching subject, the leaders of the Constitutional Republicans of 1805—Logan, Dallas, and Governor McKean—were the very circle of Philadelphia society with whom Meriwether Lewis, through his friendship with Mahlon Dickerson, had become intimately associated in his 1802 and 1803 visits to Philadelphia.

Historians of Lewis and Clark and of the PSPA during this era have so far not emphasized the significance of this set of crucial historical intersections. Richard Peters was reconstituting the PSPA at the very same moment the Constitutional Republicans were bringing Republicans such as Logan and Federalists such as Peters together in organized opposition to the radical threat of the Duane Democrats. The leaders of this conservative coalition—whom the Duane radicals derisively referred to as Tertium Quids ("third somethings")—were, in turn, the circle with whom Lewis was directly associated throughout this period, from 1802 to 1807. While I will address the significance of Lewis's connection to the Quid leaders in the next section, I want to conclude this section by suggesting the larger significance of this political contest to our understanding of the history of the PSPA during the era of Lewis and Clark.

The Memoirs of the PSPA make clear that the leading members of the PSPA viewed themselves as the privileged dispensers of scientific knowledge to a needy yeomanry they considered to be largely uneducated, ignorant, and even "indolent." Thus, as Richard Peters summarized, "it beho[o]ves every good citizen, for his own security, as well as from motives of patriotism and moral obligation, to assist in furnishing the means of warning the negligent, stimulating the indolent, and enlightening the ignorant husbandman." As Logan's break with the PSPA in the early 1790s demonstrated, the main problem the association had in achieving its goals of disseminating knowledge had everything to do with its constitutional inability to engage common farmers as equals in the work of improving the nation's agriculture.[45]

A parallel problem plagued the members of the Constitutional Republican coalition in their battle with the Duane Democrats. As the older brother of naturalist Benjamin Smith Barton wrote in one of his two pamphlets that served as briefs for the arguments of the Quids against the reforms of the radicals during these years,

> Were it not, that such wild and disorganizing notions are propagated for the most mischievous purposes, it would appear unnecessary to notice them. But it has really become an indispensable measure of prudence, and safety to the state, to caution the honest unsuspecting members of the community, against the fateful consequences of such tenets . . . [and] the seductive schemes of innovation that are attempted.[46]

Thus easily were matters of state during this era converted into matters framed in the intimate terms of seduction.[47]

In this battle over the political character of the Commonwealth of Pennsylvania, we catch a glimpse of how republican principles voiced by someone such as Logan could be turned against those who dared to challenge elite interpretations of how the republican common good should be constituted. In order to make the position and arguments of the radical democrats seem both absurd and threatening, Barton and other Quids sought constantly to represent what democrats wanted to implement as changes that would undermine the republic by destroying the traditional legal and constitutional forms upon which "the liberties of the people" rested. Just as Peters on behalf of the PSPA labeled the yeomen ignorant and indolent, Barton, Governor McKean, and the other Quids continually referred to the Duane Democrats as ignorant and attacked them for being slaves to forms of passion, rashness, pride, envy, and error that would add up to "the ruin of public liberty."[48]

Thus simultaneously with the execution of the Lewis and Clark enterprise, fundamental contests over the meaning of democratic republican political practice, the outcome of which would shape the destiny of Pennsylvania and the nation for years to come, were being decided in Philadelphia and Lancaster. While the expedition was in one sense surveying options that the development of a transcontinental Jeffersonian political economy would provide for the future of the republic, the outcome of the political debates in Philadelphia and Lancaster was determining the structure and limits of the stage upon which that political economy would play itself out long after the enterprise of Lewis and Clark had been concluded.

As stated so eloquently by Logan, republicanism was supposed to be about serving the common interest of all by binding men together into a community of reciprocally shared rights and duties. In contrast to this ideal vision, however, both the political divisions that came to a head in Pennsylvania during the period of the Lewis and Clark expedition and the limitations in the practices of improvement societies that did not allow them to win the confidence or participation of the common people help us to recognize the contradictions that haunted enterprises of republican political economy.

Lewis's "Troubles": Patrick Gass's Journal and the Intimate Contradictions of Political Economy in 1807

After sketching out some of the critical contexts for understanding the Lewis and Clark expedition as a particular enterprise of republican philanthropy and political economy, I turn now to examination of the ways such contradictions more directly haunted the historical fate of the enterprise of what Lewis called "my late tour to the Pacific ocean."[49] During Lewis's residence in Philadelphia between April 10 and July 21, 1807, the struggle between Lewis and the Pittsburgh bookseller David McKeehan over the publication of Patrick Gass's journal came to a head as McKeehan published and made it available for sale by early July 1807. Because this struggle between Lewis and McKeehan over the Gass journal is intrinsically interesting as part of the Lewis saga and also demonstrates how the contradictions of republican political economy came to shape the more intimately political aspects of the publication history of the Lewis and Clark journals, this segment of the Lewis saga deserves more careful attention than it has so far received.

For this purpose, the largely unanalyzed correspondence between Mathew Carey and David McKeehan concerning the Gass journal is a resource that adds substantially to our understanding of this journal's publication history, and thereby allows us to amend previous scholarship on the journal and its relationship to the development of Nicholas Biddle's narrative account of the expedition. While the various struggles between McKeehan and Lewis, Carey and McKeehan, and even Carey and Biddle over the Gass journal, and the larger symbolic struggle over the rights to publicity concerning the expedition, deserve more complete treatment elsewhere, space limitations here guide me to focus primarily on what a study of the struggle between McKeehan and Lewis, placed in its proper political and cultural context, might add to our understanding of the contradictions of republican political economy Lewis was having to negotiate during his 1807 residence in Philadelphia. These contradictions may have played a role in blasting Lewis's hopes for success in producing his own narrative of what he called the "darling project" of his "late tour to the Pacific ocean." A closer examination of this struggle may therefore specify and personalize the way the contradictions of republican political economy over issues of public and private interest—which I have explored in broad strokes in previous sections of this essay—could dramatically influence the historical fate of a major public enterprise such as the Lewis and Clark expedition.[50]

When the Pittsburgh bookseller David McKeehan responded to Lewis's attempt to preempt the publication of competing accounts of the expedition, McKeehan pointedly asked Lewis, in a language filled with democratic sarcasm, "by what high grant or privilege [do] you claim the right of authorizing, licensing or suppressing journals or other publications concerning it . . . where it is for the public advantage that the information collected shall be diffused as widely as possible?"[51] This dispute between McKeehan and Lewis originated in a fundamental disagreement about who had the right and obligation to diffuse information about the expedition "as widely as possible" to the public. Because McKeehan agreed with the basic republican idea that a wide diffusion of knowledge among the people would best serve the public interest, he took Lewis to task for the ways in which Lewis seemed to be subverting this principle to pursue private interests. This dispute allows us to explore how even the most ambitious philanthropic pursuits of Jeffersonian enterprise could be undermined by the intimate contradictions resulting from the inability of the agents of such enterprise to openly acknowledge and equitably reconcile competing public and private interests. By examining particular failures to reconcile such conflicts of interest, we gain insight into the contradictions that fractured not only republican enterprises but also republican individuals. For we may see in Lewis's self-division between the claims of public and private interest an intimate embodiment of the imperial contradictions that pervaded the enterprise of republican political economy. And perhaps in Lewis's tragic fate we have a reminder of the way such contradictions haunted individuals then and, through the historical legacies of the nation's imperial political economy, haunt us still.

The contest over the authority to publish expedition journals was initiated by Lewis on March 18, 1807, when, in an open letter published in the newspapers along with the first prospectus of his book project, he attempted to discourage the publication of competing expedition narratives by attacking both their public authority and legitimacy. A prospectus for the publication of the journal of expedition member Robert Frazer had much earlier (October 1806) been announced in the newspapers with the permission of Lewis. By March 1807, however, having heard that several other journals were being circulated for publication, Lewis had apparently reversed his permissive policy. His public letter not only undercut his prior authorization of the Frazer journal, which seems to have killed its publication, but warned the public against the "deceptions" that would be imposed on them by those other "unauthorized" and "spurious" publications "now preparing for the press." In their campaign to preempt competing narratives, Lewis and Clark had already purchased for three hundred dollars the journal of expedition member John Ordway, thus taking it out of circulation. When Lewis learned that Gass's journal was being prepared for publication in Pittsburgh, Lewis apparently decided to try to preempt this by having the newspapers publish his letter to the public along with a version of his own book prospectus, although he had not yet secured a publisher for his projected volumes.[52]

The man who had taken up the work of preparing the Gass journal for press was a former Pennsylvania lawyer named David McKeehan, who had graduated from Dickinson College in 1787 and had been admitted to the Pennsylvania Bar by 1792. Forced by the onset of deafness to abandon his career as a lawyer, McKeehan turned to the Philadelphia publishing firm of Mathew Carey at the end of 1804 for assistance in initiating a new career as a book and stationery store owner in Pittsburgh. At McKeehan's insistence and in response to his assurances of good prospects for sales in Pittsburgh, Carey supplied McKeehan with the stock of supplies and books needed to initiate his bookselling enterprise. Already by mid-1806, however, McKeehan was disappointed in his prospects. And by early January 1807, by which time he had obtained and begun the work of transcribing the Gass journal, McKeehan was hoping that the publication of a large edition of the journal, even against Carey's advice, would resurrect his business prospects and allow him to pay down his debts to Carey.[53]

When Lewis published his open letter of warning in mid-March 1807, McKeehan had completed his transcription of the journal and had begun the work of preparing it for the press, with some cautious advice and assistance from Carey. McKeehan probably read Lewis's letter and prospectus soon after it was published in the *National Intelligencer* of March 18 and immediately realized its potentially negative implications for his own publishing venture. Instead of being put off by Lewis's attempt to discourage competing publications, however, McKeehan used Lewis's public warning as an opportunity to respond to Lewis in kind, and immediately published his own prospectus of the Gass journal in the *Pittsburgh Gazette* of March 24.

FIGURE 3.4. Portrait of Mathew Carey, by Philadelphia artist John Neagle (1796–1865). Courtesy of the American Philosophical Society Library.

McKeehan's Gass prospectus shows evidence of being a direct though relatively restrained initial response to Lewis's attack on so-called unauthorized narratives of the expedition, since it attempts to counter Lewis's attack by emphasizing the propriety of Gass's (and thus his own) authority to produce such a narrative in several ways. McKeehan's prospectus notes by the extended title it provides his edition of the Gass journal that it contains "an *authentic* relation of the most interesting transactions during the expedition." The prospectus furthermore states the fact that Gass was employed in the expedition and that Gass's account was developed in close association with the several other journals being prepared during the expedition. And, finally, it quotes directly from the testimonial that Lewis presented to Gass and the other members of the expedition at its conclusion. This testimonial, though formulaic, includes Lewis's own words of "highest confidence and sincere thanks" for the "manly" support provided by Gass to the expedition and recommends Gass "to the consideration and respect of his fellow citizens." McKeehan's prospectus thus cites Lewis's words to good effect on behalf of the authority of Gass's journal. Just a few days after he published this prospectus, McKeehan quoted Lewis's testimonial in full for the March 26 preface he wrote for the Gass volume.[54]

McKeehan may in March have considered this relatively indirect and polite response to Lewis, provided in the form of a prospectus and preface for the published Gass journal, to be the most appropriate way to reply to Lewis's attempt to undercut public confidence in the propriety of expedition journals published without his permission. By early April, however, after the repeated publication of Lewis's preliminary prospectus and letter of warning in the pages of the *National Intelligencer* (on March 18, 25, 27, and 30 and April 1) and the Philadelphia *Aurora* (on March 23), McKeehan was spurred into publishing a much more extensive and severely pointed response to Lewis. When Carey mentioned to McKeehan his concerns about Lewis's efforts to discourage competing narratives, McKeehan's response to Carey on April 3 was blunt and self-assured: "I am not afraid of Lewis's notice, which gives me an opportunity of attacking him. There is a large edition of mine printing, and the subscription papers are filling rapidly." As if to further underline his determination, McKeehan asked Carey in this same letter to secure the copyright for his book, which Carey promptly accomplished on April 11.[55]

McKeehan's more direct and extensive "attack" on Lewis was a public letter, dated April 7, published in the *Pittsburgh Gazette* of April 14 around the time of Lewis's arrival in Philadelphia. McKeehan's criticism takes Lewis thoroughly to task for his high-handed way of dismissing those men Lewis had once both recommended to the consideration and respect of his fellow citizens and thanked for their "manly" support. Throughout his letter, McKeehan plays on the apparent betrayal by Lewis not only of his expeditionary compatriots but also of the democratic republican spirit of harmony that had sustained the expedition and made its completion possible. For this reason especially, McKeehan's response to Lewis deserves much more serious consideration than the rather dismissive treatment it has so far received.[56]

Previous scholars have noted that "Gass had no permission to publish" and—rather anachronistically since no other journals of the expedition had yet been published in 1807—that he "could add little to the scientific results," and that he gave but "a few pieces of information not found elsewhere." McKeehan's letter to Lewis has also been harshly criticized as consisting of mostly "gratuitous abuse of Lewis" because McKeehan claimed that Lewis "sought to keep all profit or benefit from the expeditions for himself." Cutright, whose essay on Gass and McKeehan gave some attention to McKeehan's letter, labels it "from beginning to end . . . injudicious, intemperate, even vicious" and implicitly labels McKeehan a "jackass." And while first drawing scholarly attention to this letter by publishing it in his *Letters* and writing a brief essay on the conflict between Lewis and McKeehan that quoted McKeehan's letter in full, even Donald Jackson referred to the McKeehan-Gass journal as "in many ways . . . a miserable piece of work." Most recently, another scholar has referred to McKeehan's publication as "the preemptive strike of an opportunist."[57]

Scholars thus seem to have echoed Lewis's defensive and possessive views of the expedition as his own "darling project," rather than as an expedition and a story that could not be rightfully owned by any one authority. Long before Donald Jackson proclaimed that "it is no longer useful to think of the Lewis and Clark expedition as the personal story of two men," McKeehan had asserted that claim as the firm basis for his publication of Gass's narrative in opposition to the efforts of Lewis to own it as his story of "*my* late tour to the Pacific ocean," a phrase that served as primary justification for McKeehan's decision to "interfere in this affair of the journals of what you very modestly call *your* late tour." Indeed, understood within the context of the democratic republican values at stake at this time, McKeehan's criticism of Lewis can no longer be considered as "merely gratuitous." When examined carefully, McKeehan's criticism expresses core expectations regarding the mutual character of democratic republican enterprises, from which all (white) men were supposed to profit equitably.[58]

McKeehan begins his attack on Lewis's preemptive strategy by lambasting the presumption of Lewis's elitist language: "Your rapid advancement to power and wealth seems to have changed the polite, humble and respectful language of *Sir Clement* into that of him who commands and dispenses favours; even your subscription lists, when you offer your learned works for publication must be '*promulgated*.'" In reviewing the content of Lewis's public letter, McKeehan gives special attention to the way Lewis granted and then withdrew the authority he had given "poor Frazer" to benefit from the publication of Frazer's journal. McKeehan also seeks to deflate Lewis's pretensions to precedence by taking explicit note of the Canadian Mackenzie's earlier exploration of much of the same area Lewis had traveled. Beyond noting that it was Mackenzie who "for the *first time* penetrated to the Pacific Ocean . . . with a party consisting of about one fourth part of the number under your command," and with much less financial support, McKeehan adds most bitingly that Mackenzie's exploration was also "without the *authority*, the *flags, or medals* of his government." And because Lewis had the advantage of being able to read Mackenzie's published journal, McKeehan suggests that Lewis was able more easily to plan for and guard against the dangers and difficulties of the journey.[59]

McKeehan then turns to address the issue of the greatly unequal rewards provided to Lewis and Clark in contrast to those given to the other members of the expedition. After noting both the land grant to Lewis and Clark of 1,600 acres (in comparison to the grants of 320 acres to the other members of the expedition) and his appointment as governor of Upper Louisiana, McKeehan comments that "these grants and rewards savour more of the splendid munificence of a Prince than the *economy of a republican government.*" After mentioning the many other honors attendant with his fame as leader of the expedition, McKeehan asks, "Who could have thought that after so much liberality shewn by the country, your Excellency would have been found contending with the poor fellows, who for their small pittance were equally exposed with yourself to the toils and dangers attending the expedition, about the publication of their journals?" McKeehan further suggests that Lewis's purchase of Ordway's journal to keep it from publication, combined with Lewis's attempt to dismiss the value of Frazer's journal, and now his additional attempt to preempt Gass's journal add up to "insatiable avarice" on the part of Lewis for both public fame and private profit.[60]

After this broad blast of criticism, McKeehan returns to his central point, which I will quote extensively because of the way it attends to what was centrally at stake on the intimate side of democratic republican political economy as it was lived by its winners and losers:

> Without thinking it worth while to ask by what right you call this tour, which you acknowledge was 'performed by order of the government,' *your* tour, let me enquire by what high grant or privilege you claim the right of authorizing, licensing or suppressing journals or other publications concerning it? Every man of sense must agree that these journals are either *private* property of the individuals who took them, or *public* property; for none but an ideot [*sic*] could for a moment suppose, that any officer upon the expedition could have a property in any but his own. If therefore they are the private property of the individuals severally who kept them, there is an end to the question. Are they public property and has the government done any act either to manifest or relinquish its claim? In my opinion there may be cases where the journals, maps, surveys, and all other documents taken during a military expedition, especially where policy and the interest of the country requires secrecy, ought to be considered the property of the public and delivered up to the government; but where no such policy, interest or secrecy exist; and where it is for *the public advantage that the information collected shall be diffused as widely as possible;* where the government never calls for any documents for their inspection but those taken by the commanding officers; . . . and where commanding officers have been allowed by the government to publish their journals, maps and other documents for their private emolument; will it be said that *in a country governed by equal laws, and where equal rights and privileges are secured to all the citizens,* these persons who have been discharged from public service and become private citizens, have not also a right to publish the documents they have taken and preserved?[61]

Finally, McKeehan suggests that in contrast to Lewis's antirepublican avarice, his own publication of Gass's journal will have three publicly beneficial results. First, it will save many the trouble of having to wait to purchase Lewis's expensive three-volume account by affording them a reasonably priced "plain and satisfactory account of the tour" without the burden of lengthy reports of scientific research, in which McKeehan asserts most of the public has little interest. Second, by providing competition, Gass's journal will work to force down the price of Lewis's publications. Third, by taking a plain "matter of fact" approach to the tour, it may "deter [Lewis] from swelling [his] work with such tales of wonder as have sometimes issued from the Ten-mile-square."[62]

After McKeehan's open letter was published on April 14, and received no public response from Lewis, the correspondence between Carey and McKeehan suggests that Philadelphia's publishers and booksellers may have taken offense and may even have worked to oppose distribution of McKeehan's book in Philadelphia. On June 16—the same day that Lewis's new prospectus for his book with the Philadelphia publisher C. & A. Conrad began to be advertised in the Philadelphia newspapers—McKeehan published a second defiant notice of his publication of the Gass journal in the *Pittsburgh Gazette* that again emphasized the bad republican manners of Lewis's attempted defaming of Gass. Finally, late in June McKeehan again advertised the Gass volume in the *Pittsburgh Gazette* and emphasized that copies of his book would be ready for sale by early July, would be very "elegantly and substantially half bound . . . in handsome marble paper with red and green leather backs," and—in contrast to the advertised price of thirty-one dollars for the set of Lewis volumes—would cost only a dollar. Jackson notes that volumes of the Gass narrative were indeed available for purchase by July 7.[63]

Given this evidence, we may ask whether there might be any connection between the early July publication of the Gass journal and what Lewis's intimate friend Mahlon Dickerson noted in his diary for July 13, 1807: "My friend Capt. L[ewis] in trouble." While Jackson suggests that this "trouble" was connected to problems Lewis was having with women in Philadelphia, the evidence sketched out here suggests that additional concerns may have been contributing to Lewis's troubled state. We need to consider more carefully the several factors that may have been unsettling Lewis at this time—factors that may have provided the substance of some of the discussions between Lewis and Dickerson on their frequent and lengthy night walks around Penn Square during the last several weeks of Lewis's residence in Philadelphia.[64] By July 13, even if no copies of the published Gass journal were yet available for purchase in Philadelphia, it seems unlikely that Lewis would not have been keenly aware of the significance of the availability of Gass's journal in Pittsburgh and the West. Given his attempts to preempt such a publication and his lack of substantial progress on his own book project, the appearance of this published narrative while he was in Philadelphia would have disturbed someone of Lewis's temperament.

But there is also one additional and more directly political matter that may have been giving Lewis serious problems by July 13. On July 4,

Lewis attended the holiday dinner of the radical democratic Society of the Friends of the People, which was presided over by William Duane, the inveterate enemy of not only Governor Thomas McKean but of the entire social circle of Quids with whom Lewis had been associated since his first visit to Philadelphia in 1802. The presence of Governor McKean's friend Lewis at the Friends of the People dinner of July 4, 1807, is all the more striking because Duane was then in the midst of a campaign to get the Pennsylvania legislature to impeach Governor McKean. The toasts at this dinner, which were published in the July 7 issue of the *Aurora* along with notice that Lewis had been in attendance, included not only a general denunciation of "Quiddism" but a specific toast proposing that the next Pennsylvania legislature should impeach McKean by convicting him of "high crimes and misdemeanors." Given the factionalized political context of Philadelphia as sketched out above, Lewis's presence at this dinner, during which he gave his own toast to Jefferson, may have contributed to undermining whatever social position Lewis had been able to retain up to that point in Philadelphia.[65]

If we add together the public doubts about the value of Lewis's mission, doubts about the viability of his writing project after the publication of Gass's journal, and the scandal that may have been raised after July 4 regarding his loyalty to the circle of Quid Republicans into whose intimate acquaintance he had formerly been welcomed, the sum is a set of circumstances that may have been haunting Lewis in serious and compounded forms by July 13 as he was beginning preparations to leave Philadelphia and return to Washington. In combination, these circumstances suggest how Lewis upon his return to Philadelphia from the West may have been engulfed by the maelstrom of contradictions that pervaded the city's and nation's political economy in 1807—contradictions that Lewis, like many others, was ill-prepared to negotiate. In their intimate effects, these contradictions may have torn Lewis's sense of accomplishment, and ultimately his sense of self, apart.

Epilogue: Intimate Legacies of the Contradictions of Imperial Political Economy

Ronda has suggested that "in many ways Lewis's prospectus was the formal announcement of a new wisdom about the expedition." Lewis's prospectus attempted to displace the expedition's failure to discover the much-desired commercial river passage to the West with a broadly literary project in natural philosophy that would detail the many significant scientific accomplishments of the expedition. If the expedition could not claim to have fulfilled its promise as an enterprise of imperial republican political economy, it could still claim its rightful place in the annals of Enlightenment science and literature.[66]

As in many enterprises of empire driven by the need for prior assurances of profitability, however, this enterprise's failure to ensure the economic value of its Jeffersonian political investment by discovering an easily exploitable commercial route to the Pacific seems to have undermined sustained support for documenting its scientific accomplishments. The failure here was thus in good part the failure of the overlapping governmental and philanthropic networks that had made the expedition possible in the first place. In spite of all the scientific ambitions held out for preparation of the volumes of the expedition outlined in both Lewis's prospectus of 1807 and Nicholas Biddle's of 1810, the two-volume narrative of the expedition, which Biddle finally published in 1814 in an edition of around fourteen hundred copies, was in many ways only a more sophisticated and expensive version of what the Gass volume had been—a "story of the expedition as a glorious western adventure." Missing from Biddle's narrative was much of the scientific documentation that would have completely distinguished it from the popular narratives that preceded it while ensuring its contemporary place in Enlightenment scientific history.[67]

The history of the Lewis and Clark journals also involved some intrigue in Philadelphia over the political economy of publication. Perhaps because of his investment in printing a "large" number of volumes of the Gass journal against Carey's advice, McKeehan's bookselling business in Pittsburgh did not considerably improve after 1807. In letters to Carey, McKeehan continually complained of financial difficulties, and in early 1810 Carey reclaimed McKeehan's remaining stock of books in Pittsburgh in order to salvage what he could from the debts McKeehan owed him. This detail may clarify the basis of Carey's claim to the right to publish four editions of the McKeehan text of the Gass journal in 1810–1812 without altering McKeehan's original copyright. Carey effectively claimed ownership of McKeehan's copyright by virtue of McKeehan's default on his debts to Carey.

And because Nicholas Biddle was at this same time in 1810 beginning work on his "official" narrative of the expedition, some competitive intrigue seems to have developed between Carey and Biddle over

FIGURE 3.5. Peale, Rembrandt. *Nicholas Biddle* (ca. 1839) (Longacre, James Barton and Welse, Thomas B, engravers. Prints and Photographs Collection, American Philosophical Society). Biddle (1786–1844) composed the two-volume *History of the Expedition under the Command of Captains Lewis and Clark to the Sources of the Missouri* (Philadelphia: Bradford and Inskeep, 1814). (See Color Plate 7.)

the "original manuscript" of the Gass journal, which had made its way from Pittsburgh to Philadelphia by way of the conclusion of Carey's business relationship with McKeehan. According to the Minutes of the Directors of the Library Company of Philadelphia for March 8, 1810, Mathew Carey gave "the original manuscript journal of Patrick Gass" to the Library Company as a gift. Carey may in part have given the Gass manuscript to the Library Company in order to place it on public display as evidence of the authenticity of the McKeehan edition of the Gass journal that Carey was then preparing to republish in its first Philadelphia edition. Meanwhile, Biddle's own letter to Clark of July 7, 1810, suggests that while Carey was preparing his edition of the McKeehan-Gass journal for publication in April and May, Biddle was trying to "stop" Carey's edition by publishing a prospectus for his own authorized narrative based on his study of *all* of the Lewis and Clark journals, including the "original manuscript" of the Gass journal "deposited in our library" (the Library Company of Philadelphia). After Biddle's mention of his use of the "original manuscript" of the Gass journal in the preparation of his narrative, however, the Gass manuscript vanishes from the Library Company's records, and from history.[68] There are thus several intriguing mysteries related to the Gass journal and Lewis's time in Philadelphia that await further investigation.

The political struggle between the Constitutional Republicans and radical democrats in Philadelphia is relevant to our search for historical understanding of the remaining mysteries of the Lewis and Clark enterprise for two reasons. First, the fate of that political contest shaped and constrained the complex sociopolitical environment of Philadelphia through which Lewis had to maneuver during his sojourn there in 1807. Lewis's inability to find his way through the intimate conflicts of private and public interest in connection with the publication of the McKeehan-Gass journal, and through the political complications of his attendance at the July 4 Friends of the People celebration, may have contributed significantly to his sense of frustration and looming failure as he departed Philadelphia for Washington around July 21. Mahlon Dickerson's last diary entry about Lewis on July 20 is ominous: "Walked at evening with Capt. Lewis, round the Centre Square—perhaps for the last time." These words, read in the context of our awareness of Lewis's "troubles," remind us of the intimate consequences of the contradictions that haunt both the institutional and sentimental structures of political economy.[69]

Second, this political struggle is relevant for the ways in which it helps to reveal the particular tensions and fractures that were present within the shaping vision and constitution of the Lewis and Clark expedition as a founding enterprise of Jeffersonian political economy. As the fractures between the Quids and the radicals demonstrate, the "civil society" of early nineteenth-century Pennsylvania was profoundly divided over issues of political economy and the definition of republican public interest. The failure of the PSPA to achieve its goals of public education and the conflict between Lewis and McKeehan over the authority to represent the expedition are only two of the ways these fractures were manifested.

While the Lewis and Clark expedition was intended to further the geopolitical aims of republican empire, it was perhaps in the day-to-day realities of its struggles as an "exploration community" that it fulfilled for at least some of its members the ideal of a "most perfect" republican harmony. The requirements of survival as an exploration community set up the framework for achieving forms of solidarity that could not be supported by the imperial architectures and hierarchical organizations of rule required for establishing and maintaining republican empire. As Ronda has observed, the discipline of military regulations and orders from above "could not build a sense of common purpose and shared destiny." That common sense of community could only be built out of shared experiences of survival, suffering, and decision making.[70] The extensive development of such a sense of community was, however, precisely what the contradictions of the political economy of republican empire precluded. A republican political economy that could serve to build a true community or union of interests thus remained little more than a Jeffersonian dream, even for Meriwether Lewis.

By reexamining details of the Lewis and Clark expedition within the larger context of this era's contradictions of political economy—explored from their intimate underside—we may be able to provide richer interpretations not only of the legacy of the expedition but also of the place of Lewis's personal tragedy within that legacy. For the contradictions and failures of political economy were then, as they continue to be now, both intimate and global in their ultimate effects. If, as Ronda has suggested, coming to terms with the Lewis and Clark expedition forces us to consider how our own present is troubled by the history of empire, then perhaps from such consideration we may gain the wisdom we need to avoid repeating the imperial mistakes of the past. For what George Logan recognized in 1800 continues to stand as warning today: "Left as we are to ourselves . . . before the nations of the earth, the cause of republican liberty shall be justified by its effects, or shall be condemned as the introducer of more calamities than it removes."

NOTES

I would like to acknowledge fellowship support from the Library Company of Philadelphia's Program in Early American Economy and Society, the American Philosophical Society, and the Rackham Graduate School of the University of Michigan, which made this paper possible. For their comments on previous versions of this essay, I would also like to thank Rob Cox, until recently the APS Library's Keeper of Manuscripts; James Green, Librarian of the Library Company of Philadelphia; and Cathy Matson, Director of the Library Company's Program in Early American Economy and Society.

1. Bernard DeVoto, *The Course of Empire* (Boston: Houghton Mifflin, 1952). Paul Russell Cutright, *Lewis and Clark: Pioneering Naturalists* (Urbana: University of Illinois, 1969). Gary E. Moulton, ed., *The Journals of the Lewis and Clark Expedition*, 13 vols. (Lincoln: University of Nebraska, 1983–2001). Much of the foregoing work, including the Moulton Journals Project, has benefited from the continuing support of the American Philosophical Society. Thomas P. Slaughter, *Exploring Lewis and Clark: Reflections on Men and Wilderness* (New York: Alfred Knopf, 2003). James P. Ronda, *Finding the West: Explorations with Lewis and Clark* (Albuquerque: University of New Mexico, 2001), 127. See also James P. Ronda, ed., *Voyages of Discovery: Essays on the Lewis and Clark Expedition* (Helena: Montana Historical Society, 1998).

2. Michael Hardt and Antonio Negri, *Empire* (Cambridge: Harvard University Press, 2000), xiv.

3. "Jefferson's Instructions to Lewis" (June 20, 1803), in Donald Jackson, ed., *Letters of the Lewis and Clark Expedition with Related Documents, 1783–1854*, 2d ed. in 2 vols. (Urbana: University of Illinois Press, 1978), 61. Ronda, *Finding the West*, 117–18. See also "Afterword" of Ronda, *Voyages of Discovery*, 327–35.

4. The first two chapters of John L. Larson, *Internal Improvement: National Public Works and the Promise of Popular Government in the Early United States* (Chapel Hill: University of North Carolina Press, 2001), provide an important overview of the ways in which many of the major projects of internal improvement (especially road and canal building) taken on by both private organizations and government during the first forty years of the nation were crippled by conflicts between competing private, local, and state interests that the federal government was powerless to resolve. Larson's narrative illustrates how the federal government failed to articulate a vision and policy for the equitable mediation of competing interests during the Federalist and Jeffersonian eras. This failure to forge a compelling sense of national common interest allowed governmental action on all levels to be distorted by the unregulated influence of private interests. Larson clarifies the multiple lines along which competing private and public interests fractured during the republican era and suggests that national government was never able to provide convincing evidence to citizens of the early republic that it could be trusted to resolve competing interests in equitable ways. Larson's history thus provides crucial context for grappling with the core problem of

republican government and political economy this essay seeks to articulate: Why was republican government in the early United States unable to create a framework for resolving these fundamental conflicts of interest? What are the deeper sources of this incapacity of republican government to resolve conflicts of interest that all the nation's republican thinkers, on the basis of the experience of the 1780s, understood would be the most essential challenge and test of the nation's constitutional framework?

5. Richard Peters, *Outlines of a Plan for Establishing a State Society of Agriculture in Pennsylvania* (Philadelphia: Charles Cist, 1794), 6, 2. The PSPA remains active today and has its own Web site, www.pspaonline.com, which provides access to information on its archives maintained by the Rare Book and Manuscript Library of the University of Pennsylvania.

6. Cathy Matson, "Capitalizing Hope: Economic Thought and the Early National Economy," in *Wages of Independence: Capitalism in the Early American Republic*, ed. Paul Gilje (Madison, Wisc.: Madison House, 1997), 127, 129, has suggested that because we still know little about how Americans changed their thinking in response to the dramatic transformations of the economy of the early republic, we would do well to pay closer attention to the thoughts and accomplishments of "boosters and funders of local experiments with field rotations, hybrid animals and plants, new kinds of outbuildings, and dairy product marketing." Because such boosters, funders, and experimenters often implemented their projects through organized association as members of agricultural and other improvement societies, we also need to pay closer attention to the work of such societies.

7. For a recent overview of the economic history of the early republic, which was written to accompany the 2003 exhibition sponsored by the Program for Early American Economy and Society at the Library Company of Philadelphia, see Cathy Matson, *Risky Business: Winning and Losing in the Early American Economy, 1780–1850* (Philadelphia: Library Company of Philadelphia, 2003). Cathy Matson and Peter Onuf provide a study of political economy in the early republic in *A Union of Interests: Political and Economic Thought in Revolutionary America* (Lawrence: University of Kansas, 1990). For an overview of the continuing efforts of Americans to hold together a "Union of Interests" into the early decades of the nineteenth century, see also Cathy Matson, "Capitalizing Hope," in *Wages of Independence*, 117–36.

8. During this era, the writing and examples of men such as Benjamin Franklin and Thomas Paine provided a crucial benchmark for understanding the necessarily controversial and politicized parameters of philanthropy.

9. For a recent overview of the distinction between the terms *charity* and *philanthropy* in the early republic, see the Introduction and first part of Lawrence J. Friedman and Mark D. McGarvie, eds., *Charity, Philanthropy, and Civility in American History* (New York: Cambridge University Press, 2003), and especially in that volume Robert A. Gross, "Giving in America: From Charity to Philanthropy," 37–41. See also Kathleen McCarthy, *American Creed: Philanthropy and the Rise of Civil Society, 1700–1865* (Chicago: University of Chicago Press, 2003), 19–29.

10. William Blackstone, *Commentaries on the Laws of England*, Vol. 4 (Chicago: University of Chicago Press, 1979), 162. In its mid-eighteenth-century manifestation, police had as much if not more to do with the extralegal enforcement of social norms, as with legal regulations. See Donna Andrew, *Philanthropy and Police: London Charity in the Eighteenth Century* (Princeton: Princeton University Press, 1989), 6–7, and see especially the writings of the British philanthropist Jonas Hanway (1712–1786), such as *The Defects of Police the Cause of Immorality . . . With Various Proposals for Preventing Hanging*

and Transportation: Likewise for the Establishment of Several Plans of Police on a Permanent Basis, with Respect to Common Beggars; the Regulation of Paupers; the Peaceful Security of Subjects; and the Moral and Political Conduct of the People (London: J. Dodsley, 1775).

11. The first major British treatise on political economy is generally recognized to be that of Sir James Steuart, *An Inquiry into the Principles of Political Economy: Being an Essay on the Science of Domestic Policy in Free Nations, In Which Are Particularly Considered Population, Agriculture, Trade, Industry, Money, Coin, Interest, Circulation, Banks, Exchange, Public Credit, and Taxes* (London: A. Millar and T. Cadell, 1767), which was written from the perspective of Steuart's own personal exposure to German police science and cameralism and focused primarily on the importance of central state activity and regulation (mercantilism). Adam Smith's *Inquiry into the Nature and Causes of the Wealth of Nations* (London: W. Strahan and T. Cadell, 1776) was written in part as a critique of the state-centered mercantilist assumptions of Steuart's treatise. It is in the movement from the thinking of Steuart to Smith that we can trace the British passage from mercantilist economic policies associated with eighteenth-century continental police science to classical political economy, with its greater skepticism concerning the value of state-centered regulation and its greater emphasis on the value of allowing private interests and the agency of civil society more play in shaping the economic policy of the state.

12. While topical limitations prevent any further consideration of the Balmis expedition here, much more than the coincidence in time of these two expeditions suggests the need for their comparative study. I am aware of no U.S. study of Lewis and Clark that recognizes the simultaneous existence of these expeditions or reflects on the numerous ways a comparative study of these expeditions would considerably increase our understanding of both. The original citation from a translation of a supplement to the *Madrid Gazette* of October 14, 1806, presented to the APS in 1806 by the Marquis de Casa Yrujo—the official Spanish representative to the U.S. government—is in John Redman Coxe, ed., *Philadelphia Medical Museum* 3(4) (1807): 237-40. A valuable historical study of this expedition's accomplishments in New Spain was written by Michael M. Smith, "The 'Real Expedicion Maritima de la Vacuna' in New Spain and Guatemala," *Transactions of the APS*, New series, Vol. 64, pt. 1 (Feb. 1974).

13. Roy E. Appleman, *Lewis and Clark: Historic Places Associated with Their Transcontinental Exploration, 1804-06* (Washington: National Park Service, 1975), 21, 28-31, 34. Benjamin Smith Barton, Professor of Natural History at the University of Pennsylvania, and a leading member of the APS, was the author of *Elements of Botany* (Philadelphia: Printed for the author, 1803), the first textbook on this subject written in the United States and one of the key scientific books Lewis carried with him on his trip west, along with a book loaned to him directly by Barton, Le Page du Pratz's *History of Louisiana* (London: T. Becket, 1774), which Lewis returned to Barton in 1807; the original du Pratz is now in the research collection of the Library Company of Philadelphia. See Cutright, *Lewis and Clark*, 25.

14. We may assume this connection because Lewis asked Jefferson to send clippings of Osage plum trees to Hamilton as early as March 1804. See Jackson, *Letters*, 170; and Cutright, *Lewis and Clark*, 370.

15. Cutright, *Lewis and Clark*, 358-63, 370-74, provides basic details on McMahon and Hamilton. See also Jackson, *Letters*, 354-57, 389-92, 583-84. Bernard McMahon (1775-1816) was an Irish immigrant to Philadelphia in 1796. In 1806 he published one of the first major U.S. works on horticulture, *The American Gardner's* [sic] *Calendar* (Philadelphia: B. Graves, 1806), a 648-page volume that according to Cutright quickly became the horticulturists' bible. Indeed, it was mentioned almost immediately

after its publication in the minutes of the meetings of both the APS and the PSPA. A copy was donated to the APS library on March 21, 1806; another was purchased for the PSPA library on April 8, 1806; and by the summer of 1807 the book was being actively borrowed by other members of the PSPA. *Minutes of the Philadelphia Society for the Promotion of Agriculture, 1785–1810* (Philadelphia: John Clark, 1854), 88–91, 102, hereafter cited as *PSPA Minutes*. According to Cutright, McMahon's *Calendar* remained the standard authority for the next fifty years. While letters between McMahon and Jefferson from April 1807 to May 1813 indicate the successful work of McMahon with Jefferson in propagating the seeds and cuttings, Hamilton sent only one report to Jefferson in February 1810, which acknowledged his relative lack of success at growing the seeds. For more richly detailed discussion of McMahon and his significance, see Rob Cox's essay in this volume.

16. For a valuable contemporary vision of agriculture as the foundation of a system of internal improvements and public economy that drew together the interests of agriculture, commerce, and manufacturing, see Richard Peters, *A Discourse on Agriculture: Its Antiquity and Importance to Every Member of the Community* (Philadelphia: Johnson and Warner, 1816), 9–17, 30–31. On Biddle and the PSPA, see Stevenson W. Fletcher, *The Philadelphia Society for Promoting Agriculture, 1785–1955*, rev. ed. (Philadelphia: The Society, 1976), 56.

17. Peter S. Onuf, *Jefferson's Empire: The Language of American Nationhood* (Charlottesville: University of Virginia Press, 2000), 68–69.

18. Onuf, *Jefferson's Empire*, 48, 53–55. As Onuf argues, belief that Jefferson completely opposed manufactures and cities is based on a one-sided misreading of his writing on the dangers of great cities as the locus for concentrations of power and wealth: "His first concern was not to forestall commercial development but rather to preempt" such concentrations of power and wealth, so that his agrarianism "was an artifact of his devotion to a republican political economy, not its fundamental premise." Jefferson understood that only the development of a great internal commerce network could "offer a viable alternative to the mercantilist regime of unequal benefits" of empire that was the context for commercial trade with Europe. Jefferson also understood that the well-being and future of his yeoman farmers depended on the commercial expansion of the interior empire (69, 71). The larger vision of Jefferson's system of inland commerce in connection with Lewis and Clark is also nicely developed in the first chapter of Ronda, *Finding the West*, 1–16, titled "A Promise of Rivers."

19. Onuf, *Jefferson's Empire*, 57–59, 63.

20. Ibid., 59, 63. We still have much work to do to grasp the importance of the Lewis and Clark enterprise and its scientific accomplishments as a founding moment for the establishment of the imperial national political economy of the United States.

21. See here especially the work of Matson and Onuf, *A Union of Interests*. The first vision of the American system of harmonious political economy developed in the thinking of the men of the APS as early as the 1760s and 1770s, but the development of actual societies for the improvement of agriculture and manufacturing occurred after the Revolutionary War. This idealism about the harmony of interests would rather quickly break down, however, during the course of factional struggles between the Hamiltonians and Jeffersonians that developed in the 1790s. Later it became clear, especially to publicists such as Mathew Carey, that maintaining any "harmony of interests" would require intense struggle to create such harmony (in opposition to passive reliance on the "invisible hand" of the market to reconcile competing interests, which not even Adam Smith actually taught). By the 1820s, as the sectional interests

of North and South increasingly diverged over trade policy, the notion of a "natural" harmony of interests became a rather archaic trope of political economists yearning for a less complicated future. See Carey's various editions of the *New Olive Branch* beginning with the first edition, *The New Olive Branch; or, An Attempt to Establish an Identity of Interest between Agriculture, Manufactures, and Commerce* (Philadelphia: M. Carey and Son, 1820), through *The New Olive Branch: Addressed to the Citizens of South Carolina* (Philadelphia: Clark and Raser, 1831). For one of the most powerful criticisms of Northern tariff policy by a Southerner, see John Taylor of Caroline's *Tyranny Unmasked* (Washington City,: Davis and Force, 1822).

22. George Logan, *A Letter to the Citizens of Pennsylvania on the Necessity of Promoting Agriculture, Manufactures, and the Useful Arts, with Constitution of the Lancaster County Society for Promoting of Agriculture, Manufactures, and the Useful Arts* (Lancaster, Pa.: W. and R. Dickson, March 14, 1800), 5.

23. James Mease, ed., *Archives of Useful Knowledge, a Work Devoted to Commerce, Manufactures, Rural and Domestic Economy, Agriculture and the Useful Arts*, Vol. 1 (Philadelphia: David Hogan, 1811), 3.

24. Here, of course, I build on the work of many other scholars, such as Carroll Smith-Rosenberg, Gina Morantz-Sanchez, Ann Stoler, Julie Ellison, Lauren Berlant, Cathy Matson, Peter Onuf, Hannah Rosen, Andrew Burstein, and Rob Cox, who have inspired me to take up the "enterprise" of reconstructing the history of political economy in the nineteenth-century United States from the intimate underside of empire's sentimental police. I provide a more comprehensive analysis of the rise of philanthropic enterprise and police out of early republican political economy in the United States in the first part of my "Freedom's Panopticon: The Rise of the Liberal Police State Out of the Theater of Civil Society in Pennsylvania, 1770–1876" (Ph.D. diss., University of Michigan, 2005).

25. Jefferson quotation cited in Onuf, *Jefferson's Empire*, 45. Indeed, this is why the special professorial chair Jefferson created at the College of William and Mary was a chair "of Law and Police," and not simply of law. My dissertation, "Freedom's Panopticon," explores the significance of this missing history of "police" to a reformed understanding of the conjoined histories of political economy and philanthropy in the early republic.

26. Peters, *Outlines of a Plan*, 6, 2. Peters claims authorship of this plan in his 1816 *Discourse on Agriculture*, 33.

27. David Brion Davis, "The Quaker Ethic and the Antislavery International," in *The Antislavery Debate*, ed. Thomas Bender (Berkeley: University of California, 1992), 50–53. In my larger project, I analyze this network of individuals and institutions as a republican system of police, understood in the important eighteenth-century sense of the term that I am working to restore to our historical memory.

28. Davis, "The Quaker Ethic."

29. Bordley had been elected to membership in the APS in 1783 and was an avid agriculturist and writer on political economy in the 1780s and 1790s. Among the other founding members, the only dedicated gentleman-farmer besides Bordley was Dr. George Logan. Like many of the gentlemen who helped found the PSPA, Logan was an avid reader of the British agricultural writer Arthur Young, who was a leader of the dissemination of new scientific methods of agriculture that had reformed British agriculture by the 1780s. The rest of the PSPA membership either had an intellectual or political interest in agricultural improvement or pursued other professions while dabbling in agricultural matters avocationally.

30. Richard Peters, *Statistical Account of the Schuylkill Permanent Bridge* (Philadelphia: Jane Aitken, 1807). Frederick Perry Powers, *The Historic Bridges of Philadelphia* (Philadelphia: City History Society, 1914), 286–93. Fletcher, *The PSPA*, 24–26.

31. *PSPA Minutes*, 96, 112.

32. Onuf, *Jefferson's Empire*, 65. Here I take up a key point noted by Onuf when he writes that "freed from metropolitan domination, independent Americans grasped and deployed the imperial idea in myriad concrete, idiosyncratic ways . . . despite or, as Tocqueville suggested, because of their diverse local loyalties and proliferating forms of association" (61).

33. Richard Peters, "Address of the Society [PSPA] to their Fellow Citizens," *PSPA Memoirs* 2 (Feb. 1810): xv. Simon Baatz briefly noted the overarching significance of the PSPA's failure to resolve during its first fifty years the "contradiction between an aristocratic patrician membership . . . and the desire . . . to impress a scientific agriculture onto the dirt farmers" in his bicentennial history of the PSPA, *"Venerate the Plough": A History of the Philadelphia Society for Promoting Agriculture, 1785–1985* (Philadelphia: PSPA, 1985), 3, 42.

34. Peters, *Outlines of a Plan*. Timothy Pickering to Rev. Samuel Dean of Portland, Maine (March 8, 1794), PSPA Collection, Folder 300, Rare Book and Manuscript Library, University of Pennsylvania. Richard Peters, *A Discourse on Agriculture*, 33. John B. Bordley, *Essays and Notes on Husbandry and Rural Affairs* (Philadelphia: Thomas Dobson, 1799), 450. Baatz, *Venerate the Plough*, 3. Donald B. Marti, *To Improve the Soil and the Mind* (Ann Arbor: UMI, 1979), 5, 8.

35. Though qualified as a medical doctor, Logan chose not to take up practice; Frederick B. Tolles, *George Logan of Philadelphia* (New York: Oxford University Press, 1953), 53.

36. Ibid., 67–69.

37. Ibid., 76, 78, 81–82.

38. Ibid., 88–89. The relatively short life of this association may be the best indicator of the limits of Logan's ability to bridge the divide between his own social position and interests and those of the common farmers he wished to serve. But this only makes more worthy of note the fact that, unlike many like him who claimed to possess democratic sympathies, Logan invested significant energy in attempting to make such sympathies productive, and—a full decade before Jefferson came to Washington—invited common farmers into his household to try to found with them a philanthropic association that would serve their interests. Logan's failure here, and his eventual conservative political turn after 1800, only further underline the severity of the social and political chasm that troubled the early life of the republican nation.

39. Tolles, *George Logan*, 101–6, 115–16.

40. Richard Sylla used this phrase recently in a talk at the Annual Meeting of the Library Company of Philadelphia, May 13, 2003, titled "The Federalist Financial Revolution." Tolles, *George Logan*, 111–25. On Bordley as a Hamiltonian, see John B. Bordley, *National Credit and Character* (Philadelphia: Daniel Humphreys, 1790), and Olive Moore Gambrill, "John Beale Bordley and the Early Years of the Philadelphia Agricultural Society," *Pennsylvania Magazine of History and Biography* 66 (Oct. 1942): 410–39, at 414.

41. See George Logan's May 1793 handbill, which summarized his major principles and was distributed to the farmers of Pennsylvania and beyond, in Misc. Mss., Logan Papers, Historical Society of Pennsylvania (hereafter HSP). Tolles, *George Logan*, 123, 131.

42. Logan, *Letter to the Citizens of Pennsylvania*, 5–6.

43. George Logan, *An Address on the Natural and Social Order of the World, Delivered Before the Tammany Society* (Philadelphia: Benjamin Franklin Bache, May 12, 1798).

44. Andrew Shankman, "Malcontents and Tertium Quids: The Battle to Define Democracy in Jeffersonian Philadelphia," *Journal of the Early Republic* 19 (Spring 1999): 43–72. An overview of the history of the battle between the Quids and radicals in Pennsylvania from 1800 to 1808 is provided by Richard Ellis, *The Jeffersonian Crisis: Courts and Politics in the Young Republic* (New York: Oxford University Press, 1971), 157–83.

45. Peters, *Discourse on Agriculture*, 17. On the antagonism of common farmers to the work of the PSPA during these years see Fletcher, *The PSPA*, 30–31, 41–42. This problem would continue to haunt the PSPA long after the era of Lewis and Clark. While even Peters (*Discourse on Agriculture*, 32) recognized that the Berkshire County Agricultural Society in Massachusetts had by 1816 begun to demonstrate the value of annual cattle and agricultural exhibitions for bridging the divide between common farmers and the work of agricultural societies, it was not until 1822 that the PSPA authorized such an exhibition. But even this one attempt to open itself to the participation of common farmers stirred up such controversy that the leading members of the PSPA split over it, causing the society to fall into inactivity for more than a decade until it was renewed in 1838 under the leadership of Nicholas Biddle, with a new generation of members; Fletcher, *The PSPA*, 45–47, 53, 56. On the transforming influence of the Berkshire model, see Marti, *To Improve the Soil*, 15–27.

46. William Barton, *The Constitutionalist: Addressed to Men of All Parties in the United States* (Philadelphia: H. Maxwell, 1804), 7, 46.

47. See also William Barton, *Observations on the Trial by Jury: with Misc. Remarks concerning Legislation & Jurisprudence, and the Professors of the Law; Also, Shewing the Dangerous Consequences of Innovations, in the Fundamental Institutions of the Civil Polity of a State* (Strasburg, Penn.: Brown & Bowman, 1803). The key statement of the position of the Constitutional Republicans is contained in their *Address of the Society of Constitutional Republicans . . . to the Republicans of Pennsylvania* (Philadelphia: William McCorkle, 1805), of June 10, 1805, signed by George Logan as president and Israel Israel as vice president of the party.

48. William Barton, *The Constitutionalist*.

49. "Lewis to the Public" (March 14, 1807), in Jackson, *Letters*, 385.

50. I plan to give more extended consideration to these matters in a paper focused on the intriguing publication history of the Gass journal in Pennsylvania from 1807–1812. Previous accounts of the McKeehan-Gass and Lewis contest are by Donald Jackson, "The Race to Publish Lewis and Clark," *Pennsylvania Magazine of History and Biography* 85 (April 1961): 163–77; Paul Russell Cutright, "Patrick Gass and David M'Keehan," in *A History of the Lewis and Clark Journals* (Norman: University of Oklahoma, 1976), 19–32; "Introduction" to the McKeehan-Gass journal in Moulton, *Journals*, 10:xiii–xviii; Carol Lynn MacGregor, ed., *The Journals of Patrick Gass: Member of the Lewis and Clark Expedition* (Missoula, Mt.: Mountain Press, 1997); and Stephen Dow Beckham, "Patrick Gass, First in Print," in *The Literature of the Lewis and Clark Expedition: A Bibliography and Essays* (Portland, Ore.: Lewis and Clark College, 2003), 89–103.

51. Jackson, *Letters*, 403–4.

52. Lewis's original prospectus, before he contracted with Philadelphia's C. & A. Conrad as publisher, was printed in the *National Intelligencer* on March 18, 23, 25, 27, and 30 and April 1 and in Philadelphia's *Aurora* on March 23 (Jackson, *Letters*, 386). Some confusion regarding the two different versions of Lewis's book prospectus has been caused by Jackson's initial April 1 dating of the second prospectus issued by the Philadelphia

publishing firm of C. & A. Conrad, which Jackson later admitted to be too early because the Conrad prospectus was not published in the newspapers until June 16 (*Letters*, 682). It should also be noted that what Jackson published under heading of the "The Conrad Prospectus" as item 262a in *Letters*, 394–97, is actually the first Lewis prospectus of March 1807, not the Conrad prospectus. The Conrad prospectus appeared in the Philadelphia *Aurora* from June 16 through the end of July. It was also separately published by Smith and Maxwell of Philadelphia, possibly as advertising supplement for the *Port Folio*, on July 18 and 25 and August 1 (copies held at Yale and the University of Pennsylvania), as noted by Beckham, "Patrick Gass," 91. Careful examination of the available evidence allows us to conclude that Lewis published his own version of the prospectus in the newspapers from March 18 to April 1, before he had secured a publisher (a common practice, according to Jim Green), and did not begin to publish the prospectus he had worked out with the publisher C. & A. Conrad until at least early June 1807. The earliest date on an available copy of the Conrad prospectus appears to be June 3. This may indicate that Lewis had more difficulty securing a publisher in Philadelphia than has been previously supposed and suggests that he may have secured his Philadelphia publisher only after the announcement of McKeehan's publication of the Gass journal in Pittsburgh became well known in Philadelphia, especially by those in the book trade. On Lewis's permission granted to Frazer, see Lewis's letter to the public in Jackson, *Letters*, 386, and Moulton, *Journals*, 10:xiii, xvi.

53. Since McKeehan was already at work transcribing the journal by January 7, 1807, he must have obtained the journal manuscript from Gass sometime before late December in 1806. One possibility is that Gass and McKeehan met up in Wellsburg, (West) Virginia, just south of Pittsburgh, in order to exchange the manuscript. Gass may have traveled through Wellsburg on the way to Washington, D.C., where he would meet up with Lewis. Wellsburg was once McKeehan's home while he was a schoolteacher. Jackson, *Letters*, 391n; Cutright, *Journals*, 21–22, 24–25; Appleman, *Lewis and Clark*, 236; and James J. Holmberg, ed., *Dear Brother: Letters of William Clark to Jonathan Clark* (New Haven: Yale University, 2002), 115. That Lewis skipped a planned stop in Vincennes, where Gass had been waiting for him in late October, suggests there may already have been some difficulties in the relationship between Gass and Lewis; John G. Jacob, *The Life and Times of Patrick Gass* (Wellsburg, Va.: Jacob and Smith, 1859), 108–9. Incoming and outgoing correspondence (1804–1807), Lea and Febiger Records, HSP.

54. Jackson, *Letters*, 345–46. McKeehan's prospectus for the Gass journal is dated March 23, 1807, the same day as the appearance of Lewis's prospectus in the Pennsylvania papers. Compare the nearly identical wording of Lewis's testimonials to Gass and Bratton; Jackson, *Letters*, 347–48, 391.

55. McKeehan's letter is dated April 7 but was not printed in the *Pittsburgh Gazette* until April 14 and apparently received no additional circulation after this (Jackson, *Letters*, 399–408). McKeehan to Carey (April 3, 1807), Lea and Febiger Records, HSP.

56. James P. Ronda, "'A Most Perfect Harmony': The Lewis and Clark Expedition as an Exploration Community," in Ronda, *Voyages of Discovery*, 77–88.

57. Moulton, *Journals*, 2:36 and 10:xvi. Cutright, *Journals*, 27. Jackson, "The Race to Publish" (1961), republished in Ronda, *Voyages of Discovery*, 222. Last comment cited in Beckham, "Patrick Gass," 90.

58. Even Jefferson called the expedition "Mr. Lewis's tour" and "Lewis's journey to the Pacific"; Ronda, *Finding the West*, 123, and Jackson, *Letters*, 596. For Lewis's reference to his "darling project," see Moulton, *Journals*, 4:10; Jackson, *Letters*, v, 385–86, 400; Ronda, *Voyages*, 327–30. Albert Furtwangler's essay, "Captain Lewis in a Crossfire of

Wit" (in Ronda, *Voyages*, 229–51), discusses the treatment Lewis received from the poet Joel Barlow and the critic John Quincy Adams. The "wit" of McKeehan's criticism of Lewis should be understood in relation to the contexts analyzed by Furtwangler.

59. Jackson, *Letters*, 399–402 (emphasis in original). See also Slaughter, *Exploring Lewis and Clark*, 38–39, on the point of Mackenzie's precedence a decade before Lewis and Clark.

60. Jackson, *Letters*, 402 and n380 (my emphasis).

61. Ibid., 403–4 (with McKeehan's emphasis on individual words near beginning of the passage; my emphasis on long phrases near end). Matson, *Risky Business*.

62. Jackson, *Letters*, 405–6.

63. On the offense that Philadelphia booksellers took to McKeehan, see Incoming Letters, McKeehan to Carey (May 22, 1807), Lea and Febiger Records, HSP; Jackson, *Letters*, 407–8, n2.

64. Jackson, *Letters*, 683.

65. *Aurora* (July 7, 1807). The passages concerning Lewis from Mahlon Dickerson's diary for 1802–1803 and 1807 are printed in Jackson, *Letters*, 677–84. After Governor McKean defeated his Democratic opponent Simon Snyder in the fall 1805 gubernatorial election, Duane mounted a major public campaign against McKean in the newspapers and persuaded the legislature to begin impeachment proceedings, which ultimately failed.

66. Ronda, *Finding the West*, 120.

67. Lewis had to struggle to ensure adequate compensation for the members of his expedition and then had to struggle continually to cover his own debts. For a myriad of reasons, including the failing health of the two leading Philadelphia naturalists (Barton and Hamilton) who had provided initial support and Jefferson's own inability to reward Lewis financially except by burdening him with a governorship for which he was poorly prepared, Lewis never had the resources he needed to organize himself or others to write up the scientific accomplishments of the expedition. Our own era's philanthropic, educational, and governmental agencies have given major support to the completion of scholarly research on the Lewis and Clark expedition, especially the publication of the Moulton edition of the Lewis and Clark journals that was sponsored by the American Philosophical Society and the Center for Great Plains Studies at the University of Nebraska and was published with the support of a grant from the federally funded National Endowment for the Humanities. Ronda, *Finding the West*, 123.

68. Not only did McKeehan publish a "large" Pittsburgh edition of the Gass journal in 1807, but at least seven additional editions of the Gass journal were published before Biddle's official narrative of the Lewis and Clark expedition was published in 1814: a London edition in 1808; four Philadelphia editions published by Mathew Carey in 1810, 1811, and 1812; and two more international editions published in Paris and Weimar (Cutright, *Journals*, 29). Contrary to Cutright (*Journals*, 29–31), however, the Gass journal's publication did not substantially help McKeehan's financial position, since he continually complains of hardship to Carey (Incoming and Outgoing Correspondence between Carey and McKeehan [1807–1810], Lea and Febiger Records, HSP). Because of Carey's business relationship with McKeehan, the fact that he began publishing the first of four editions of the Gass journal in Philadelphia in 1810 shortly after concluding his business association with McKeehan, and Biddle's mention of having used the "original manuscript" of the Gass journal "deposited in our library" in preparing his narrative, I theorized that it may have been Carey who obtained the original manuscript from McKeehan and brought it to the Philadelphia

Library Company. I mentioned this possibility to the Library Company of Philadelphia's Librarian James Green and wondered whether there might be some evidence of the Gass journal having found its way to Philadelphia in the Library Company's records for 1810. Jim's subsequent communication confirmed this idea by noting that the Minutes of the Directors of the Library Company for March 8, 1810, include under the list of recent gifts the notation "the original manuscript journal of Patrick Gass by Mathew Carey." Thank you to Jim Green for providing this citation and also for suggesting the rationale that might have prompted Carey to make this gift to the Library Company. As Jim also clarified, however, this "gift" was never formally accessioned by the Library Company, nor is there any evidence to confirm that it was ever made available for borrowing at the library. The question of what happened to the Gass manuscript is therefore only made more intriguing by the fact that Nicholas Biddle seems to have been the last person to have mentioned having physical contact with the "original manuscript" of the Gass journal in preparing his narrative. On Biddle's reference to the Gass manuscript and his attempt to "stop" Carey's republication of the Gass journal, see Biddle's letter to Clark (July 7, 1810) in Jackson, *Letters*, 550–51.

69. Jackson, *Letters*, 684.

70. Ronda, *Voyages of Discovery*, 82, 87. See also the last chapter of Ronda, *Finding the West*, 117–29.

4

"I Never Yet Parted"

Bernard McMahon and the Seeds of the Corps of Discovery

Robert S. Cox

The chief objects of your journey are to find the shortest & most convenient route of communication between the U.S. & the Pacific ocean, within the temperate latitudes, & to learn such particulars as can be obtained of the country through which it passes, it's productions, inhabitants & their interesting circumstances.
    Thomas Jefferson, instruction to André Michaux, April 1793

The object of your mission is to explore the Missouri river, & such principal stream of it, as, by it's course and communication with the waters of the Pacific ocean . . . may offer the most direct & practicable water communication across this continent for the purposes of commerce.
    Thomas Jefferson, instruction to Meriwether Lewis, June 20, 1803

Looking west from Monticello, Thomas Jefferson envisioned the shadows of an Empire of Liberty spreading to the Pacific shore, growing out of "the mutual interest and natural sociability of liberty-loving republicans" to overcome fragility and faction in the nation and forge a durable and "harmonious union of free states in America."[1] In part, Jefferson's hopes for a new and expansive nation drew upon the heft of Scots philosophers such as Adam Smith, and particularly upon their theories of sympathetic and commercial exchange in promoting harmonious union. For Smith, fiscal and emotional exchange famously produced networks of reciprocal indebtedness and expectancy that made the very idea of societies and nations possible. Like many others in the new national government, Jefferson shared in the belief that commercial exchange held an almost mystical capacity for promoting peace in international affairs, while in domestic affairs commercial ties were "the equivalent to affection among people," person and nation converging in unity.[2]

Lewis and Clark have meant many things to many historians over the years, but the two notions that their expedition was somehow a manifestation of Jefferson's Empire of Liberty and that it was somehow tied to commerce have been remarkably persistent, even though the ultimate origins are rather more complex. The Corps of Discovery, as it turns out, was the last in a series of expeditions conceived at the American Philosophical Society (APS), and the only one to be brought to full fruition, and in some sense it may be traced back not to Jefferson but to the Quaker botanist and seedsman Humphry Marshall. As early as 1778, Marshall was rumbling about a "journey to the Missis-

FIGURE 4.1. Silhouette of Thomas Jefferson. American Philosophical Society. (See Color Plate 8.)

sippi westward" in the halls of the APS, and in 1785 he lobbied his fellow members to organize an expedition under his botanically inclined nephew Moses Marshall and his cousin William Bartram. When that effort, too, withered on the vine, Marshall turned across the Atlantic to Joseph Banks in an attempt to persuade the British Royal Society to send either Moses or himself to "explore the western regions in Search of minerals, fossils or inflammables and objects of natural History &c." When this, too, passed, Marshall renewed his efforts with the APS in 1792 and found that his views at last intertwined with those of a person, Jefferson, who was capable of transforming idea into practice. The end result, a failure by most measures, was an expedition led by the young French botanist André Michaux that was intended to descend the Ohio River to the Mississippi and from there to ascend to the Missouri westward to the Pacific. Although Michaux was recalled before reaching terra incognita, the instructions that Jefferson drafted for him served as a conceptual template for Lewis and Clark a decade later.[3]

Although a certain continuity connects these earlier efforts to the Corps of Discovery, they are, at least in one regard, distinct. True, when he dusted off Michaux's instructions for Lewis's all-observing eye, Jefferson still entertained hopes of finding herds of mastodons roaming the western wilds and still suggested that taking notes on birch paper would best ensure their survival in unfavorable conditions.[4] But between the time of Michaux and Lewis, Jefferson added five crucial words to the instructions that subtly recast the primary goal of the expedition: "for the purpose of commerce." At several levels, as Ralph Guinness first argued seventy years ago, the expedition of Lewis and Clark was a "politico-commercial" enterprise, an essential step in capturing markets and resources for future Americans. For Guinness and many who have pursued this line of reasoning, politico-commercial entailed locating trade routes; expanding markets; subverting English or Spanish competitors; creating demand, alliances, and dependencies; and, of course, creating profit. Yet even this list does not capture the layers of meaning attached to the phenomenon of commerce as understood in 1800. Because of the socially poetic valence of commerce in the eighteenth century, because Adam Smith's commercial and social sympathy held such sway in the minds of American intellectuals, the expedition entailed more than a mere assessment of trade routes and commercial potential, more than the possibility of disrupting or usurping British and Spanish dominion—it held the potential for stitching the nation together on a continental scale through an exchange of explorers, goods, and knowledge. The syndetic function of commerce and the long-term goal of promoting the American nation within its continental frame provide a crucial context for interpreting the instructions to Lewis and Clark and, as I will suggest, for the subsequent history of the seeds and plants they collected. Politics, nationalism, and seedsmanship were co-conspirators in the Corps of Discovery.[5]

By way of illustration, the implications of exchange in this putative Empire of Liberty can be seen particularly vividly in Jefferson's instructions on Indians, which formed another key part of his larger plans for the continent. Adopting the "benevolent" face that had informed American Indian policy since the Washington administration, Jefferson instructed Lewis to acquaint those he encountered with the "peaceable & commercial dispositions" of the government and of the government's wish to be "neighborly, friendly, & useful to them." Useful, in this case, meant providing the means for Indians to elevate their sociocultural status as laid out by the stadial historians of the Scottish Enlightenment, to help lift the "children of the forest" from barbarism to agrarianism and, ultimately, mercantilism. By encouraging Indians to "abandon" hunting—that cause and effect of barbarity—and to take up sedentary agriculture, Jefferson believed he could drive home to them a central advantage of civilization, that "less land and labor will maintain them . . . better than in their former mode of living." At the same time, the federal government would instill a desire for ownership and consumer goods among Indians through well-placed trading houses, designed to "place within their reach those things which will contribute more to their domestic comfort, than the possession of extensive, but uncultivated wilds." No fools, Indians would soon recognize "the wisdom of exchanging what they can spare & we want, for what we can spare and they want," and would be drawn ever deeper into the circulatory system(s) of white America.[6] Indians would exchange goods and desires with whites, forging ever stronger social bonds, and Jefferson predicted that they would exchange physical bodies as well. "If any of them should wish to have some of their young people brought up with us," he wrote to Lewis, "& taught such arts as may be useful to them, we will receive, instruct & take care of them."[7]

All of this exchange would bring Indians within the white economy, which in turn, as Jefferson wrote to Henry Dearborn, would allow the government to "cultivate an affectionate attachment from them." Once agriculture had elevated Indians from barbarity, Jefferson would perform the final integral in his benevolent calculus. "When they withdraw themselves to the culture of a small piece of land," he wrote, "they will perceive how useless to them are their extensive forests, and will be willing to pare them off from time to time to exchange for necessaries for their farms and families. To promote this disposition to exchange lands, which they have to spare and we want, we shall push our trading uses, and be glad to see them run in debt, because we observe that when these debts get beyond what the individuals can pay, they become willing to lop them off by a cession of lands."[8]

There is crassness in this view of life, but for all that, it would be a mistake not to recognize the logic of commerce and exchange in which it was rooted. At least in the abstract, the lopping off of lands was only the beginning of a process of integration by exchange, not the end: transforming Indians from *Homo americanus* into *Homo economicus* was only the first stage in an evolutionary progression with few limits. In 1802, Jefferson revealed how far he thought it might proceed, informing a visiting delegation of Indians that if they chose to live under American laws and institutions, they might one day "join in our great councils and form one people with us, and we shall all be Americans." Although I would hesitate to ascribe any foolish consistency to Jefferson's thoughts on race, in this instance he drew few limits to the meaning of one people. "You will mix with us by marriage," he exclaimed, "your blood will mix with ours, and will spread, with ours, over this great island." By luring Indians within the economy, bringing them within the very blood of white America, Jefferson's harmonious union would become reality, a true world unto itself.[9]

The role of plants in this grand union may be less easily discerned, but plants were indeed crucial to the exchange that promised to integrate and bind the nation. The controlled culture of plants, of course, was the key signifier that distinguished the civilized from the savage; it was the indispensable element in promoting the sociocultural elevation of Indians, but beyond this plants served as commodities within several overlapping economies. As ornamentals, food crops, or materia medica, plants and seeds circulated across the continent, working westward as well as eastward in the wake of Lewis and Clark, and to and fro throughout the Atlantic world. They circulated among friends and political allies, coreligionists, gardeners, botanists, and other curious colleagues to bind relationships and communities of knowledge. They served as gifts binding individuals in webs of reciprocity, as tokens of scientific prestige, and as signifiers of a cultivated intellect. Plants were tangible and fungible, a commercial and intellectual product to be possessed, co-opted, and sometimes subverted.

The convoluted history of the seeds and plants collected by Lewis and Clark, their passage from Washington and Oregon into the botanical record, was nearly as arduous as the journey itself, involving the conflicting personalities, premature deaths, and interests and disinterests of half a dozen men. Beginning with Jefferson and Lewis, the seeds and plants passed through the grasp of the physician-naturalist Benjamin Smith Barton (Lewis's mentor in botany and a professor of materia medica at the University of Pennsylvania), through the tilled fields of the gentleman-gardener William Hamilton into the sketchbook and (ink) bottle of the wayfaring Frederick Pursh before at long last germinating into print.[10] Working largely behind the scenes, one obscure figure, Bernard McMahon, assumed a primary role in nurturing the seeds from field to page.

The Expedition

Even before the Corps of Discovery headed west from St. Louis, the first botanical specimens were heading east. In March 1804, Lewis shipped back several slips of the Osage orange and wild plum to Jefferson, requesting that some of each be given to the Philadelphia gardener William Hamilton for cultivation, a suggestion that was well conceived.[11] Having received his botanical training in Philadelphia, Lewis knew well the communities of botanists and gardeners in the city and was well aware of Hamilton's reputation as a master hand with unusual plants. Lewis's choleric mentor in botany, Barton, regularly took his classes from the University of Pennsylvania to Hamilton's estate, the Woodlands, to tour the greenhouses that overflowed with thousands of rare and tender exotics.[12]

Blessed with wealth and social standing, the grandson of the illustrious attorney who had defended Peter Zenger, Hamilton was responsible for transforming the Woodlands into the nation's first great example of picturesque landscape design in the English style, ruling over its grounds with grace and enthusiasm. Situated on almost six hundred acres of land on the west bank of the Schuylkill River near the Gray's Ferry bridge, the Woodlands was designed to dazzle, not only in its rambling romantic vistas and river views, but in the sheer profusion of species and varieties grown there, culled from all the corners of the New World and Old. Tended by a succession of talented gardeners that included the Scots immigrant John Lyon and Frederick Pursh, the German, the displays at the Woodlands were so impressive in greenhouse and grounds that one writer quipped, "The curious person views it with delight, the naturalist quits it with regret." Aspiring naturalists such as Barton and his students were repeatedly regretful for their frequent departures, but the estate was a delight for almost any visitor of stature, intellect, and curiosity during the 1790s and 1800s and was de rigeur for any scientifically inclined visitor to Philadelphia, including Thomas Jefferson.[13]

Yet in Hamilton, grace and enthusiasm were wedded to a pronounced miserliness, expressed, in McMahon's words, as a "jealousy of any person's attempt to vie with him in a collection of plants." While Hamilton gladly accepted specimens from his fellow enthusiasts, he was notoriously reticent to part with any of his own, choosing to engage in exchange only on select occasions. The arrival of specimens as important as the Osage orange seems to have qualified as just such a select occasion for Hamilton, who sent his nephew Andrew Hamilton to Jefferson citing "the strength of our long acquaintance" and bearing gifts of some of his greatest treasures. The gift of a gingko, paper mulberry, and delicate silk tree of Constantinople were noteworthy not only for being so unusual but for concisely expressing four disparate facts: Hamilton's gratitude, his botanical and horticultural connoisseurship, his esteem for the president's own botanical knowledge, and his attachment to their budding relationship.[14]

Indeed, there were compelling reasons for Hamilton to be concerned for his relationship with Jefferson and for his meticulous care in cultivating it through the exchange of such exotic plants. Although Hamilton and Jefferson shared an interest in botanical curiosities, in most other ways they were an unlikely pair. During the Revolution, for instance, while Jefferson labored in the cause of independence, Hamilton was reputed to harbor Loyalist sympathies, even earning "banishment" from Philadelphia in 1780. Although he never forfeited his property, as many Loyalists did, the tour that Hamilton took of England in 1784 and 1785—the tour in which he first learned to garden like an Englishman—seems to fall conveniently near the settlement of peace and at a time when many American Loyalists went, or were driven, into exile. Certainly, Jefferson and Hamilton were never truly close, and a certain reserve and defensiveness on both their parts marks their correspondence. When Jefferson wrote to Hamilton in April 1800 after a three-year hiatus, he apologized at unusual length for his neglect. Complaining of the battering he had sustained in recent partisan struggles and of the falsity of some friendships it had exposed, he reassured Hamilton that their differences would never undermine their friendship. "I never considered a difference of opinion in politics, in religion, in philosophy, as cause for withdrawing from a friend," he assured, noting that even during the Revolution, "which was trying enough," he had "never deserted a friend because he had taken an opposite side." Loyalist Virginians, Jefferson said, were his best witnesses and could "attest my unremitting zeal in saving their property, and can print out the laws in our statute book which I drew, and carried through in their favor." Scientific union, in Jefferson's formula, trumped political division.[15]

As a grateful Hamilton tendered the Osage oranges to the care of David Landreth, the seedsman and nurseryman, a more likely Jeffersonian entered the picture. Bernard McMahon was a "regularly educated gardener" of considerable skill and experience, an Irish immigrant who, in the half decade after he arrived in Philadelphia, established himself as one of the nation's most adventurous seedsmen. Although the details of his life remain shrouded by the fogs of temporal distance and discretion, McMahon developed a strong trade in seeds and plants in the decade prior to the War of 1812, earning a reputation among his wide circle of peers and friends for his horticultural and botanical acumen. He was so well connected in the networks of botanists and gardeners in Philadelphia as supplier, colleague, or client that the historian Liberty Hyde Bailey accepted that the Lewis and Clark expedition itself was "planned at his house."[16]

McMahon shared little with Hamilton and, as his snide remark about Hamilton's jealousy toward other plantsmen suggests, Hamilton shared little with McMahon. But on several levels, McMahon saw eye to eye with their mutual friend Jefferson, and despite the brevity of McMahon's residence in the United States, a set of social, political, and botanical relationships soon brought the two together.

The precise year of McMahon's arrival in the United States, like many facts of his life, remains difficult to fix, but he appears to have washed ashore with the wave of radical refugees who fled Ireland after the suppression of the United Irishmen in 1798. In 1857, the botanist William Darlington recalled meeting McMahon for the first time in Dilworthtown, Chester County, "In the autumn, I think, of 1799," where McMahon had gone to escape "the ravages of yellow fever." More distinctly, he recalled McMahon as one of the "*Exiles of Erin* who sought refuge in our country." Although McMahon's political affiliations are elusive, the evidence suggests that he swam in the radical stream. Even in the 1850s, at a time when radicalism was a sensitive subject, one writer remembered that McMahon had fled Ireland "from political motives," adding coyly that "what these were has not been determined; most probably it was necessary to fly from the persecution of government" (always a fine motive in American circles).[17]

If McMahon was, as he seems, typical of his fellow refugees, he was an Ulsterman and a Protestant by birth who mixed a Painite egalitarianism and antipathy to religious establishment with a rabid Anglophobia. Regardless of the details, he, his skills, and his beliefs found abundant company in a city that sponsored both a thriving seed trade and an embracing community of radical Irish refugees. By the late 1790s, the Philadelphia Irish had formed several well-organized benevolent societies and had already entrenched themselves as a force in the rough and tumble of partisan politics, and in 1800 they would be credited with delivering the razor-thin majority that secured the presidency for Jefferson. Although the city's Democracy fractured into more and less radical camps shortly thereafter (the Quids and radicals), McMahon's associates seem uniformly derived from the more radical camp. Two other details point to the radical inclinations of this shadowy man: in all likelihood, first, his younger son bore the bellwether name Thomas Paine McMahon—or least so Jefferson believed—and second, the two books that he donated to the American Philosophical Society were his own *American Gardeners' Calendar* and Ezra Stiles's *History of Three of the Judges of King Charles I*, an account of the English regicides who had escaped the Restoration by fleeing to the more congenial shores of America.[18]

Upon his arrival in the city, McMahon was buoyed by support from the community of Irish radicals in Philadelphia, and particularly from William Duane, the Irish immigrant publisher of the newspaper *Aurora*. Although McMahon was said to have been "bred" to the seed trade and implies that he had extensive training in gardening before his emigration, his first employment in the city was probably with Duane. Although his precise activities are difficult to determine, there are hints: McMahon signed a receipt to William Bartram on January 1, 1800, for a year's subscription to the *Aurora*, and two years later when he first appeared in the Philadelphia city directories, he was listed as an "accomptant" living at 69 New Street.[19]

These slender clues, however, only begin to hint at Duane's importance for McMahon. Duane was more than just a generous printer and more than a helpful fellow countryman; he was a staunch political ally of Jefferson's, a man with an unalloyed radical pedigree who had risen to the head of the radical wing of the city's fractious Democratic Party. A former member of the London Corresponding Society, he enjoyed the distinction of earning expulsion from two continents for his radical screeds before arriving in Philadelphia. Even these experiences, however, did not daunt him. After succeeding to sole editorship of the *Aurora* in 1798 following the death of Benjamin Franklin Bache (grandson of Benjamin Franklin), Duane became a particular target of the authorities during the alien and sedition fury, but once again he came through with press (and body) intact and his pen still razor sharp.[20]

FIGURE 4.2. Charles Balthazar Fevret de St. Memin. William Duane. Engraving, ca. 1802? St. Memin Collection, American Philosophical Society. (See Color Plate 9.)

With Duane's help, McMahon had prospered enough by 1802 to return to his old profession, if he ever really left it, opening a seed store that was remembered as a gathering place for an "informal fraternity" of young and aspiring botanists in Philadelphia, including Thomas Nuttall, William Baldwin, William P. C. Barton (Benjamin Smith Barton's nephew), and William Darlington. The vivid presence behind the counter of Ann McMahon, Bernard's second wife, co-worker, and successor, added to the congenial atmosphere. Over the next decade, he developed and diversified his trade, adopting a succession of new titles as he tilled the fields of intellectual ambition and social prestige. His first seed catalog, published in 1804, is testimony to his ambition, spreading over thirty pages and offering more than eight hundred annuals and perennials for sale, but his entries in the city directories provide an even better indication of the course he calculated to the top of the seed trade. Beginning as a simple "garden and grass seeds merchant" at 129 Chestnut, McMahon added "florist" to his title when he moved around the corner to 39 S. 2nd Street in 1807. Six years later, he became "botanist, grass and garden seed merchant," before settling on "botanist, nurseryman, grass and garden seed merchant" when he removed to 13 South Second Street in 1815.[21]

The key term in this metamorphosis was "botanist," with its implications that McMahon offered more than the applied work of a seedsman or nurseryman and that he was more than a merchant or collector: he was, he implied, a skilled observer with a facility in theory as well as practice. Subtly underscoring this notion, when McMahon purchased nearly twenty acres in December 1808 for a "nursery and botanic garden" halfway between Germantown and Philadelphia, he named it

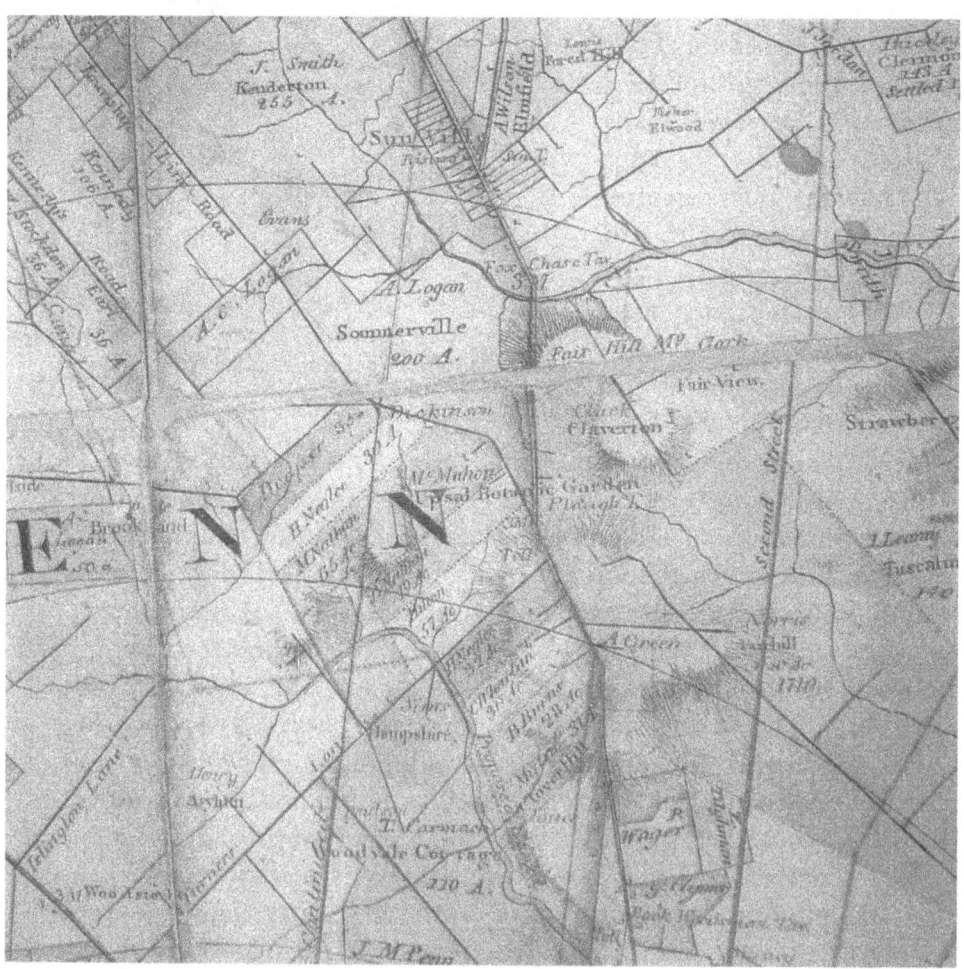

FIGURE 4.3. Detail of John Hills, *Plan of the City of Philadelphia and its Environs*, 4th ed. (Philadelphia, ca. 1815). Historical Society of Pennsylvania. Township Line Road crosses the eastern edge of Upsal and the major road to the east is Germantown Avenue. (See Color Plate 10.)

Upsal in homage to the city of Linnaeus's birth, cleverly signifying his allegiance to the world's greatest systematist and to the cutting edge of botanical theory. Calling Upsal a botanic garden further emphasized his pretensions to scientific status and civic concern.[22]

McMahon thus presented himself as no mere seedsman, no mere merchant of goods, but as a merchant of knowledge. He joined Barton in teaching summer courses at Mme Rivardi's Seminary, one of the city's elite schools for girls, and enlisted with the city's elite in the philanthropic Philadelphia Society for Promoting Agriculture in 1811. But it was through his store and pen that his public face emerged. By late in the winter of 1805–1806, McMahon had opened "a Botanical, Agricultural, and Horticultural Book-Store" at his seed store, "the more effectively to accommodate his customers," claiming that he offered "every valuable book, ancient or modern," on the subject "on moderate terms"

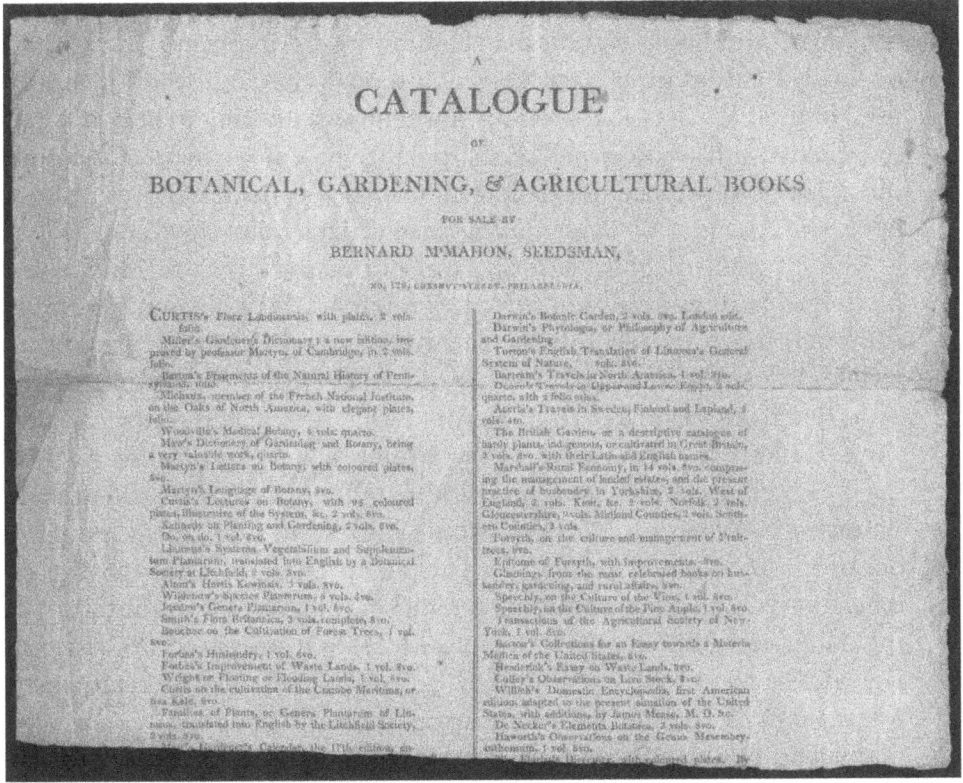

FIGURE 4.4. Bernard M'Mahon, *A Catalogue of Botanical, Gardening, and Agricultural Books* (Philadelphia: s.n., 1805?). Benjamin Smith Barton Papers, American Philosophical Society. (See Color Plate 11.)

along with a wide range of gardening implements and supplies. Though sometimes said to be more for show than sale, these books were—and were designed to be—impressive. Offering European and American titles alike, McMahon's shelves brimmed with Erasmus Darwin's *Botanic Garden*, Adrien de Jussieu's *Genera Plantarum*, and Linnaeus's *Systema Vegetibilium;* he offered Barton's *Collections for an Essay Towards a Materia Medica of the United States* and his *Fragments of the Natural History of Pennsylvania*, William Bartram's *Travels*, William Woodville's *Medical Botany*, and all fourteen volumes of William Marshall's *Rural Economy*.[23]

Connections with books and authors were more than casual for McMahon—they were a leitmotif running throughout his life. His daughter by his first marriage, Mary, married a bookbinder, Abraham Ogden; Bernard served with Duane as co-executors and managers of a trust established by the estate of the printer Patrick Mulligan; and his own executors included his neighbor William Y. Birch, a stationer and bookseller, and William John Duane, William Duane's son. Like the self-applied title "botanist," the books signified a standing in the intellectual world not normally held by a mere tradesman, a status reiterated when he advertised himself as a sort of patron for horticulture, offering to link prospective clients with trained gardeners looking for employment. Of course the pièce de résistance of intellectual display for McMahon was his own book, the *American Gardener's Calendar,* to which I will return shortly.[24]

The effusion of guile, energy, and enthusiasm that McMahon exhibited in building his seed store was rewarded by a blossoming trade. Although there are few reliable records of sales, McMahon's was stunningly diverse, including "Tree, Shrub, and Flower Seeds and Roots, procured from various parts of Europe, Asia, Africa, and America," that were "suitable for cultivation in the United States, and in the West Indies." There are hints that his trade extended to Boston, New York, Baltimore, Pittsburgh, Norfolk, and Charleston, and on at least two occasions he shipped substantial packets to Europe. Through the intermediary of another republican émigré, John Vaughan, librarian of the American Philosophical Society, McMahon prepared an order in December 1804 for one hundred dollars' worth of American seeds for a client in Amsterdam and, again through Vaughan, exchanged plants and books with François André Michaux, son of André, accepting twenty-five copies of Michaux's treatise on oaks for resale and six of the elder Michaux's *Flora Boreali*.[25]

More than anyone, though, it was Duane, the publisher, who furthered McMahon's professional relationships. The *Aurora* was a prime outlet for McMahon to advertise in, and rather unusually for him, Duane published McMahon's second catalog of seeds, but it was Duane's personal connections that produced the greatest yields. When McMahon and Jefferson struck up a warm correspondence during the spring 1806, primed by the exchange of botanical gifts, it was Duane who acted as go-between, carrying greetings, letters, and gifts. In March, after McMahon donated a copy of his newly published *American Gardener's Calendar* to the APS (of which Jefferson was still president), Duane delivered a second copy to Jefferson personally, accompanied by McMahon's suitably humble request for specimens collected by Lewis in "Missouri." Although Jefferson did not immediately comply—the specimens, he noted, had already been placed at the APS—he returned his thanks (through Duane), throwing in "a few of the most valuable" seeds he had recently received from a European correspondent.[26]

The role of the *Calendar* in fostering this relationship is noteworthy in several respects, not only for its obvious function in currying favor with a potential patron, but for the light it sheds on McMahon's ideas of nation and its tacit claim to community with Jefferson's expansionist Empire of Liberty. In his study of the United Irish in America, David Wilson remarks how many of the radical émigrés of the 1790s channeled their frustrated energies on behalf of an independent Ireland into a fervent American nationalism and intense political activism, a caricature that suits both McMahon and Duane. Although the evidence for McMahon's participation in formal politics is slight—a note to Barton regarding the status of "our lottery bill" before the state legislature comprises the sum total—his *Calendar* is a concise evocation of sentiments that would have resonated with his fellow Irish radicals, not to mention with Jefferson.[27]

The *Calendar* opens with a paean to the glorious future to be expected from an agrarian country populated with an "intelligent, happy and independent people, possessed so universally of landed property," a people "unoppressed by taxation or tithes, and blest with consequent comfort and affluence." That this future remained largely theoretical bothered McMahon not a whit. What excused America's delay in realizing it, he wrote, was the lack of anything to read on agriculture and horticulture other than "works published in foreign countries" (conveniently offered for sale by McMahon), works that had only the tendency to "mislead and disappoint the young American Horticulturist." Fine horticulture, he implied, was not necessarily fine American horticulture. To rectify this grave deficiency, McMahon was prepared "to contribute my mite to the welfare of my fellow-citizens," he wrote, "and to the general improvement of the country" by placing his *Calendar* at his adopted nation's disposal.[28]

What distinguishes the *Calendar* from most similar works, and what made it so popular that it ran through eleven editions over fifty years, was the striking breadth of its ambition. Specifying month by month the chores to be performed by the gardener, the *Calendar* attached itself to all the divisions of the garden, from kitchen to orchard, vineyard to pleasure garden, nursery, and greenhouse, seeming to penetrate every aspect of life for men and women alike. In each section, the emphasis fell upon the spectacular abundance of the native flora, though never to the exclusion of the equally abundant imports that could be adapted to flourish in American soils. McMahon presented methods for collecting wild plants and cultivating root vegetables, discussed the most promising fruit trees "which can be cultivated with us to advantage, or even to indulge curiosity," and laid out the virtues of live hedges, licorice, rhubarb, sea kale, cork, mulberry, and silk worms. The most striking feature to emerge through this proliferation of detail is how McMahon, unlike his contemporary garden writers, conceived of horticulture as a national project on a continental scale, drawing men and women, young and old, into a common national enterprise. Emphasizing the adjustments that each gardener would need to make to meet the demands of regional climates, of southern heat and northern winter, and emphasizing the ways in which the garden entered into every facet of life for every citizen, McMahon's *Calendar* became coextensive with the American continent and the conceptual American nation.[29]

Through discussions of fecundity, industry, and adaptability, McMahon made it clear that his sentiments were nationalist, not nativist. In the *Calendar*, he argued that native plants possessed a particular value for the gardener (and nation) that was often overlooked due to their familiarity. "Here," he wrote,

> I cannot avoid remarking, that many flower-gardens, &c. are almost destitute of bloom, during a great part of the season; which could be easily avoided, and a blaze of flowers kept up, both in this department [the flower garden], and in the borders of the pleasure-ground, from March

to November, by introducing from our woods and fields, the various beautiful ornaments with which nature has so profusely decorated them. Is it because they are indigenous, that we should reject them? ought we not rather to cultivate and improve them? . . .

In Europe plants are not rejected because they are indigenous, on the contrary they are cultivated with due care; and yet here, we cultivate many foreign trifles, and neglect the profusion of beauties so beautifully bestowed upon us by the hand of nature.[30]

Yet emulating European attitudes was not McMahon's goal, for Americans, he reasoned, could improve upon European models and, through trade, could strengthen their nation to the universal advantage of its citizens. That the native plants were beneficial did not suggest that imported ones could not be so, too. When properly adapted to American circumstances, imports were every bit as worthy as natives, and with the vast extent of the American empire expanding before them, nearly every plant could become a naturalized American. McMahon was particularly exercised about viticulture, which had long suffered in America, it was believed, because of the poverty of native grape varieties and the inadaptability of European ones. Writers who had denigrated American prospects for viticulture, citing the poor climate in the States, were a particular provocation.

What do they perceive insalubrious, in the air, or unfriendly to vegetable life in the soil of America, any more than in transatlantic countries; or are they led astray by prejudiced European writers, whose envy, or want of knowledge, or perhaps both, had prompted them to assert, that neither animals or vegetables arrive at as good or as great perfection in America, as Europe? However, a little time and some industry, will show that the prejudice is erroneous, and that the *Vine* can be cultivated, in the far great part of the *Union*, to immense national, as well as individual advantage.[31]

McMahon's point was not simply that America could support a vigorous and valuable biota—Jefferson had long ago demonstrated as much—but that adaptability was a peculiarly American virtue. When the pseudonymous "Columella" wrote a letter to the *Daily Advertizer* denigrating the African Cape of Good Hope grape for American viticulture, for example, McMahon felt compelled to respond, motivated "by the interest I feel for the independence and welfare of my country, and fellow citizens." As a "manager" of the Vine Company of Pennsylvania for "several years"—a commercial endeavor devoted to the cultivation of grapes "to *national* as well as individual advantage"—he defended the utility of the foreign grape. "From whence it came originally, I will not pretend to say, nor is it of much importance," he insisted. "If it be indigenous, is it to be despised on that account? if foreign, and likely to answer the end, why discourage its cultivation?" While most European grapes thrived in "cities and large towns," they had proven less successful elsewhere and could therefore not be expected to satisfy the demands for domestic wine consumption. What was needed, he concluded, were new varieties, naturalized or native, that were as well adapted to American conditions as they were to American tastes. "There is not the least doubt," he wrote in his *Calendar,* "but the Vines of any temperate climate, can be naturalized in any state of the Union, in a very short time." Beyond naturalizing and hybridizing, McMahon is said to have been the first to advocate grafting European scions on American rootstock.[32]

While it is tempting to resort to psychology here—the transplant expatiating on the value of transplants—exchange offers a more fruitful framework for analysis. The key to the American future, McMahon suggested, was unfettered and extensive trade, the force that binds society, and from early in his time in Philadelphia, he exhorted American plantsmen to do just that. In announcing publication of the *Calendar* in Duane's *Aurora,* McMahon appended a statement in which he "*earnestly*" solicited the "admirers of plants in every Nation or Country, as well as in every State or Territory of the Union, to an exchange of mutual services," requesting them to consider exchanging plants of any sort that "grow wild, or are indigenous in their respective countries or neighbourhoods."[33]

In his second seed catalog, McMahon again inveigled those who had "the prosperity and welfare of his country at heart," as well as "the lovers of improvement in every part of the United States, and the territories thereto belonging" to exchange seeds with him. Any "trees, shrubs, grasses and other herbaceous plants (with or without names)," he wrote, that were "growing in an indigenous state in their respective vicinities, or obtained by them from friends in other places," would be gratefully received and compensated for by the exchange of vegetables, grasses, fruits, or whatever else might be available and desired.[34] The exchanges were to be promiscuous—to and from every part of the nation and even beyond:

> What I can spare of those [seeds] from my own course of experiments, I mean to exchange with other nations, for such plants as are adapted to, or capable of being naturalized in the different regions of the Union; and by this means, make an effort to introduce into the country, for permanent cultivation, all the important vegetable productions of the temperate zones, as well as several of the torrid.[35]

With its immense geographic scope and diverse climates, the United States would, in short, become a vast botanical garden, an experiment in agriculture benefiting from the most beneficial plants regardless of origin, properly selected, tended, and adapted by American hands, male and female.

Jefferson's response to the *Calendar* is not recorded in detail, but the initial exchange of books and seeds precipitated a long string of similar exchanges, several years' worth. McMahon immediately thanked Jefferson for the gift of Mediterranean seeds by promising to do his best to make them "as well as any other kinds that you will please to favour me with in future, useful to the country." At the same time, he took pains to further cement their relationship by including a gift of his own of some roots and plants of tarragon, an act that soon begat Jefferson's gift of some "quarantine" corn (corn that matures in forty days), which begat in turn McMahon's gift of tulip roots. By July, Jefferson was staking a claim on McMahon for a shipment of plants for Monticello, to be delivered once he retired from the presidency. By the end of the year, with Lewis having returned from the West, Jefferson informed McMahon that his name had been added to Hamilton's "as the persons most likely to take care" of the precious seeds of the Corps of Discovery.[36]

Lewis, of course, was responsible for preparing the botanical results of the expedition, perhaps in collaboration with Barton, but while Lewis might conceivably describe the specimens that he had seen and collected in the field, tending the seeds was another matter. The prestige and expertise of a botanist such as Lewis, or even Barton, were not insignificant, but the opportunity to raise the seeds to maturity and examine living specimens up close, alive, and at leisure demanded a person of consummate horticultural skill.

Entirely apart from the technical demands, the seeds placed an additional burden on those who would cultivate them: confidentiality.

Scientific laurels accrue to the first to publish, and Lewis and Jefferson were concerned that the growing plants would be exposed to some fame-starved botanist who might rush to press before Lewis could reap his justly earned scientific rewards. The seeds could therefore be entrusted only to someone who would preserve them from such subversive eyes, and on both counts, skill and discretion, Hamilton and McMahon passed muster. Thus after giving a parcel of seeds to Jefferson for his personal use, Lewis agreed to divide the remainder between Hamilton and McMahon and promised to deliver them in person.

The story, however, quickly took a turn. Having formed a particular attachment to his trading partner, McMahon, Jefferson decided that he would give him the packet of western seeds that had been earmarked for Monticello, in order, he said, to get them into the ground at once rather than await Lewis's delivery. That this explanation is incomplete seems perhaps too obvious. Jefferson advised McMahon to say nothing of the arrangement to Lewis, "lest it might lessen the portion he will be disposed to give you, and believing myself they will be best in your hands, I wish to increase the portion deposited with you." Two days later, with Lewis delaying his departure for Philadelphia, Jefferson circumvented his protégé again, though perhaps with his consent, sending McMahon and Hamilton their halves of the seed trove directly.[37]

McMahon set immediately to work sowing seeds and offering commentary on botanical affinities and other related matters. In short order he had proved his horticultural mettle. While Hamilton, as Rodney True observed, "seems to have taken his share of the seeds less seriously," McMahon boasted within a month that his fields were sprouting with seven varieties of western plants, and by June he reported success with "*all* the varieties of Currants (7) and Gooseberries (2) brought by Govr. Lewis, and of about 20 other *new species* of plants, as well as five or six new *genera*." All the while, his exchanges with Jefferson continued: a handful of western gooseberries sent to Washington were matched with a packet of seven hundred seeds that Jefferson had recently received from the French botanist André Thouïn, collected from "every country" in the world except the United States. McMahon was humbled by the lavish gift. "I have pleasure and pride in the successful cultivation of plants," he wrote, "but in proportion to the actual or probable good I can render thereby to my fellow-men; and indeed I do not begrudge a share to such of the brute animals as can possibly be benefitted thereby."[38]

COLOR PLATE 1. *See Vitiello essay, page 17.*

COLOR PLATE 2. *See Vitiello essay, page 20.*

COLOR PLATE 3. *See Vitiello essay, page 27.*

COLOR PLATE 4. *See Vitiello essay, page 44.*

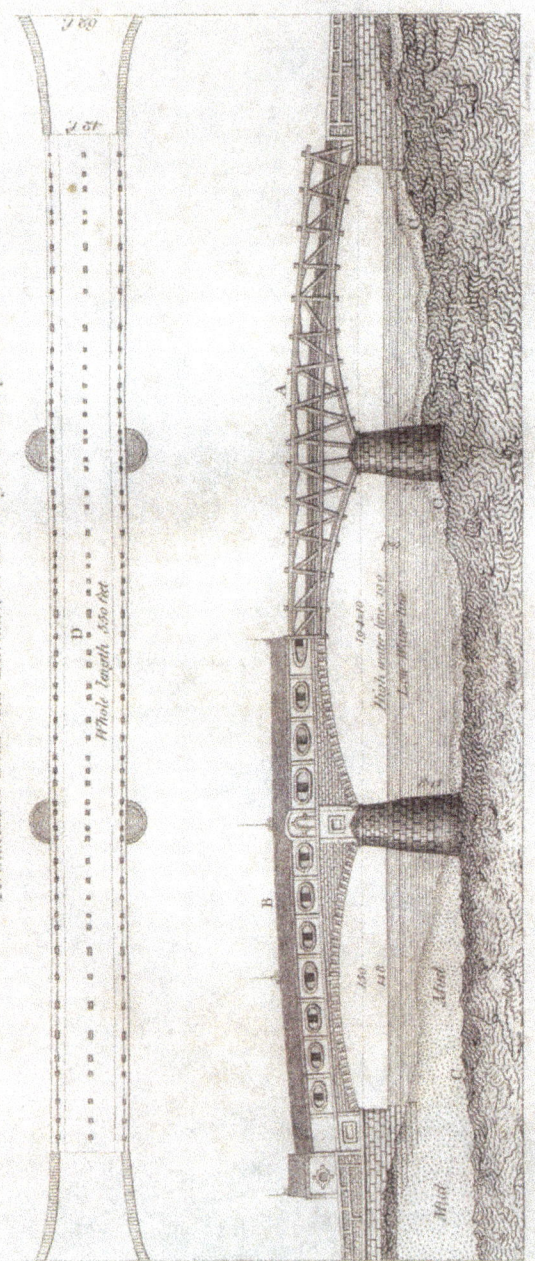

COLOR PLATE 5. See Kimmel essay, page 67.

COLOR PLATE 6. *See Kimmel essay, page 69.*

COLOR PLATE 7. *See Kimmel essay, page 89.*

COLOR PLATE 8. *See Cox essay, page 103.*

COLOR PLATE 9. *See Cox essay, page 111.*

COLOR PLATE 10. *See Cox essay, page 112.*

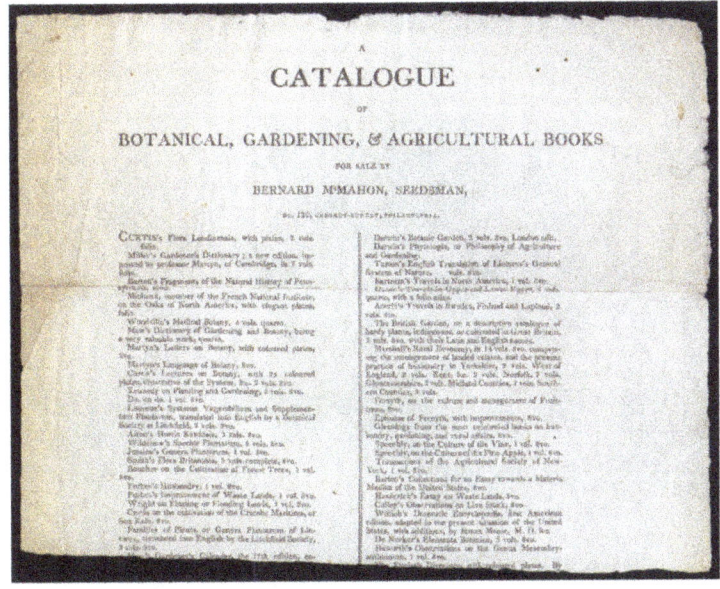

COLOR PLATE 11. *See Cox essay, page 113.*

COLOR PLATE 12. *See Cox essay, page 122.*

COLOR PLATE 13. *See Cox essay, page 128.*

COLOR PLATE 14. *See Jengo essay, page 146.*

COLOR PLATE 15. *See Jengo essay, page 152.*

COLOR PLATE 16. *See Jengo essay, page 169.*

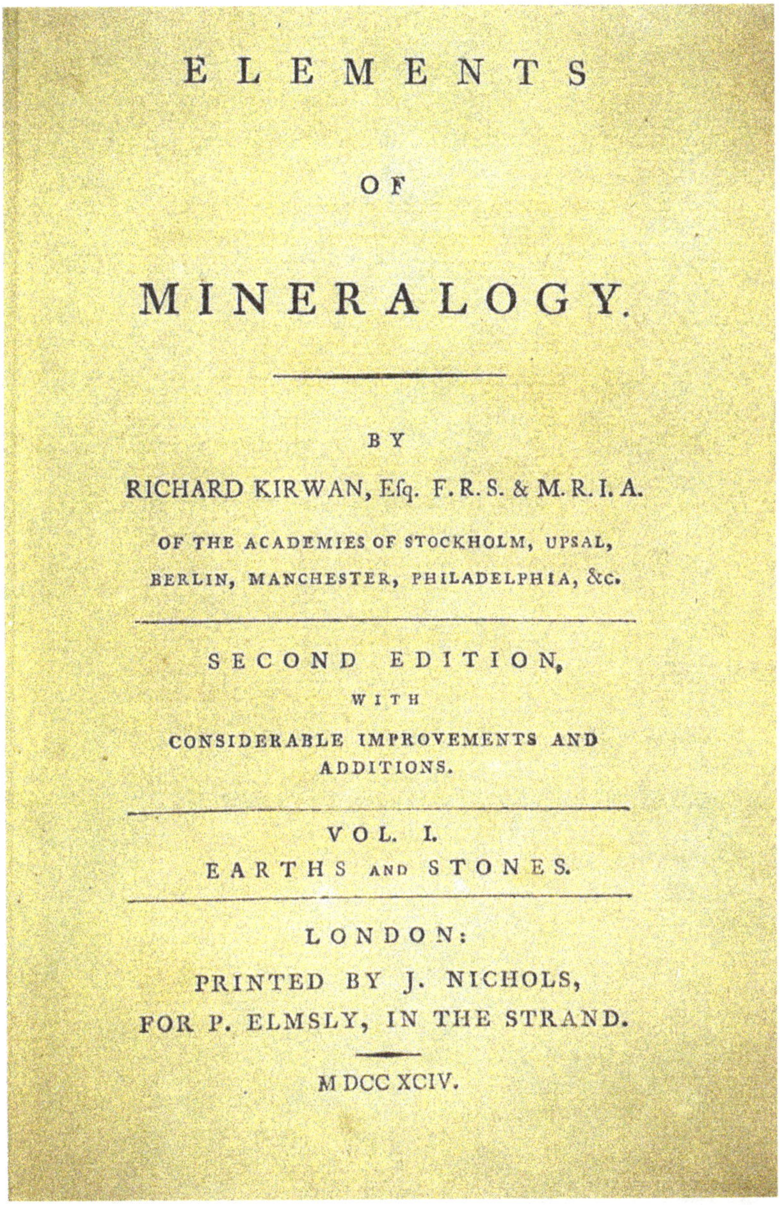

ELEMENTS

OF

MINERALOGY.

BY

RICHARD KIRWAN, Esq. F.R.S. & M.R.I.A.

OF THE ACADEMIES OF STOCKHOLM, UPSAL,
BERLIN, MANCHESTER, PHILADELPHIA, &c.

SECOND EDITION,
WITH
CONSIDERABLE IMPROVEMENTS AND
ADDITIONS.

VOL. I.
EARTHS AND STONES.

LONDON:
PRINTED BY J. NICHOLS,
FOR P. ELMSLY, IN THE STRAND.

MDCCXCIV.

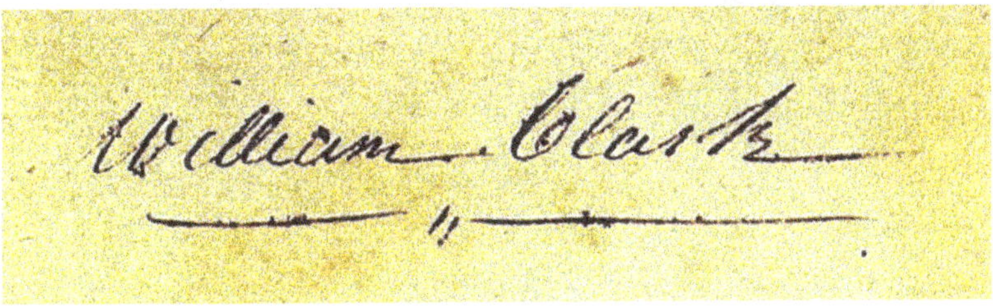

William Clark

COLOR PLATE 17. *See Jengo essay, page 195.*

Color Plate 18. *See Mizelle essay, page 221.*

Color Plate 19. *See Mizelle essay, page 225.*

While the propagation of Lewis's plants moved rapidly forward, there was little sign that Lewis and Barton were keeping pace. Month after month, Lewis delayed visiting Philadelphia and seems to have done little toward realizing the goal of publishing the botanical results of the expedition. Barton, whom both Lewis and Jefferson had assumed would collaborate in this work, was equally dilatory, setting aside the plants that had been entrusted to him in November 1805 in order to complete his massive botanical survey of the eastern states. All the while, McMahon continued to raise the western specimens in secret, keeping them well concealed from the poachers of the scientific world.

Applying a spur, the ever-discreet McMahon suggested to Lewis in April 1807 that he hire an assistant to help with the western plants and, stepping into his horticultural patron's role, nominated a young man for the job then staying at his house. Frederick Pursh, the German immigrant and Hamilton's former gardener, was "better acquainted with plants, in general, than any man I ever conversed with on the subject," as McMahon suggested, and was equally well capable of preparing the illustrations for publication, and Pursh had the added advantage of being well known to Barton. "*Between you and me,*" he added, not wishing to let a dig at a rival go undug, Hamilton did not "use him well" at the Woodlands. What McMahon did not take into account was that whenever Barton was involved, personal relationships would never be easy, and whenever Pursh was involved, they were sure to be volatile.[39]

Barton's direct involvement with Pursh had begun the year before, when he hired the German in April 1806 to botanize in Virginia and North Carolina in hopes of collecting additional specimens for his comprehensive floral survey. Although Barton may have respected Pursh's abilities, tensions cropped up between them from almost the beginning. When Barton wrote to his brother William in Virginia to alert him that Pursh would visit, for instance, he was anything but coy. "In the course of about fifteen or eighteen days," he wrote, "you will if he don't die drunk on the way, receive a letter from me by the hand of a Mr. Fred: Pursch. When you see him, dont let on that you had ever heard of the man before. He is an excellent gardener & a good botanist, who is traveling, *at my expence,* in search of plants, &c." The allegation of Pursh's bibulous tendencies was not unique to Barton, but the lengths to which he went to describe it were. Barton harped upon the drinking, virtually insisting that William never let Pursh far from his sight, keeping him home if it meant keeping him sober. "I think you need not be ashamed to admit him to

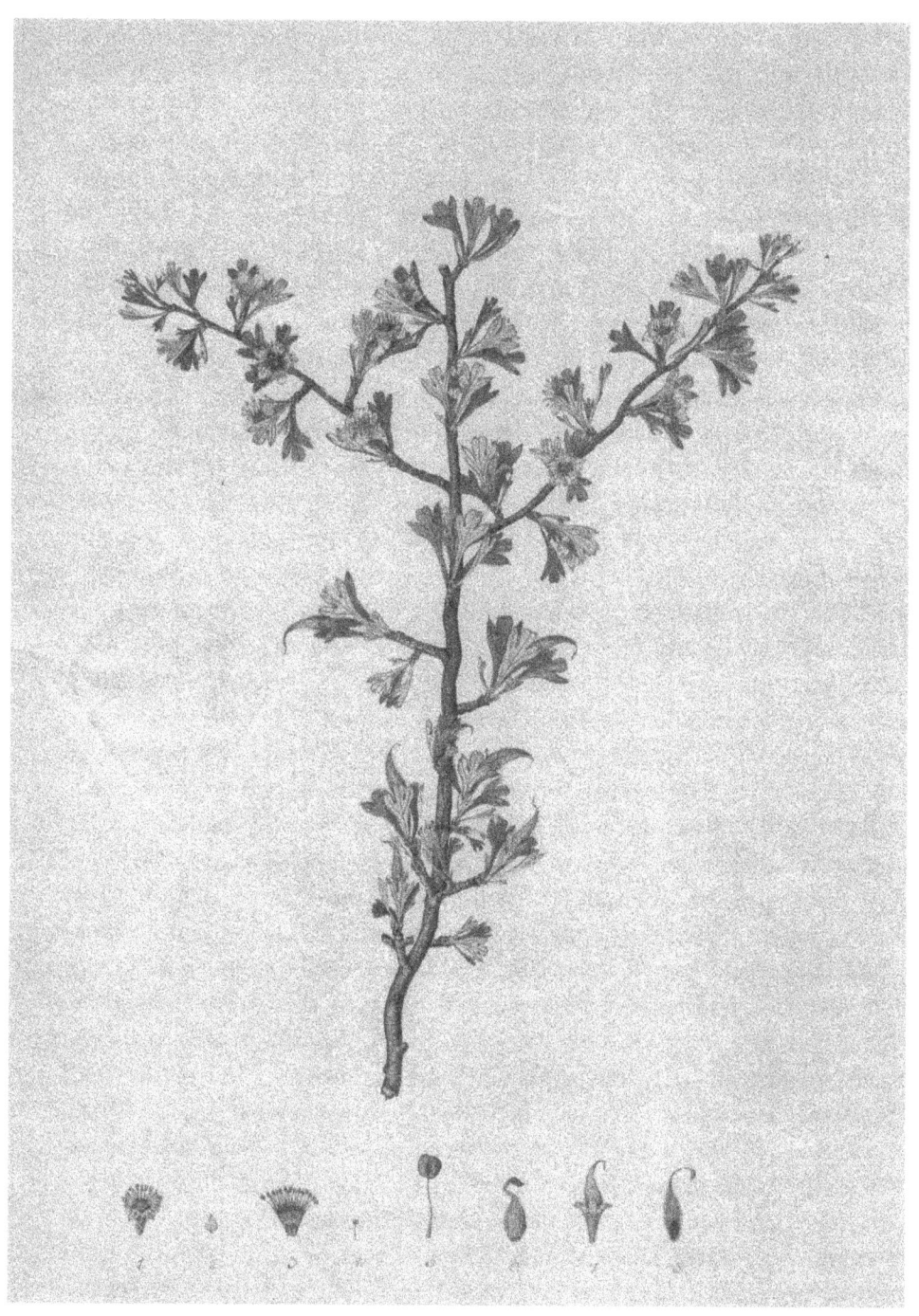

FIGURE 4.5. Frederick Pursh, *Purshia tridentata* (originally described by Pursh as *Tigarea tridentata*). Benjamin Smith Barton Papers, American Philosophical Society. Watercolor on paper. (See Color Plate 12.)

your table," he wrote, "but when you give him toddy, pray, I beseech you, let the proportion of water be very great. Drinking is his greatest failing (and God knows it is a big one), but the poor fellow, who has been well educated, has merit, and I verily believe would not steal anything in the [illegible], rum, gin, whisky, or the like excepted."[40]

Despite Barton's qualms and Pursh's fear of snakes, the southern excursion ended profitably in the early fall, yielding 895 specimens, and after he returned to Philadelphia, Pursh settled in with McMahon to work on Barton's herbarium, possibly including the Lewis and Clark specimens. When Barton called upon Pursh to undertake a second botanical tour in May 1807, this time northward into New York State, it appears that the tensions not only remained unresolved but had been exacerbated by a problem with which Barton was all too familiar—nonpayment for services rendered. Before Pursh departed for the north, Barton consented to sign a contract committing to the "honorable & just payment" of eighty dollars due from the previous year in compensation for Pursh's "attention to my herbarium." Naturally prone to malcontentedness, Pursh now had a reason.[41]

Nearly a year later, Pursh was still complaining that he had not been paid. He had gone to New York filled "with the disinterested view on my side & my own inclination & love to the science" and had been especially frugal throughout while working diligently on Barton's behalf. Claiming (perhaps falsely) that he had a position lined up near Baltimore, Pursh demanded immediate settlement of the debt, even as he understood that Barton's feelings for him had hardened (a condition typical of the obstreperous botanist). "The reserved conduct which you have shown to me this last season," Pursh wrote, "must necessaryly make me a great deal of uneasiness, as I wished & pursued nothing with more zeal than to merit your esteem & thanks in every step I have taken; but should I be so unfortunate as to be disappointed in this I must satisfy myself with the consciousness of my own good will & consider myself treated in the same manner, as I most allways had the misfortune to get no thanks as the reward of my labour."[42]

Barton's reserve had many sources, including friction with both Lewis and McMahon, not to mention Pursh. He seems to have taken umbrage that McMahon had succeeded in securing all the dried specimens, both Lewis's and those that had been delegated to Barton in 1805, following the suggestion (just prior to the New York trip) that Pursh be engaged to work on them. And he was no doubt uneasy to find that in the months following his return from New York, Pursh busied himself "drawing & describing" them, even though Pursh was ostensibly working for him. After another year passed with too little attention from Lewis, and even less hope of payment from Barton, Pursh himself became "very uneasy," and by December 1808 wrote sarcastically that he was "exceeding sorry" that Barton had found it "not convenient . . . to comply at present with my wishes of an immediate settlement between us." With the situation degrading and no sign of Lewis, McMahon recommended Pursh for a position with David Hosack's Elgin Botanical Garden in New York, and with a festering resentment over nonpayment, Pursh left Philadelphia in April 1809, taking all "his drawings and descriptions with him."[43]

On its own, any one of these situations might have delayed publication of the botanical results, but Lewis's unexpected demise in October 1809 derailed even the delay. After the baton passed to William Clark, who was neither available nor able to the task, the obvious choice to assume responsibility for the project was Barton, slow and acerbic but expert in botany. In May 1810, Barton was asked to prepare a natural historical appendix to the journals of Lewis and Clark that Nicholas Biddle had begun to edit.[44]

Yet Barton informed Stephen Elliott, a botanical colleague from South Carolina, that things were not right even before Lewis's death. "In consequence of a dispute between Gov. L. and [Barton]," Elliott informed Henry Muhlenberg, "the work was suspended and no person could be engaged to conduct the Scientific part of it." Without further elaboration, Barton complained of "ill usage, and seemed pa[rticularly?] displeased with McMahon," presumably over McMahon's role in the retrieval of the herbarium. Elliott, however, seems to have suspected that Barton's pique was merely a case of Barton being Barton. Without quite stating the obvious, Elliott told Muhlenberg that the young ornithologist Alexander Wilson offered an entirely different account of events. "The Botanical part is progressing under the care of a German named Bursh or Bursch," he wrote, "and is nearly completed." Adding punch, he predicted "that the whole work will probably be ready for the press in the course of this winter," though McMahon, he concluded, "could probably give you the best information on the subject." It seemed possible, therefore, that both out-of-sorts botanists, Barton and Pursh, were stalking the same quarry.[45]

For his part, even after Lewis's death, McMahon continued to keep his confidences, as he had promised Jefferson he would. He held tightly to the dried specimens until he was requested to pass them along to Clark, and he continued to care for the "several kinds of *new* living plants" that he had grown. Through all the vicissitudes of the project, McMahon never let these "new" plants out of his sight. "I never yet parted with one of the plants raised from his seeds," he told Jefferson in December 1809, "nor with a single seed the produce of either of them, for fear they should make their way into the hands of any Botanist, either in America, or Europe, who might rob Mr. Lewis of the right he had to first describe and name his own discoveries."[46]

Elliott's suspicions of Pursh and McMahon's worries about Lewis's "rights" turned out to be well founded. In January 1810, Clark requested that all of the specimens and illustrations in Pursh's hands be turned over at once, while Jefferson informed McMahon that "whatever is honorable, & whatever may be useful to the work," to settle Pursh's account would be done. Pursh later claimed that he complied with Clark's request, but it is not clear whether his accounts were ever satisfactorily settled. Later that year, he curtailed his stay with Hosack, departing for a West Indian winter (1810–1811) to recover his health, and although he returned briefly to the United States, he was off again before the end of the year.[47]

On this second departure, rumors of Pursh's whereabouts quickly became grist for the botanical gossip mill, leading observers into wild speculation. Zaccheus Collins, a rising Philadelphia botanist, heard that Pursh had died but soon learned that the wayward German had turned up in England, not the afterlife. "As to the plants of Lewis & Clark's journey," Collins wrote Muhlenberg, "we know as little about them as you do, other than that we may soon look for a description of some of them by Bursh now in London, who has in hand Prodromus Florae Americanae on the eve of publication. . . . So far therefore from Bursh being dead as Dr. Hosack told me was reported in N. York two months ago, he is *actively* alive and means to add to the number of foreigners who describe our productions & publish the same beyond our limits."[48]

The idea that a foreigner might abscond with the scientific honors due to Lewis and Clark was too much for young and aspiring American botanists to handle, confirming their worst fears about their status relative to their European colleagues. Following Pursh's trail backward, Collins paid a visit to McMahon's "little room," which he described to Muhlenberg with scarcely concealed contempt.

> His dried specimens chiefly consist of Hamilton's exotics and from their including some of the more rare or new plants scarcely to be met with

[or] even figured in this country are chiefly to be valued. The books of American plants seemed not to have been opened for a great while—specimens named by Burch—much ravaged by insects, and offered. I think nothing that would to *you* have imparted novelty or interest.[49]

Collins feared that with the collections of the Linnean Society at his disposal, Pursh could be well on his way to completing a description of the western plants, whatever the ethics of the situation demanded. Pursh, he felt, could not "in honour or honesty avail himself of Lewis's plants or drawings from them, if he received pay for any service required of, or performed by him." Yet suspecting that pay might just be the issue, Collins left room for Pursh's reputation to escape unblemished: "if, in the sphere of events or management this pay were withheld Bursch might consider himself free to use the drawings as he pleased." With all the delays and obstructions that had afflicted the publication of Lewis and Clark's plants, Collins was beginning to worry that the results would never see the light of day. "A mystery and fatality," he wrote, "seems to have attended the affair throughout."[50]

The suspense lingered for several months, perhaps because Pursh "fell into one of his old fits of intemperance," but it finally came to an end with the appearance of the two-volume *Flora Americae Septentrionalis* in December 1813. In preparing the *Flora*, Pursh apparently worked from duplicates he had withheld when returning the specimens to Clark, and he apparently retained a set of his own sketches. The trepidation that Collins and his peers felt over the failure to keep these most American plants within the ambit of American science came to the worst possible outcome—a European scientist had published the results in Europe. American botanists such as Jacob Green lamented that while Americans "neglected the botanical examination of this country, foreigners have immortalized themselves by doing it." More succinctly, Muhlenberg carped, "John Bull is fat and pays well."[51]

McMahon's End

The slide from a search for national unity into division and international despair took nearly a decade and ended ignominiously. The mystery and fatality that Collins had noted seems to have exerted its curse to all who touched the seeds. Lewis's death in 1809 was followed by Hamilton's in 1813 and by Barton's two years later, and the plants themselves fared little better. Still concerned with the fate of Lewis and Clark's plants after Pursh's coup and Hamilton's demise, Collins sought out whatever remained at the Woodlands, only to find that these too had fallen to fate. "I am informed the present gardener is a clever industrious man but so fraught with making fine cauliflowers, so careful to procure fine *showables,* as not to be likely to know much 'about plain western mere varieties of the backwoods.'" McMahon, he reported, "does not seem fond of talking about Lewis's plants."[52]

Ever discreet, McMahon did not begin to sell the potentially lucrative western plants until 1812, when he began advertising the fragrant currant (*Ribes odoratissimum*) and other species of *Ribes* that "were collected by Messrs. Lewis and Clarke, on the shores of the rivers *Columbia* and *Jefferson,* and in the *Rocky Mountains,* on their expedition to the Pacific Ocean." Pointedly, McMahon noted that these varieties of *Ribes* had been sent to him by Jefferson personally, "to whose love of country and science, the advertiser is indebted for several hundred important species of plants, now in his possession, and in a successful state of cultivation."[53]

Three years later, on September 16, 1816, McMahon died. His passing was lamented in the *Aurora* in words that echoed McMahon's political economy of horticulture:

> From his previous experience and industry, and great enthusiasm in the profession to which he was bred, [McMahon] has rendered very eminent service to the United States, more indeed than all who had preceded him, by applying the principles of agricultural science to the varieties of the climates of this continent; pointing out the errors which had retarded improvement, he contributed to the comforts, and the most delightful of human recreation, planting the shrub, nursing the buds into bloom, and tendril into vigor. His book of gardening is a precious treasure, and ought to occupy a place in every house in the country; its principles are eternal, and its instruction fruitful of advantage.[54]

Although McMahon may never have fully reaped the financial rewards from the Lewis and Clark plants, he nevertheless died in comfortable circumstances, leaving to his wife his lot and store on Second Street and to his son James Upsal and all its appurtenances. Enough money remained in the estate to hold in trust for daughter Mary and to bequeath two hundred dollars to his three servants upon the expiration of their terms.[55]

Within two weeks of her husband's death, Ann McMahon assumed responsibility for the business "in all its branches," and with the assistance of their son Thomas (recently discharged from the army) guided the firm for at least another quarter century, periodically issuing new editions of the *American Gardener's Calendar*. In 1831, a special committee of the Pennsylvania Horticultural Society reported that McMahon's collection still seemed "good," and the firm was said to possess a sixty-foot-long greenhouse and a "small nursery" on Camac Street, while the seed store on Second Street still boasted more than two thousand varieties. After James McMahon's death in 1818, Upsal was offered for sale, though it appears to have been retained in the family, and Thomas seems to have left the firm before 1827 to try his hand as an attorney and notary, applying to fill a vacancy under Philadelphia's wealthiest merchant, Stephen Girard. When Ann's sight dimmed as she grew older, she too sold out. In the end, Bernard's longest-lived legacy was the genus *Mahonia*, which Thomas Nuttall named after him, but even this fell to mystery and fatality: the name has been suppressed as a junior synonym of *Berberis*.[56]

FIGURE 4.6. *Berberis nervosa* from Frederick Pursh, *Flora Americae Septentrionalis*, vol. 1 (London, 1814). *B. nervosa* was assigned to the new genus *Mahonia* by Thomas Nuttall in 1818. (See Color Plate 13.)

Yet neither the demise of McMahon's firm nor the suppression of the genus *Mahonia* nor the persistence of hard feelings over Pursh's usurpation negate a central fact of the legacy of the Lewis and Clark seeds: the degree to which a community of self-consciously American botanists had formed in their wake. The mystery and fatality that afflicted Lewis and Clark seems to have galvanized American botanists to attend even more ardently to their native flora. Prompted by Pursh's injury to his sense of national pride, Muhlenberg wrote to his botanical correspondent Manasseh Cutler to envision a new future for an American botanical community linked through the exchange of specimens and ideas. "Let each one of our American Botanists do something and soon the riches of America will be known," he wrote.

> Let Mechaux describe South Carolina and Georgia; Kramsch, North Carolina; Greenway, Virginia and Maryland; Barton, Jersey, Delaware, and the lower parts of Pennsylvania; Bartram, Marshall, Muhlenberg, their Neighborhood; Mitchell, New York; and You, with the northern Botanists, your states—how much could be done! If, then, one of your younger Companions (I mention Dr. Barton, in particular, whose business it is) would collect the different Floras in one, how pleasing to the botanical world![57]

Muhlenberg betrays not a hint of irony in naming a Frenchman, two German-speaking Moravians, and a physician trained in Europe as his Prometheans for American botany. In all the fitfulness of fate, McMahon's nationalist American botany had been realized.

NOTES

I am grateful to several persons for their valuable comments and suggestions, particularly Joel Fry, Peter Hatch, Shawn Kimmel, Charles Laverty, Peggy Cornett, Jim Green, and Rachel Onuf.

1. Peter S. Onuf, "The Scholars' Jefferson," *William and Mary Quarterly* 50 (1993): 697; Merrell Peterson, "Jefferson and Commercial Policy, 1783–1793," *William and Mary Quarterly* 22 (1965): 584–610; Doron S. Ben Atar, *The Origins of Jeffersonian Commercial Policy and Diplomacy* (New York: St. Martin's Press, 1993). McMahon's name was usually spelled M'Mahon in the early nineteenth century, but I have chosen to use the more common modern form McMahon.

2. Gordon S. Wood, "The Trials and Tribulations of Thomas Jefferson," in *Jeffersonian Legacies*, ed. Peter S. Onuf, 408 (Charlottesville: University Press of Virginia, 1993). The socially poetic function of exchange, affective and monetary, is particularly well outlined in Adam Smith, *The Theory of Moral Sentiments*, ed. D. D. Raphael and A. L. MacFie (New York: Oxford University Press, 1976); Jean-Christophe Agnew, *Worlds Apart: the Market and the Theater in Anglo-American Thought, 1550–1750* (Cambridge: Cambridge University Press, 1986); Julie Ellison, *Cato's Tears and the Making of Anglo-American Emotion* (Chicago: University of Chicago Press, 1999).

3. John W. Harshberger, *The Botanists of Philadelphia* (Philadelphia: T. C. Davis & Sons, 1899), 102; Humphry Marshall to Joseph Banks, Nov. 14, 1786, Humphry Marshall Papers, William L. Clements Library, University of Michigan; Henry Savage and Elizabeth J. Savage, *André and François André Michaux* (Charlottesville: University Press of Virginia, 1986). Technically, William Bartram was Marshall's first cousin once removed.

4. Donald Jackson, *Letters of the Lewis and Clark Expedition* (Urbana: University of Illinois Press, 1962), 15–16; Paul Semonin, *American Monster* (New York: New York University Press, 2000).

5. Ralph B. Guinness, "The Purpose of the Lewis and Clark Expedition," *Mississippi Valley Historical Review* 20 (1933): 90–100.

6. Jackson, *Letters of the Lewis and Clark Expedition*, 11; Guinness, "The Purpose of the Lewis and Clark Expedition."

7. Jackson, *Letters of the Lewis and Clark Expedition*, 64; R. S. Cox, "Supper and Celibacy: Quaker-Seneca Reflexive Missions," in *Sixty Years' War for the Great Lakes, 1754–1814*, ed. David C. Skaggs and Larry Nelson, 243–74 (Lansing: Michigan State University Press, 2000).

8. Thomas Jefferson to Henry Dearborn, Aug. 12, 1802, in *Territorial Papers of the United States. Vol. VII. Indian Territory 1800–1810*, ed. Clarence Edwin Carter, 68 (Washington, D.C.: National Archives, 1936); Robert M. Owens, "Jeffersonian Benevolence on the Ground: The Indian Land Cession Treaties of William Henry Harrison," *Journal of the Early Republic* 22 (2002): 405–35.

9. Saul K. Padover, *The Complete Jefferson* (New York: Duell, Sloan & Pearce, 1943), 503; Anthony F. C. Wallace, *Jefferson and the Indians: The Tragic Fate of the First American* (Cambridge: Harvard University Press, 1999); Bernard W. Sheehan, *Seeds of Extinction: Jeffersonian Philanthropy and the American Indian* (Chapel Hill: University of North Carolina Press, 1973); Francis Paul Prucha, *American Indian Policy in the Formative Years: The Indian Trade and Intercourse Acts, 1790–1834* (Cambridge: Harvard University Press, 1970). Jefferson was no more consistent in his views on Indian miscegenation than he was on black miscegenation, and it is as possible to view Jefferson's benevolent policies as laying the groundwork for the removals of the 1830s, as Anthony Wallace does, as it is to view them as precursors to racial union.

10. The custodial history of the plants collected on the Lewis and Clark expedition, now housed at the Academy of Natural Sciences of Philadelphia, has received considerable attention. Earle E. Spamer and Richard M. McCourt, "The Lewis and Clark Herbarium" [CD-ROM], *Special Publications of the Academy of Natural Sciences of Philadelphia* 19 (2002); Earle E. Spamer, Richard M. McCourt, Robert Middleton, Edward Gilmore, and Sean B. Duran, "A National Treasure: Accounting for the Natural History Specimens from the Lewis and Clark Expedition (Western North America, 1803–1806) in the Academy of Natural Sciences of Philadelphia," *Proceedings of the Academy of Natural Sciences of Philadelphia* 150 (2000): 47–58; Gary E. Moulton, *The Journals of the Lewis and Clark Expedition*, Vol. 12 *Herbarium of the Lewis and Clark Expedition* (Lincoln: University of Nebraska Press, 1999); James L. Reveal, Gary E. Moulton, and Alfred E. Schuyler, "The Lewis and Clark Collections of Vascular Plants: Names, Types, and Comments," *Proceedings of the Academy of Natural Sciences of Philadelphia* 149 (1999): 1–64.

11. Harshberger, *Botanists of Philadelphia*; Meriwether Lewis to Thomas Jefferson, March 26, 1804, Jefferson Papers, Library of Congress (hereafter LC). Lewis also requested specimens be given to John Mason of D.C., whom Donald Jackson identifies as an attorney, banker, and farmer, and later a superintendent of Indian Affairs. Jackson, *Letters of Lewis and Clark Expedition*, 170–72.

12. Townsend Ward, "A Walk to Darby," *Pennsylvania Magazine of History and Biography* 3 (1879): 150–66.

13. *Port Folio* 2 (1809): 505; Benjamin H. Smith, "Some Letters from William Hamilton, of the Woodlands, to his Private Secretary," *Pennsylvania Magazine of History and Biography* 29 (1905): 70–78, 143–59, 257–67; Sarah P. Stetson, "William Hamilton and His 'Woodlands,'" *Pennsylvania Magazine of History and Biography* 73 (1949): 26–33; Richard J. Betts, "The Woodlands," *Winterthur Portfolio* 14 (1979): 203–34. Pursh was hired as gardener to the Woodlands in September 1803. C. S. Rafinesque to Henry Muhlenberg, July 10, 1803, H. E. Muhlenberg Papers (no. 443), Historical Society of Pennsylvania (hereafter HSP); Joseph Ewan, "Frederick Pursh and His Botanical

Associates," *Proceedings of the American Philosophical Society* 96 (1952): 599–628.

14. Bernard McMahon to Thomas Jefferson, Jan. 3, 1809; Bernard McMahon to Thomas Jefferson, July 1806; William Hamilton to Thomas Jefferson, Oct. 1805 and July 7, 1806. Jefferson Papers, LC.

15. Thomas Jefferson to William Hamilton, April 22, 1800, Jefferson Papers, LC.

16. Bernard M'Mahon, *American Gardener's Calendar*, 11th ed. (Philadelphia: Lippincott, 1857), xiii; Bernard M'Mahon, *American Gardener's Calendar*, 1st ed. (Philadelphia: B. Graves, 1806), v; L. H. Bailey, *Cyclopedia of American Horticulture*, vol. 2 (New York: MacMillan, 1900), 963; Joseph Ewan, "Bernard M'Mahon (c. 1775–1816), Pioneer Philadelphia Nurseryman, and His American Gardener's Calendar," *Journal of the Society for the Bibliography of Natural History* 3 (1960): 363–80. Bailey's claim that the Lewis and Clark expedition was planned at McMahon's is repeated in U. P. Hedrick, *A History of Horticulture in America to 1860* (New York: Oxford University Press, 1950). Contra Ewing, McMahon's claim of thirty years' experience as a gardener makes it unlikely that he was born in 1775. If McMahon passed through a fairly typical apprenticeship in the trade, a more likely birth date would be between 1755 and 1760. In the federal census of 1810, McMahon's household included two males over forty-five years old (one, presumably, himself) and one female between twenty-six and forty-five. The two youngest children listed were under ten.

17. M'Mahon, *American Gardener's Calendar*, 11th ed., xiii, xii, xi. McMahon's obituary in the *Aurora* (Sept. 19, 1816) states that he had emigrated "about twenty years since" and may be the source of Ewan's claim that McMahon arrived in 1796.

18. Michael Durey, *Transatlantic Radicals in the Early American Republic* (Lawrence: University of Kansas Press, 1997); Michael Durey, "Thomas Paine's Apostles: Radical Emigres and the Triumph of Jeffersonian Republicanism," *William and Mary Quarterly* 44 (1987): 661–88; David Wilson, *United Irishmen, United States: Immigrant Radicals in the Early American Republic* (Ithaca, N.Y.: Cornell University Press, 1998); Seth Cotlar, "Joseph Gales and the Making of the Jeffersonian Middle Class," in *The Revolution of 1800,* ed. James Horn, Jan Lewis, and Peter S. Onuf, 331–59 (Charlottesville: University Press of Virginia, 2002); Edward C. Carter, "A 'Wild Irishman' under Every Federalist's Bed: Naturalization in Philadelphia, 1789–1806," *Pennsylvania Magazine of History and Biography* (1997): 331–46; Edward C. Carter, "The Political Activities of Mathew Carey, Nationalist, 1760–1814" (Ph.D. dissertation, Bryn Mawr College, 1962). The key works for recreating McMahon's life include William Darlington's reminiscence in M'Mahon, *American Gardener's Calendar,* 11th ed.; Ewan, "Bernard M'Mahon"; and Sarah Pattee Stetson, "American Garden Books Transplanted and Native, Before 1807," *William and Mary Quarterly* 3 (1946): 343–69. When Jefferson responded to Thomas P. McMahon's request for assistance in securing a government position in 1813, he addressed him as Thomas Paine McMahon; however, Thomas is listed as Thomas Patrick McMahon in military records. Jefferson replied that he no longer assisted in securing patronage appointments, yet Thomas was commissioned as a lieutenant in the army less than two weeks later, an outcome that Thomas later explicitly attributed to Jefferson's influence. Thomas Jefferson to Thomas Paine McMahon, April 3, 1813, Jefferson Papers, LC; Francis B. Heitman, *Historical Register of the United States Army,* vol. 1 (Washington, D.C.: Government Printing Office, 1903); Thomas P. McMahon to Stephen Girard, July 13, 1827, Stephen Girard Papers, Girard College. In 1816 Bernard McMahon donated Ezra Stiles's *A History of Three of the Judges of King Charles I, Major-General Whalley, Major-General Coffe, and Colonel Dixwell: Who, at the Restoration, 1660, Fled to America and Were Secreted and Concealed, in Massachusetts and Connecticut, for Near Thirty Years* (Hartford, Conn.: Elisha Babcock, 1794). It is interesting to note that there were other

contemporary politically active, perhaps radical, seedsmen, including William Cobbett and Grant Thorburn, who engaged in a priority dispute over who had introduced rutabagas. Hedrick, *History of Horticulture*.

19. William Bartram, receipt book, microfilm copy at the APS. Thanks to Joel Fry for bringing this to my attention. Ewan concludes that McMahon initially worked for Duane. Ewan, "Bernard M'Mahon (c. 1775–1816)."

20. Duane was born in New York to an Irish family and raised in Ireland. He was expelled from both India and Ireland before landing in Philadelphia and became sole editor of the *Aurora* after Bache's death by yellow fever in 1798. Duane's political influence was surely not harmed by his marriage in 1800 to Bache's widow, Margaret Hartman, and his ties to the Franklin name.

21. James Robinson, Philadelphia Directory, City and County Register for 1803 (Philadelphia: Printed for the publisher and sold by William Woodhouse, 1803); James Robinson, Philadelphia Directory for 1807 (Philadelphia: Printed for the publisher and sold by William Woodhouse, 1807); James Robinson, Philadelphia Directory for 1813 (Philadelphia: Printed for the publisher and sold by William Woodhouse, 1813); and James Robinson, Philadelphia Directory for 1815 (Philadelphia: Printed for the publisher, 1815).

22. Bernard McMahon to Thomas Jefferson, Jan. 3, 1809, Jefferson Papers, LC. McMahon's estate was situated between the Logan estate, Stenton, and the Norris estate, Fairhill, three and a quarter miles north of Centre Square, near the intersection of Germantown Avenue and Township Line Road (at or near present-day Fotterall Square). It should not be confused with Upsala, the mansion built by John Johnson between 1797 and 1801 in Germantown on Germantown Avenue near the intersection with Upsal Street. Tinkcom et al. suggest that Johnson's Upsala was named in honor of the birthplace of the Swedish writer Fredrika Bremer; however, the name was already in use when the fourth edition of John Hills's map of Philadelphia was printed in 1815, when Bremer was only fourteen years old. On Upsala, see Harold Donaldson Eberlein and Cortlandt Van Dyke Hubbard, *Portrait of a Colonial City: Philadelphia, 1670–1838* (Philadelphia: Lippincott, 1939); Robert I. Alotta, *Street Names of Philadelphia* (Philadelphia: Temple University Press, 1975); Harry M. Tinkcom, Margaret B. Tinkcom, and Grant Miles Simon, *Historic Germantown* (Philadelphia: APS, 1955); John Hills, *Plan of the City of Philadelphia and Its Environs*, 4th ed. (Philadelphia: John Hills, 1815). When put up for sale in 1818, Upsal was advertised as having a two-story brick house with frame stable, a greenhouse with about three thousand plants, many "peculiar, valuable, and far sought for" implements, and a "fish pond and island . . . having therein Gold and Silver fish." *Poulson's American Daily Advertiser*, April 4, 1818. I am grateful to Joel Fry for this reference.

23. Mary Johnson, "Madame Rivardi's Seminary in the Gothic Mansion," *Pennsylvania Magazine of History and Biography* 104 (1980): 3–38; "Sketch of the History of the Philadelphia Society for Promoting Agriculture," *Memoirs of the Philadelphia Society for Promoting Agriculture* 6 (1939); *Aurora*, Feb. 12, 1806; Bernard M'Mahon, *A Catalogue of Garden, Herb, Flower, Tree, Shrub, and Grass Seeds* (Philadelphia: William Duane, 1807), 4; Stetson, "American Garden Books Transplanted and Native, Before 1807"; Ewan, "Bernard McMahon"; Bernard M'Mahon, *A Catalogue of American Seeds* (Philadelphia: Bartholomew Graves, 1804); Bernard M'Mahon, *A Catalogue of Botanical, Gardening, and Agricultural Books* (Philadelphia: s.n., 1805?). Interestingly, the Library Company of Philadelphia has a copy of Thomas Martyn, *The Language of Botany*, 2d ed. (London: J. Davis for B. and J. White, 1796), which McMahon sold to William Hamilton in

December 1803, suggesting that he may have been selling books at a fairly early date. The book was later owned by John W. Bartram.

24. *Aurora*, Sept. 30, 1816; Philadelphia Registrar of Wills, Abstracts of Wills for Philadelphia County, Book 6, no. 87 (1816), 4596. Though not an infallible guide to his social status, in the Mulligan will McMahon is identified as "gentleman." William Y. Birch, yet another radical émigré, is often confused with the artist and engraver William Birch; another neighbor was the encyclopedia publisher Thomas Dobson. McMahon offered to link clients with gardeners in ads placed in the *Aurora* (for example) on February 12, 1806, and March 11, 1813. McMahon's son Thomas joined the PSPA in April 1819.

25. *Aurora*, Feb. 12, 1806; *Aurora*, Mar. 12, 1813 (in which McMahon warns clients in those cities not to pay money to anyone but him and his wife); Bernard McMahon, Invoice to American Philosophical Society, Dec. 8, 1804, American Philosophical Society (APS) Archives; François André Michaux to John Vaughan, Sept. 25, 1815; François André Michaux to John Vaughan, May 1, 1815; François André Michaux to Bernard McMahon, Aug. 23, 1815, Michaux Papers, APS.

26. M'Mahon, *A Catalogue of Garden, Herb, Flower, Tree, Shrub, and Grass Seeds;* Thomas Jefferson to Bernard McMahon, April 25, 1806, Jefferson Papers, LC. Although the letter has not survived, McMahon was presumably requesting specimens of plants that Lewis had sent back from Fort Mandan during the spring of 1805 that were entered into the donation book at the American Philosophical Society on November 16, 1805, and placed in Barton's hands for "nomination." On December 22, 1806, Michael Leib, the German-American leader of another radical faction in Pennsylvania, wrote to Jefferson to request specimens of western plants for the well-known botanist Henry Muhlenberg, but without success. Interestingly, Jefferson appears to have requested another copy of McMahon's book through Duane a year and a half later. Donation Book, Nov. 16, 1805, Lewis and Clark Collection, APS; Jackson, *Letters of the Lewis and Clark Expedition*, 353–54; "Letters of William Duane," *Proceedings of the Massachusetts Historical Society* 20 (1907): 303. McMahon's second catalog is usually dated as either 1806 or 1815 but lists McMahon's address as 39 S. 2nd Street, where he resided between 1807 and 1813. The *Calendar* was published on February 14, 1806. *Aurora*, Feb. 12, 1806, Feb. 19, 1806, and Feb. 22, 1806.

27. Bernard McMahon to Benjamin Smith Barton, n.d., Barton-Delafield Collection, APS.

28. M'Mahon, *American Gardener's Calendar*, 1st ed., iii. The lottery bill probably refers to one of the attempts to fund a canal between the Susquehanna and Delaware Rivers. Asa Earl Martin, "Lotteries in Pennsylvania Prior to 1833," *Pennsylvania Magazine of History and Biography* 47 (1923): 307–27; 48 (1924): 66–96, 159–80.

29. McMahon, *American Gardener's Calendar*, 1st ed., iv. McMahon was particularly noted for his innovative methods of propagating Quickset hedges. *Aurora*, Sept. 19, 1816.

30. McMahon, *American Gardener's Calendar*, 1st ed., 72.

31. McMahon, *American Gardener's Calendar*, 1st ed., 227.

32. Bernard M'Mahon, "Cultivation of the Vine," *Niles Weekly Register* 2 (1812): 181; McMahon, *American Gardener's Calendar*, 1st ed., 228; Hedrick, *A History of Horticulture in America to 1860*. McMahon had a heated dispute with Peter Legaux of the Vine Company over the sale and distribution of 3,150 vines that was ultimately settled by submitting it to arbitration by a group of three men, including William Duane. Peter Legaux, Journal of the Vine Company of Philadelphia, Aug. 13, 1813, APS. Legaux

was founder of the Vine Company, and Duane (a colonel in the army at the time) was a long-time member.

33. *Aurora*, Feb. 12, 1806.

34. McMahon, *A Catalogue of Garden, Herb, Flower, Tree, Shrub, and Grass Seeds*, 3.

35. Ibid.

36. Bernard McMahon to Thomas Jefferson, April 30, 1806; Bernard McMahon to Thomas Jefferson, July 12, 1806; Thomas Jefferson to Bernard McMahon, July 15, 1806; Thomas Jefferson to Bernard McMahon, Jan. 6, 1807. Jefferson Papers, LC. Bailey (*Cyclopedia of American Horticulture*, vol. 2, 963) states that McMahon and Landreth "were instrumental in distributing the seeds which those explorers collected," though at least with reference to the period before 1815 distribution seems not to have occurred. Landreth's involvement beyond the cultivation of the Osage orange is uncertain.

37. Thomas Jefferson to Bernard McMahon, March 20, 1807, Jefferson Papers, LC.

38. Rodney H. True, "Some Neglected Botanical Results of the Lewis and Clark Expedition," *Proceedings of the American Philosophical Society* 67 (1928): 9; Bernard McMahon to Thomas Jefferson, June 28, 1808; Thomas Jefferson to Bernard McMahon, Dec. 28, 1808; Bernard McMahon to Thomas Jefferson, Jan. 3, 1809. Jefferson Papers, LC. Because McMahon did not yet own Upsal, it is not clear where the crops for 1807 and 1808 were raised.

39. Jackson, *Letters of the Lewis and Clark Expedition*, 398–99. On Pursh, see Ewan, "Frederick Pursh and His Botanical Associates"; True, "Some Neglected Botanical Results of the Lewis and Clark Expedition"; Stetson, "American Garden Books, Transplanted and Native, Before 1807."

40. Benjamin Smith Barton to William Barton, April 18, 1806, Barton-Delafield Collection, APS. Barton appears to have hired Pursh to make botanical drawings as early as 1801 (see Pursh to Barton, Sept. 14, 1801, Barton-Delafield Collection, APS, in which Pursh complains of having his gardening work interfere with his agreement to finish the drawings). The impressive results of Pursh's efforts in Virginia can be judged by his "Catalogus plantarum quas collegit & observavit in Itinere Virginiano," 1806, Barton-Delafield Collection, APS.

41. Frederick Pursh, "Journal of a Botanical Excursion in the Northeastern Parts of Pennsylvania & in the State of N.Y.," 1807, APS; Benjamin Smith Barton, Agreement with Frederick Pursh, May 26, 1807, and Frederick Pursh, Memorandum of expenses on the journey in 1807, May 26–Oct. 5, 1807, Barton-Delafield Collection, APS; Whitfield J. Bell, "Benjamin Smith Barton, M.D. (Kiel)," *Journal of the History of Medicine and Allied Sciences* 26 (1971): 197–203. Pursh's memorandum indicates that he had received a total of $125 during the trip on a total of just over $135. Bell uncovered Barton's questionable claims about his medical degrees and makes reference to potential financial embarrassments during his education in England.

42. Frederick Pursh to Benjamin Smith Barton, March 10, 1808, Barton-Delafield Collection, APS.

43. Bernard McMahon to Thomas Jefferson, Jan. 17, 1809, and Bernard McMahon to Thomas Jefferson, Dec. 24, 1809, Jefferson Papers, LC; Frederick Pursh to Benjamin Smith Barton, Dec. 13, 1808, Barton-Delafield Papers, APS.

44. Charles Willson Peale to Rembrandt Peale, Feb. 3, 1810, Peale Papers, APS; Jackson, *Letters of the Lewis and Clark Expedition*, 548–49.

45. Stephen Elliott to Henry E. Muhlenberg, Oct. 21, 1809, H. E. Muhlenberg Papers (No. 443), HSP.

46. Jackson, *Letters of the Lewis and Clark Expedition*, 485.

47. Thomas Jefferson to Bernard McMahon, Jan. 13, 1810, Jefferson Papers, LC; Jackson, *Letters of the Lewis and Clark Expedition*, 490–91.

48. Zaccheus Collins to Henry E. Muhlenberg, Sept. 24, 1812, H. E. Muhlenberg Papers (No. 443), HSP.

49. Zaccheus Collins to Henry E. Muhlenberg, Oct. 15, 1812, H. E. Muhlenberg Papers (No. 443), HSP. Collins's hand is difficult to discern here, and he may have written "Macran." There was a Philadelphia nurseryman named McArran; however, he does not appear to have set up shop until several years later. The context of Collins's comments also suggests McMahon.

50. Zaccheus Collins to Henry E. Muhlenberg, Oct. 15, 1812, H. E. Muhlenberg Papers (No. 443), HSP.

51. Zaccheus Collins to Henry E. Muhlenberg, Jan. 18, 1813, H. E. Muhlenberg Papers (No. 443), HSP; Green and Muhlenberg cited in Ewan, "Frederick Pursh, 1774–1820, and His Botanical Associates," 617; John C. Greene, "American Science Comes of Age, 1780–1820," *Journal of American History* 55 (1968): 22–41; Jeannette E. Graustein, *Thomas Nuttall, Naturalist: Explorations in America, 1808–1841* (Cambridge: Harvard University Press, 1967), has a lucid description of Pursh's activity in London at the time of publication.

52. Zaccheus Collins to Henry E. Muhlenberg, Aug. 11, 1814, H. E. Muhlenberg Papers (No. 443), HSP.

53. *Aurora*, March 11, 1812.

54. *Aurora*, Sept. 19, 1816.

55. Philadelphia Registrar of Wills, Abstracts of Wills for Philadelphia County, Book 6, no. 87 (1816), 4596.

56. *Aurora*, Sept. 30, 1816; *Poulson's American Daily Advertiser*, April 4, 1818; Pennsylvania Horticultural Society, *Report of the Committee . . . for Visiting the Nurseries and Gardens in the Vicinity of Philadelphia* (Philadelphia: William F. Geddes, 1831), 10, 11; Thomas P. McMahon, Receipt to Thomas McAtee, 1818, Morris Family Papers, APS; Thomas P. McMahon to Stephen Girard, July 13, 1827, Stephen Girard Papers, Girard College. The labels (in Pursh's hand) on the Lewis and Clark herbarium specimens suggest that *Mahonia* was originally to be named *Lewisia*. Moulton, *The Journals of the Lewis and Clark Expedition*, vol. 12. Although Upsal was offered for sale in 1818, it is not certain whether it left the McMahon family's hands. An 1831 advertisement for Hibbert & Buist indicates that they had purchased the "Greenhouse and Nursery Grounds, established by the late Mr. McMahon." *Poulson's American Daily Advertiser*, July 12, 1831.

57. Cited in Greene, "American Science Comes of Age," 36.

5

"Mineral Productions of Every Kind"

Geological Observations in the Lewis and Clark Journals and the Role of Thomas Jefferson and the American Philosophical Society in the Geological Mentoring of Meriwether Lewis

John W. Jengo

Introduction

THE EXPEDITION to explore the Louisiana Purchase and the lands beyond, led by Captains Meriwether Lewis and William Clark, is an enduring story of adventure, teamwork, and peerless leadership. The outcome is well known: the loss of only one man over a twenty-eight-month long, eight thousand-mile trek to the Pacific Ocean and back by keelboat, pirogues, horses, and canoes and on foot. The scientific discoveries by Lewis and Clark in the fields of geography, botany, zoology, and ethnology have been justly celebrated: they measured the width of the continent, produced a map considered to be a cartographic masterpiece, and established American claim to Oregon, Washington, and Idaho; they described 178 plants and 122 animals that were new to science, including western signature species such as the ponderosa pine, the prairie dog, the coyote, and the grizzly bear; and they recorded priceless ethnological baseline data of native American cultures, the Shoshoni and Nez Perce among others, that were still untouched by the impending influence, disease, and debasement of Manifest Destiny.

Although the fame of the Lewis and Clark expedition, formally known as the Corps of Volunteers for North-Western Discovery, comfortably rests on the aforementioned achievements and the vivid images of an untouched, and now largely vanished, wilderness, what about geology? That geology was an important aspect of the expedition goals is irrefutable, because the task of documenting the "mineral productions of every kind" was included in President Thomas Jefferson's preexpeditionary instructions and was slated to be an essential part of the postexpeditionary second volume of the never-completed Conrad and Company edition of the journals. Why did Jefferson have mineralogy included in the expedition instructions? What role did Jefferson and other members of the American Philosophical Society (APS) play in Lewis's, and by extension Clark's, geological education and their use of appropriate scientific terminology? What did Lewis and Clark, the first American explorers of the West, emphasize in their journal observations and why? Are there useful, perhaps even insightful, observations of geology in the captains' journals, safeguarded by APS for nearly two hundred years, that have gone unappreciated by historians and scientists alike? And have Lewis and Clark been judged fairly by historians with regard to their geological and mineralogical observations, given the state of these sciences at the dawn of the nineteenth century?

Mineralogy, Geology, and Thomas Jefferson's "Instructions to Lewis"

Consistent with his Enlightenment ideals that science should be applied to serve mankind in order to further progress and ensure human happiness, Thomas Jefferson undoubtedly viewed the natural productions of the land as one of the most essential elements of this philosophy.[1] While it has been recognized that climate, soils, flora, and fauna were of principal interest to Jefferson, it bears noting that Jefferson never failed to have mineralogy included in any set of instructions he developed for exploration of the trans-Mississippi West. There is also much evidence that Jefferson had been thinking about geological concepts and the vast mineral potential of the new nation in the decades that preceded the Lewis and Clark expedition.

In a handful of Jefferson's prodigious correspondence, minerals appear to have been an ephemeral curio that Jefferson enjoyed sharing with his contemporaries, particularly his friends in Europe. Desiring to obtain specimens prior to his impending voyage to Europe to begin his tenure as minister plenipotentiary to France, Jefferson enlisted the assistance of George Rogers Clark in his November 26, 1782, letter to provide "[d]escriptions of animals, vegetables, minerals, or other curious things."[2] Fourteen years later, Jefferson found himself facilitating the exchange of mineral specimens, among other natural history items, with Prince Louis, heir to the Spanish throne, who was creating a personal "cabinet," or museum.[3] And upon Jefferson's final retirement in Monticello, minerals and other geological specimens were included in his valued natural history collection displayed in the entrance hall.[4]

On the other hand, a substantial body of letters indicates that Jefferson's interest in geology and mineralogy was more than just mere curiosity. Jefferson's correspondence with Charles Thomson, a trusted friend and the secretary to the Continental Congress, during the period when Jefferson was formulating replies to the queries of François de Barbé Marbois (the secretary of the French legation to the United States), which would result in Jefferson's celebrated *Notes on the State of Virginia* (*Notes*),[5] indicates that Jefferson thought mineralogy was an important natural production of the country. Thomson shared this view and articulated to Jefferson in a March 9, 1782, letter that "This Country opens to the philosophic view an extensive, rich and unexplored field. It abounds in roots, plants, trees and minerals, to the virtues and uses of which we are yet strangers."[6] The theme of the unrealized potential of these mineral resources would continue to arise over the next twenty years in Jefferson's geology-related correspondence.

Jefferson's continued correspondence with Charles Thomson in 1786–1787 on rock strata is revealing because it indicates that Jefferson was interested in resolving how rocks could be found in a variety of inclinations and determining what mechanism was responsible for these upheavals and the formation of mountains and valleys.[7] There was a lively exchange of ideas and theories between the two men, after Thomson asked Jefferson his opinion on John Whitehurst's *An Inquiry into the Original State and Formation of the Earth* (1778), perhaps triggered by the publication of another edition of this book in 1786.[8] Jefferson's response is remarkable because it reveals the depth of his analyses of Whitehurst's book. While acknowledging that there were "many interesting facts brought together, and many ingenious commentaries on them," Jefferson methodically dissected the flaws in Whitehurst's theory that steam was the mechanism for creating mountains and valleys, unequivocally stating that "there are great chasms in his facts, and consequently in his reasoning," and that a "sceptical reader therefore, like myself, is left in the lurch." (Jefferson also took particular issue with the theorist's use of a divine creator and the failure to reconcile this with "the millions of ages necessary" to form the earth.)[9]

Thomson must have realized that he hit a nerve and in a following letter submitted that "in referring you to Mr. Whitehurst I did not mean to recommend him as an Author on which you were to build your faith."[10] Thomson then attempted to deflect the discussion away from the unproved theory and toward the observable result, one with potential future implications for the Lewis and Clark expedition, "His eruption will tolerably well account for the oblique position of the strata of rocks which is observable in most parts of the world. But what are we to think of their horizontal position in our Western country?"[11] When Jefferson replied, he cataloged the variety of rock inclinations he had observed in his travels and offered a diplomatic resolution to this unresolved question. "They may indeed have been thrown up by explosions, as Whitehurst supposes, or have been the effect of convulsions."[12] Although Jefferson demurred from further debate—asking "Why seek further the solution of this phaenomenon?"[13]—it's obvious he had done some serious thinking on the matter, including the effort on his trip through the European Alps and Apennines (a southern extension of the Alps in Italy) to note the positions of the rock formations. Jefferson's familiarity and confidence in stratigraphic concepts would be exhibited in his careful and groundbreaking archaeological work[14] and in casual correspondence with family members—for example, his letter to Thomas Mann Randolph on June 5, 1791, that discussed strata and limestone.[15]

Despite his interest in determining the extent of the country's mineral resources, Jefferson's position that any mineralogical exploration be a privately funded venture was well illustrated in his response to a letter from a B. Francis that had been directed to President George Washington. Francis had requested governmental support to conduct a study of the country's geological strata to facilitate the mining of metals. Jefferson replied on June 22, 1792, that although he was confident that there was great "subterranean riches in this country," the exploration of the "mineral kingdom, as that of the vegetable and animal, is left by our laws to individual enterprize, the government not being authorised by them to interfere at all."[16] Six months later, Jefferson would play a leadership role in such a private enterprise, the APS's sponsorship of the French botanist André Michaux's western expedition.

Minerals were specifically included in the signed text of the APS subscription agreement (ca. January 22, 1793), which stated that upon Michaux's return he would communicate to APS "the information he shall have acquired of the geography of the said country it's inhabitants, soil, climate, animals, vegetables, minerals and other circumstances of note."[17] The Michaux instructions (ca. April 1793), often considered to be the rough draft of Jefferson's instructions to Meriwether Lewis a decade later, directed Michaux to take notice of "productions animal, vegetable, and mineral so far as they may be new to us and may also be useful or very curious."[18] As we all know, the Michaux expedition unraveled, and it is believed that the political intrigues that doomed it convinced Jefferson that only a federally funded expedition could ensure a successful exploration of the trans-Mississippi West.[19]

In the mid-1790s, Jefferson received several remarkable requests from European correspondents for his assistance in gathering information about American natural history, with mineralogy and geology prominently mentioned. Marc Auguste Pictet, a Swiss natural scientist and professor of natural philosophy at the Academy of Geneva, wrote Jefferson on January 1, 1795, during a time when transplanting this institute to America was seriously being considered. Pictet stated that he was "indulging in the mean time the thought of Mineralogical and Geological excursions in a world entirely new to me" and cited Jefferson's *Notes* as a significant inspiration.[20] Jefferson's reply on October 14, 1795, clearly indicated his opinion on where the country stood on exploiting those resources: "Our geology is untouched, and would have been a precious mine for you, as your views of it would have been precious to us. . . . Our country is but beginning to develope it's resources."[21] On July 30, 1795, Christoph Daniel Ebeling, a German scholar and educator, sought Jefferson's assistance in compiling information for a multivolume history of America, essentially a "Notes on America," that would closely mirror the eclectic scope of Jefferson's *Notes*, which Ebeling openly admired. Ebeling stated that he intended to include in his work "the Mineralogy of each State. This, you know, is still the most defective part of American Natural History."[22] Surely, these objective opinions from respected correspondents only reinforced for Jefferson that a well-planned and expertly executed exploration was needed to fully ascertain the unknown mineral resources that lay to the west.

Finally, we can look at Jefferson's role as president of the APS, particularly his involvement in the Historical and Literary Committee, for evidence of his interest in the natural history of the earth. This committee, under Jefferson's direction, submitted a report in late 1798 that laid out priorities for research into what were then termed American "antiquities" (principally, but not exclusively, archeological and paleontological artifacts). An important portion of this document was a "circular letter" (essentially a "call for papers") that was widely distributed to the scientific community. This letter, which was signed by Jefferson, Caspar Wistar, Charles Willson Peale, and several other APS members, listed the types of "antiquities" that the committee believed merited particular attention; prominent among them was the desire to "invite researches into the Natural History of the Earth, the changes it has undergone as to Mountains, Lakes, Rivers, Prairies, &c."[23]

By the time Jefferson finalized the now-famous instructions to Lewis, he intended these directives to be read as both a guidebook and checklist, specifying the type of observations that were needed to identify and roughly map the geographic extent of these heretofore undiscovered resources. As such, Jefferson included very specific mineralogical objectives in the list of objects he considered worthy of note: "the remains or accounts of any [animals] which may be deemed rare or extinct; the mineral productions of every kind; but more particularly metals, limestone, pit coal, & saltpetre; salines & mineral waters, noting the temperature of the last, & such circumstances as may indicate their character; volcanic appearances."[24] These same objectives were repeated nearly verbatim, but the mineral list was expanded slightly, in the draft instructions for what would become the Freeman-Custis expedition of the Red River in the spring and summer of 1806: "the mineral productions most worth notice, but more particularly metals, limestone, gypsum, pitcoal, salt petre, rock salt & saltsprings."[25] Additionally, Jefferson's correspondence with William Dunbar, a Scottish-born scientist, inventor, and prominent Mississippi planter, during the time the two men were planning a potential Arkansas–Red River expedition, also reflected Jefferson's view that the leaders selected for other Louisiana Purchase explorations should also have an expertise in "the departments of botany, natural history & mineralogy," yet another example of the importance he placed on these particular natural resources.[26]

What Were These "Mineral Productions of Every Kind"?

It is important to clarify what Jefferson meant by "mineral productions of every kind." For most people, their primary exposure to mineralogy is through the attractive mineral and gem collections in museums throughout the world. Of course, Jefferson had something entirely different in mind, and he phrased his instructions perfectly. Although a mineral is defined as a naturally occurring, inorganic substance with a range of chemical compositions and a very specific crystalline form that can often possess a striking beauty, the word is also used to describe ordinary rocks, stones, gravels, sands, clays, and other materials such as coal and iron ore. When such materials lie undisturbed in concentrations or amounts that merit and justify commercial use, they are termed "mineral resources." Only when these resources are removed from the ground and subsequently utilized are they truly termed "mineral products." So clearly, Jefferson was thinking well ahead of just identifying the location of these resources; he was focused on the economic value and usefulness of these anticipated "mineral productions."

A glance backward at life in the early nineteenth century in America, particularly as related to agriculture and manufacturing, reveals why Jefferson thought certain mineral productions such as coal, limestone, clays, and metals were essential (which would also explain why they were given such prominent mention in Jefferson's *Notes*). For example, it was discovered in England in the 1700s that coal produced a hotter burning fuel than wood charcoal. The technologies that were subsequently developed during the Industrial Revolution anticipated utilizing a more reliable supply of energy, and coal filled that role in many different capacities. Additionally, during his time in Europe, Jefferson witnessed pit coal being used in France to generate hot air to lift balloons[27] and observed how coal was put to use in England to generate steam to operate gristmills, which Jefferson described in several letters to Charles Thomson in 1786.[28] Important as a building material, limestone was also indispensable to the success of Jefferson's beloved agriculture because its chemical properties reduced the acidity of soil, improving the soil's potential in growing crops. Limestone also had a very crucial use as flux in smelting iron ore, serving as an essential catalyst to remove impurities from the molten iron. Clays were the principal raw materials for making bricks, perhaps the single most important building material in Jefferson's era other than wood and fieldstone. One need look no further than eighteenth-century colonial architecture and the extensive use of brick in Jefferson's Monticello and Poplar Forest homes to recognize the importance of this raw material.

It is well beyond the scope of this paper to detail the myriad uses of metals in the era of Jefferson; a list of just the kitchenware and eating utensils alone could fill pages.[29] However, a review of the supplies that Meriwether Lewis purchased in Philadelphia in the spring of 1803 to outfit the expedition provides a representative example of the varied uses of these metals and why they were so important to the young nation. For example, Lewis purchased brass thimbles, brass wire, brass inkstands, brass boat and pocket compasses, copper kettles, gold scale weights, flints and whetstones, iron bound kegs, iron corn mills, iron spoons, cast iron combs, iron weights (for the steelyard), lead canisters, sheet lead for bullets, pewter looking glasses, a silver-plated pocket compass, writing slates, steel for striking fire, steel plate hand saws, tin horns, tin saucepans, and tin canisters. Also purchased were metallic items such as adzes, augers, awls, axes, brads (thin wire nails), bullet molds, buttons, chains, chisels, files, fishing hooks, gimlets, hatchets, knitting pins, knives, lanterns and lamps, lancets, needles, pliers, rasps, scissors, shears, spikes for setting poles, steelyards, and vices. Metals were the essential component of the all-important scientific instruments, including the chronometer, sextant, microscope, pocket telescope; the invaluable rifles; and the star-crossed iron-framed boat. Nor were essential minerals forgotten in Lewis's medical kit, which included copperas, Glauber's salt, magnesia, and niter.[30] Even some of the Indian gifts were comprised of metals, including broaches, earrings, lockets, and rings.[31]

One of the more definitive indications that mineral productions were not simply an afterthought in the Jefferson instructions came during the time the expedition was bunkered down in Camp Dubois outside of St. Louis in the winter of 1803–1804. Lewis apparently circulated a census/survey form letter in early January 1804 to the leading merchants and citizens of St. Louis inquiring about populations, demographics, imports and exports, and natural resources. Mineralogy is prominently mentioned in this inquisitive letter: "What are your mines and minerals? Have you lead, iron, copper, pewter, gypsum, salts, salines, or other mineral waters, nitre, stone-coal, marble, lime-stone, or any other mineral substance? Where are they situated, and in what quantities found? . . . Which of those mines or salt springs are worked? and what quantity of metal or salt is annually produced?"[32] These inquiries yielded at least fifteen donated mineralogical specimens that Lewis relayed to Jefferson four days after the departure of the expedition from Camp Dubois.[33]

An Assessment of Geological Observations in the Journals of Lewis and Clark

Capt Lewis went out with a View to see the Countrey and its productions.
WILLIAM CLARK, September 17, 1804

On May 14, 1804, the time had finally come for Lewis and Clark to proceed on to the Pacific Ocean and discover for themselves the true occurrence and extent of those anticipated "mineral productions of every kind." In order to ascertain the source of the captains' geological learning and to fully appreciate the extent to which they applied this knowledge, I thoroughly reviewed and appraised the journals of Lewis and Clark for evidence of geological observations. Given the daunting number of geologically related observations, which exceed some fifty thousand words, I have attempted to group the captains' most significant remarks in broad categories to facilitate the discussion of their most insightful and informative entries.[34] But first, a word about William Clark.

William Clark's Contribution

It is recognized by Lewis and Clark scholars that Lewis was the recipient of two years of scientific interaction with Thomas Jefferson while serving as his secretary and intensive schooling by APS members Benjamin Smith Barton, Caspar Wistar, and Andrew Ellicott (often referred to as the APS mentors) in Lancaster and Philadelphia in the spring of 1803, and that Jefferson viewed Lewis as the principal scientist of the expedition. However, the written record indicates that Lewis immediately engaged Clark as an equal partner in the expedition's scientific objectives. In Lewis's very first correspondence with Clark regarding the expedition, the now-famous letter inducing Clark "to participate with me it's fatiegues, it's dangers and it's honors," Lewis describes in detail the scientific aspects of their mission, including ascertaining "the soil and face of the country . . . the miniral productions of every discription."[35] Once together, Lewis undoubtedly shared his expertise with Clark, and it's not difficult to imagine the captains reviewing the reference books and discussing what to emphasize in their journals. The journals are the best evidence that Clark proved a quick study. So while Lewis clearly dominated in many of the technical geological observations to follow, it is important to remember that Clark's contributions are invaluable. For example, consider the following two journal entries:

> the high lands juts to the river and form a most tremendious Clift of rocks near the Commencement of this Clift I saw a Cave, the mouth of which appeared to be about 12 feet Diameeter, and about 70 foot above the water. . . . The chanel which forms the Island next to the fort is intirely dry, and appears to be filling up with Sand and mud. (Clark, December 4, 1803)

> In this Course I observed (1), Several caves, also a number of Indented Arches of deferent sises in the Clifts on the Larbd. Side, which gave it a verry romanteck appearance. . . . a Streen suficient large to aford water for mills (several of which are now established on the Creek) at all Sea-

sons. . . . the Current of the river sets imedeately against this rock, we had some difecualty in passing it- this Rock appears to be Composed of Grit well calculated for Grind Stones. (Clark, December 5, 1803)

These entries were written during the time that Lewis was in Kaskaskia and then traveling by horseback to Cahokia, so only Clark was witness to this portion of the Mississippi River and these observations were his alone. Already Clark was noting the character of the river, unique geological features, and economical uses of the waterways and rocks. Thus, it is imperative to acknowledge that Clark bought to the expedition his own unique skills, which would be demonstrated time and again in the years ahead.[36]

Technical Terms
STRATA

Overall, Lewis and Clark did not utilize many technical geological terms, especially when compared to Lewis's impressive command of botanical terminology. But the terms they did use were appropriately applied. For example, the captains utilized the word "strata," defined as a tabular or sheetlike layer of rock visually distinguishable from other underlying and overlying rock units, in at least twenty-eight different daily journal entries, and they occasionally attempted to use the word in its singular form "stratum" (e.g., see Lewis's description of Fort Mandan mineralogical specimen No. 59).[37] The first recorded usage of the word "strata" was in Lewis's October 3, 1803, letter to Jefferson describing the mammoth bone and teeth specimens recovered from the Big Bone Lick, a rich paleontological site in Boone County, Kentucky, twenty miles southwest of Cincinnati, Ohio.[38] The word was first applied in relation to rock units in Lewis's Ohio River journal:

> the flint appears to ly in stratas yet reather divided by the *limestone* even in those stratas, they appear to be from six inches to a foot asunder. all the stone of whatever discription which I have observed in this country appere to lye in horizontal stratas except where they have been evedently been forced or removed from their origional beds. (Lewis, November 25, 1803)

Clark only mentions "strata" once on the journey up the Missouri River from St. Louis to the Mandan villages (calling the rock layers "Straters" on August 22, 1804, the same day as Lewis's near-toxic encounter testing for minerals). It is revealing that the use of the word "strata" did not become prevalent in the journals until Lewis took up his journal on a consistent basis after departing Fort Mandan in April 1805. Lewis correctly used the term to describe the various layers of rock he was observing, but he also showed his command of the general concept of stratigraphy (the science of understanding the spatial arrangement of strata) when he described the frustrating process of freeing the expedition boats from the grip of river ice at Fort Mandan, the winter 1804–1805 encampment in North Dakota:

> The ice which incloses them [the keelboat and perogues] lyes in several stratas of unequal thicknesses which are seperated by streams of water. this peculiarly unfortunate because so soon as we cut through the first strata of ice the water rushes up and rises as high as the upper surface of the ice thus creates such a debth of water as renders it impracticable to cut away the lower strata which appears firmly attatched to, and confining the bottom of the vessels. (Lewis, February 3, 1805)

FIGURE 5.1. Meriwether Lewis's most detailed stratigraphic observations were of the White Cliffs and Missouri Breaks region in present-day Montana, including the rocks that comprise the Judith River Formation here at river mile 97 in the Upper Missouri River Breaks National Monument. As Lewis described on May 27, 1805, "the bluffs are very high steep rugged, containing considerable quantities of stone and border the river closely on both sides. . . . the bluffs are composed of irregular tho' horizontal stratas of yellow and brown or black clay, brown and yellowish white sand, of soft yellowish white sand stone and a hard dark brown free stone." Photograph by John W. Jengo. (See Color Plate 14.)

After Lewis began to use "strata" frequently, Clark adopted its usage, albeit with his characteristically fearless spelling flair (e.g., stratias, straturs, stratiums, stratums, strater, stratus, straters, strates, and stratea!). Lewis never spelled strata incorrectly (he only abbreviated it once in his January 10, 1806, journal entry), always applied the word in the proper context, and utilized it in his journal entries, his mineralogical specimen descriptions, and his geographic description of the affluents of the Missouri River, believed to have been composed at Fort Mandan (often referred to as Codex O).

Lewis's finest achievement in describing stratigraphic relationships took place on May 31, 1805.[39] On this day, Lewis penned a most memorable description of the Virgelle Sandstone Member of the Eagle Sandstone, the inspiration for his famed "seens of visionary inchantment" and "most romantic appearance" passages describing the White Cliffs of the Missouri River:

> The bluffs of the river rise to the hight of from 2 to 300 feet and in most places nearly perpendicular; they are formed of remarkable white sandstone which is sufficiently soft to give way readily to the impression of water; two or thre thin horizontal stratas of white free-stone, on which the rains or water make no impression, lie imbeded in these clifts of soft stone near the upper part of them. (Lewis, May 31, 1805)

Lewis went on to note the change in lithology from sandstone (which forms steep cliffs) to shale (which weathers to form gradual slopes), and then he lucidly described how this sandstone is weakly cemented and quite vulnerable to percolating water, the principal agent of erosion, so as to form "a thousand grotesque figures, which with the help of a little immagination and an oblique view at a distance, are made to represent eligant ranges of lofty freestone buildings, having their parapets well stocked with statuary."[40] Lewis finishes his account of the geology of this area by carefully describing discordant, freestanding stone walls, a most unusual feature heretofore not noted on the journey up the Missouri River:

> for here it is too that nature presents to the view of the traveler vast ranges of walls of tolerable workmanship, so perfect indeed are those walls that I should have thought that nature had attempted here to rival the human art of masonry had I not recollected that she had first began her work. These walls rise to the hight in many places of 100 feet, are perpendicular, with two regular faces and are from one to 12 feet thick, each wall retains the same thickness at top which it possesses at

> bottom. . . . These walls pass the river in several places, rising from the water's edge much above the sandstone bluffs, which they seem to penetrate; thence continuing their course on a streight line on either side of the river through the gradually ascending plains, over which they tower to the hight of from ten to seventy feet untill they reach the hills, which they finally enter and conceal themselves. these walls sometimes run parallel to each other, with several ranges near each other, and at other times interscecting each other at right angles, having the appearance of the walls of ancient houses or gardens. (Lewis, May 31, 1805)

From Lewis's deliberate narrative, one can easily visualize the scale and geometry of these stone walls, technically termed "dikes."[41] The dikes are resistant to erosion, and thus they emerged to form freestanding walls as the other rocks in the White Cliffs area eroded at a faster rate. Lewis's graceful description of the walls disappearing into the hillsides and the mental image that invoked cannot be improved upon.[42]

INTERSTICES

In the geological vernacular, the term "interstice" is defined as an opening or space in a rock. The use of the word "interstices" is another instance of Lewis using a technical scientific term that probably originated from his interaction with Jefferson and the APS mentors:

> The stone of which these walls are formed is black, dence and dureable. . . . these are laid regularly in ranges on each other like bricks, each breaking or covering the interstice of the two on which it rests. thus the purpendicular interstices are broken, and the horizontal ones extend entire throughout the whole extent of the walls. (Lewis, May 31, 1805)[43]

> several fine springs burst out at the waters edge from the interstices of the rocks. (Lewis, July 19, 1805)

> these springs issue from the bottoms and through the interstices of a grey freestone rock. (Lewis, June 29, 1806)

Lewis not only used the word correctly when describing the joints in the stone walls in the White Cliffs area (May 31, 1805), the fractures that yielded groundwater (July 19, 1805, and June 29, 1806), and in several mineralogical specimen descriptions,[44] but he also appropriately applied the term when describing the timber construction of Indian hunting lodges (May 4, 1805), the narrow cracks in bark specimens he examined while at Fort Clatsop (February 5–6, 1806), and how the Nez Perce filled the spaces between stones that covered their burial graves (June 2, 1806). It does not appear that Clark ever used the term independently.

BITUMINOUS

The term "bitumen" is a generic term that is used to describe a naturally inflammable substance that can possess a wide variety of colors and degrees of volatility.[45] A substance said to be bituminous is defined as a sediment or strata that contains a noticeable amount of organic or carbonaceous matter, which appears to be what Lewis and Clark were describing in the following journal entries:

> Capt. Clark found on the Lard shore under a high bluff issuing from a blue earth a bittuminus matter resembling molasses in consistance, colour and taste. (Lewis, September 9, 1804)

> In maney of those hills forming bluffs to the river we procieve Several Stratums of bituminious Substance which resembles *Coal.* (Clark, April 11, 1805)

> considerable quantities of bitumenous water, about the colour of strong lye trickles down the sides of the hills. (Lewis, April 14, 1805)

> The appearance of Salts, and bitumun Still Continue. (Clark, May 25, 1805)

Lewis thought at least one specimen of a bituminous substance was worth collecting, Fort Mandan mineralogical specimen No. 44, which was part of the shipment of specimens Lewis sent back to Jefferson from Fort Mandan.[46]

CALCAREOUS

When applied to rock identification, the term "calcareous" requires that at least 50 percent of the chemical composition of the rock be calcium carbonate.

> on the lard. shore at the commencement of the big bend observed a clift of black porus rock which resembled *Lava* tho' on a closer examination I believe it to be calcarious and an imperfect species of the French *burr-* preserved a specemine, it is brownish white, or black or yellowish brown. (Lewis, September 20, 1804)

Here we see Lewis at his best. He thought initially that these rocks were lava but reassessed his judgment of this weathered zone of the Pierre Shale, which does contain calcareous zones.[47] This was also the only time Lewis used the somewhat obscure term "burr," which is defined as a nodule or other hard mass of rock (normally siliceous) encased in a softer rock.[48] It's an appropriate application of the term, because the Pierre Shale does have zones of concretions or nodules. The specimen Lewis collected on this day may have been Fort Mandan mineralogical specimen No. 59, described as "A Specimen of calcareous rock," which was also included in the shipment of mineralogical specimens sent to Jefferson from Fort Mandan.[49]

Lewis only uses the term "calcareous" one other time in the journals, on February 3, 1805, when he attempted to explain why rocks of the "calcarious genus" were exploding when exposed to fire. Lewis may not have realized that it wasn't the calcium carbonate that caused the rocks to shatter but rather the connate (trapped) water within the rock that expanded in the heat and broke the rocks apart.

Mineral Productions — Economical Minerals and Building Materials
IRON AND LEAD

Although Lewis and Clark had success in identifying the presence of iron (e.g., see Clark's description of "yellow oaker [ochre] creek" on July 5, 1804), largely because of the distinctive brick-red to reddish-brown staining that results when iron oxidizes (i.e., weathers or "rusts"), they misidentified strata as an iron "ore" several times on the lower Missouri River (e.g., July 18–19 and August 27, 1804). They did not realize that these rocks were merely stained with hematite or limonite, which are secondary iron oxide minerals. Their recognition of actual iron occurrences improved in 1805 during their passage through the Missouri River Breaks and White Cliffs, where they noted the presence of

> large round kidneyformed and irregular seperate masses of a hard black Iron stone, which is imbeded in the Clay and sand. (Lewis, May 27, 1805)

These roughly circular, iron-rich concretions, which have partially protected the underlying creamy white, weakly cemented sandstone from the myriad of erosional forces, are responsible for the "most romantic appearance" of columns, pulpits, toadstools, pedestals, and other unique features of the White Cliffs.[50] After the White Cliffs, iron is only mentioned in the context of its coloration of soils and rock strata:

> the colour of the hills and bluffs in the neighbourhood indicate the existence of that metal [iron]. (Lewis, June 16, 1805)

"MINERAL PRODUCTIONS OF EVERY KIND" 151

about my Camp the Cliffs or bluffs are a hard red or redish brown earth containing Iron. (Clark, June 25, 1805)

One would suppose that iron was one of the important minerals that Jefferson had in mind when he listed "metals" as an object worthy of note in his instructions, so it's a bit surprising that it was not more emphasized in the captains' journals.

The only references to lead ore in the journals were comments made to Lewis and Clark by George Drouillard[51] or the engagés:

> assended a hill of about 170 foot to a place where the french report that Lead ore has been found, I saw no mineral of that description. (Clark, June 4, 1804, describing Lead Mine Hill)

> The french inform that Lead Ore has been found in defferent parts of this river. (Clark, June 8, 1804, describing the Lamine [Mine] River)

> in this country the Indians as well as some of the French hunters report the existence many mines. some of lead, others of a metal resembleing lead, but of a lighter colour more dense & equally malleable; it is not stated to be silver. (Lewis, Codex O, undated, Winter 1804–1805, describing the watershed of the Niobrara River)[52]

Lewis recorded the effort to gather more information about these lead occurrences:

> a high hill which is said to contain lead ore, our surch for this ore however pruved unsuccessfull and if it does contain ore of any kind, it must be concealed. (Lewis, Codex O, undated, Winter 1804–1805)[53]

> lead mines which are said to have been discoved on it, tho' the local situation, quality, or quantity of this ore, I could never learn. (Lewis, Codex O, undated, Winter 1804–1805)[54]

Although Lewis and Clark failed to confirm the presence of the lead ore in the vicinity of Lead Mine Hill, it's clear they attempted to gather as much information as they could within the limited time they had to explore the backcountry.[55]

LIMESTONE

There were at least twenty daily journal entries in which Lewis and Clark identified the presence of limestone. When the captains identified a rock type as a limestone in the journals, they had a perfect track record, whether the limestone was part of a stratigraphic outcrop exposed along the river:

FIGURE 5.2. Of all of the rock types that Lewis and Clark attempted to identify on the expedition, they had the greatest success with limestone. The captains correctly identified that limestone was the dominant lithology here at the Three Forks of the Missouri, where Lewis noted on July 27, 1805, that "the river was again closely hemned in by high Clifts of a solid limestone rock which appear to have tumbled or sunk in the same manner of those discribed yesterday. the limestone appears to be of an excellent quality of deep blue colour when fractured and of a light led colour where exposed to the weather. it appears to be of a very fine gr[a]in the fracture like that of marble." This view of the limestone cliffs about the Gallatin River was taken from Fort Rock, which Lewis accurately described as, "between the middle and S.E. forks near their junctions with the S.W. fork there is a handsom site for a fortification it consists of a limestone rock of an oblong form; it's sides perpendicular and about 25 ft high." Photograph by John W. Jengo. (See Color Plate 15.)

> the rock which compose these clifts is a singular one tho' not uncommon to this country it is a Limestone principally.... I was informed at Cape Jeradeau where the same rock appears, that it makes a very good lime. (Lewis, November 24, 1803)

> the limestone appears to be of an excellent quality of deep blue colour when fractured and of a light led colour where exposed to the weather. it appears to be of a very fine gr[a]in the fracture like that of marble. (Lewis, July 27, 1805)

or scattered on the plains adjacent to the Missouri River:

> a suficient quantity of limestone may be readily procured for building near the junction of the Missouri and yellowstone rivers.... it is of a light colour, and appears to be of an excellent quality. (Lewis, April 26, 1805)

or part of the rocky bed of the Missouri River approaching the Three Forks:

> I obseve some limestone also in the bed of the river which seem to have been brought down by the current as they are generally small and woarn smooth. (Lewis, July 25, 1805)

Despite this achievement, Lewis and Clark occasionally missed the presence of limestone, perhaps because they were not able to examine the rock closely enough or, in the case of Lewis misidentifying the limestone at Gates of the Mountains (he called it a granite), the shadows may have affected his view.[56] It appears from the journal record that Clark may not have been entirely comfortable with identifying limestone independently. For example, he chose to describe the limestone outcrops encountered on his return route from the Three Forks to the Yellowstone River as "hard white rock" rather than limestone (see Clark's journal entries for July 13 and 15, 1806). This seems odd given the experience he must have gained in identifying this rock type on the outbound journey with Lewis. Perhaps it's an indication of Lewis's more extensive training or practice in describing limestone. For example, Lewis truly demonstrated his command for rock lithology description in his geographic description of the Affluents of the Missouri River (Codex O) when he described the occurrence of limestone between the mouth of the Missouri and the confluence of the Missouri and Gasconade Rivers:

> I have observed in ascending the Missouri to this place ... large quarries of this stone, lying in horizontal stratas, from ten to 40 feet in thickness.

> this stone is of light brown colour, with a smal tint of blue; fracture imperfect conchoidal; when broken it presents the appearance of a variety of small shells and other marine substances, of which it seems to be entirely composed. in this solid and massive rock, are inclosed stones of yellowish bron flint, of bulbous and indeterminate shapes, from an ounce to ten or twelve pounds weight. . . . this stone produces lime of an excellent quality, and is the same-with that, which makes it's appearance on the Mississippi from Cape Gerrardeau, to the entrance of the Missouri. (Lewis, undated, Winter 1804–1805)[57]

This is one of the few times Lewis and Clark documented the geographic extent of the rock units they were encountering. The mention of "small shells and other marine substances" is also one of the few references to fossil occurrences in the journals. Two other noteworthy examples are:

> in this Hill is limestone & Seminted rock of Shels &c. (Clark, July 21, 1804)

> a hard freestone of a brownish yellow colour shews itself in several stratas of unequal thicknesses frequently overlain or incrusted by a very thin strata of limestone which appears to be formed of concreted <cemented> shells. (Lewis, May 26, 1805)

Both Clark's "Seminted rock of Shels" and Lewis's "concreted shells" describe an occurrence of limestone formed by densely packed, cemented masses of fossil shells. The captains may have been instructed to note such occurrences because of Jefferson's long-standing interest in the origin of fossil shells.

CLAYS AND "SLATES"

Due to its prevalence in the riverside strata east of the Rocky Mountains, fine-grained rocks and sediments were often noted by Lewis and Clark. The captains proved to be very adept at identifying clays in recent glacial terraces, loess, and river alluvium deposits, and they had an excellent grasp of recognizing clays within suspended-sediment load in the rivers and creeks they traversed and passed.

On the other hand, it appears Lewis and Clark never used the word "shale," which was one of the most common rock lithologies they encountered traveling up the Missouri River. The captains were apparently unaware of the distinction between shale and slate, because they used the word "slate" on at least ten occasions to describe shale deposits (e.g., July 18, August 27, September 12–13, 15, and October 8, 1804;

June 13–14 and July 23–24, 1805).[58] Clark even referred to some of these exposures as "Soft Slate Stone" or "resembling Slate much Softer," which indicated that he had no difficulty recognizing shale lithologies. It is also evident that Clark knew how to recognize chalk even though he preferred to identify these chalk exposures as "clays":

> Several mile in extent of white Clay Marl or Chalk. (Clark, August 27, 1804)

> proceeded on pass the Bluffs Compsd. of a yellowish red, & brownish White Clay which is a hard as Chalk. (Clark, September 1, 1804)

It is evident that Lewis and Clark used the words "clay," "soft rock," or "soft stone" in the journals interchangeably to describe the weathered material derived from bluff-forming shale, chalk, or bentonite. While this is also true of some of the captains' clay observations on the Upper Missouri, Jefferson, Beaverhead, Lemhi, and the Marias Rivers, they also correctly identified the clay that was contained within the glacial tills, river alluvium, and upland soil profiles along these stretches of river.

As always, Lewis and Clark had the usefulness of clay and other fine-grained "earths" in mind:

> on the lard. qutr. is a large bank of white clay that appears to be excellent *Spanis whiting*. (Lewis, November 25, 1803)[59]

> those Bluffs afford good Clay for Brick, a great quantity on the 3 points one Opsd. one abov & one below. (Clark, August 3, 1804, describing the area of Council Bluffs)

> there are several small sand-bars along the shores at no great distance of very pure sand and the earth appears as if it would make good brick. (Lewis, July 28, 1805, describing the area of Three Forks)

So as to leave no doubt, Lewis reiterated in Codex O about the scarcity of useable timber in the vicinity of Council Bluffs to build a trading post; thus, he recommended,

> I concieve that the cheepest and best method would be to build of brick, the ea[r]th appears to be of an excellent quality for brick, and both lime and sand are convenient. (Lewis, undated, Winter 1804–1805)[60]

COAL

It is quite likely that Lewis and Clark needed no instruction on how to recognize coal. Given the number of journal entries where it is mentioned, the captains were particularly attuned to the occurrence of "carbonated wood" and coal, sometimes referred to as "pit" coal in the journals.[61] There were more than forty daily journal entries where the presence or absence of coal is mentioned, a testament to Lewis and Clark dutifully following Jefferson's implicit instructions. In one of Lewis's first journal entries, he noted the economical uses of this valuable resource:

> there are many fine mines of *pitt* Coal on this stream [Big Muddy River], and one not far from its mouth whence boats asscend in common and high tide are loaded with and transport it the Saline on W. of mississippi and to Kaskaskias & elsewhere for the use of the blacksmiths and other artizans. (Lewis, November 25, 1803)

It was no doubt fortuitous that the distinctly brownish-black to black, vitreous appearance of coal, especially when contrasted with the light-colored rock strata that typically encased it along the expedition route, made coal deposits visible from just about every vantage point and that this ease of recognition played a major role in the prominent mention of coal in the journals. Of all the captains' lithologic observations, the distribution of coal is the easiest to piece together from the journals, particularly its prevalence in the region above the confluence of the Missouri and Yellowstone Rivers and the variability in its quality:

> passed a Coal-mine, or Bank of Stone Coal ... this bank appears to Contain great quantity of fine Coal, the river being high prevented our Seeeing that contained in the Cliffs of the best quallity. (Clark, June 25, 1804)

> Camped on the L.S. above a Bluff containing Coal (5) of an inferior quallity. (Clark, October 20, 1804)

> all the hills have more or Less indefferent Coal in Stratias at different hites. (Clark, April 9, 1805)

> this Coal or Carbonated wood is like that of the Missouri of an inferior quallity. (Clark, July 28, 1806)

Lewis and Clark did not technically rank the coal deposits that they were encountering,[62] but when the captains remarked that a deposit was of an "inferior" or indifferent quality, such as they did on October 20, 1804, April 9, 1805, and July 28, 1806, they were correctly identifying lignite coal. They often called lignite deposits "carbonated wood," an excellent description of this soft material that often retains its original wood texture. Given that modern-day coal rankings have rather rigidly defined parameters that include ascertaining the volatile organic matter percentage and specific calorific or BTU value of a deposit, Lewis

"Mineral Productions of Every Kind"

and Clark could not have feasibly ranked the various coal deposits that they encountered to the degree that is possible today.

Additionally, Lewis and Clark often estimated the thickness of the coal deposits along their route:

> many horizontal stratas of carbonated wood, having every appearance of pit-coal at a distance; were seen in the the face of these bluffs. these stratas are of unequal thicknesses from 1 to 5 feet, and appear at different elivations above the water some of them as much as eighty feet. (Lewis, April 9, 1805)

> there is more appearance of coal today than we have yet seen, the stratas are 6 feet thick in some instances; the earth has been birnt in many places, and always appears in stratas on the same level with the stratas of coal. (Lewis, April 29, 1805)

> I passd. Straters of Coal in the banks on either Side those on the Stard. Bluffs was about 30 feet above the water and in 2 vanes from 4 to 8 feet thick, in a horozontal position. the Coal Contained in the Lard Bluffs is in Several vaines of different hights and thickness. (Clark, July 28, 1806)

Lewis and Clark should also be credited with disproving the belief that active volcanoes existed in the Louisiana Territory (a speculation that arose to explain the so-called pumice and lava stone observed floating down the Missouri River) by noting the close interrelationship between the coal beds and layers of burnt earth that they had been observing along the Missouri River:

> Those Bluffs appear to have been lately on fire, and at this time is too hot for a man to bear his hand in the earth at any debth, gret appearance of Coal. (Clark, August 24, 1804)

> I believe it to be the stratas of Coal seen in those hills which causes the fire and birnt appearances frequently met with in this quarter. where those birnt appearances are to be seen in the face of the river bluffs, the coal is seldom seen, and when you meet with it in the neighourhood of the stratas of birnt earth, the coal appears to be presisely at the same hight, and is nearly of the same thickness. (Lewis, April 16, 1805)

As Lewis's April 16, 1805 (and April 29, 1805, as well) journal entries illustrate, the captains had determined that the burning of coal beds not only caused the burnt appearance of cliffs and bluffs but also slightly metamorphosed the adjacent strata into what they termed "pumicestone." Nor did Lewis forget this cause-and-effect relationship on the return journey when he noted sixteen months later that at or just below the entrance of this river we meet with the first appearance of Coal birnt hills and pumicestone, these appearances seem to be coextensive. (Lewis, August 7, 1806)

As if to accentuate this discovery and put an end to speculations about chimera volcanoes along the Missouri River, Lewis composed a cleverly concise and witty comment to accompany a "Lava & pummice Stone" specimen (Fort Mandan mineralogical specimen No. 67) that he sent back from Fort Mandan: "The tract of Country which furnishes the Pummice Stone seen floating down the Misouri, is rather burning or burnt plains than burning mountains."[63] Jefferson must have been pleased to see this question, one that he seriously contemplated in *Notes*, so neatly resolved.[64]

SALT

Lewis and Clark leave no question about the essential economical role of salt (naturally occurring sodium chloride) in their early journal entries. During the winter 1803–1804 layover in Camp Dubois, Clark noted traders and commercial traffic involving salt (e.g., December 16, 1803, and January 1 and April 18, 1804, journal entries) and made other notations on either the commerce of salt or its relative yield in bushels:

> this landing is the place that Boats receive Salt from the Saline Licks which is one mile and 2½ miles S W from the River, and is worked at present to great advantage. (Clark, November 28, 1803)

> a Salt works is establish[ed] on a Small river 30 miles up the river 10 miles from the mississippi. (Clark, undated, placed after the January 3, 1804, journal entry in Moulton, *Journals*, 2:147)

> passed the mouth of a Creek Called *Saline* or Salt <Creek> R . . . has So many Licks & Salt Springs on its banks that the Water of the Creek is Brackish, one Verry large Lick is 9 ms. up on the left Side the water of the Spring in this Lick is Strong as one bushel of the water is said to make 7 lb. of good Salt. (Clark, June 6, 1804)

> Capt. Lewis took four or five men & went to Some Licks or Springs of Salt water from two to four miles up the Creek on Rt. Side the water of those Springs are not Strong, Say from 4 to 600 Gs. of water for a Bushel of Salt. (Clark, June 7, 1804)

In addition, just a few weeks prior to leaving Camp Dubois, Lewis composed a detailed "Notes on Salines" for Jefferson based on information that he had gathered from a French waterman and fur trader describing the location and the quality of salt deposits.[65] Lewis appears to have been particularly persistent in his inquiries about salt deposits, as evidenced by his report issued a year later from Fort Mandan:

> I have obtained no satisfactory account of any fossil salt being found in Louisiana, altho' repeated enquiries have been made off such as possess the best information of the interior parts of the country. (Lewis, Codex O)[66]

Lewis and Clark noted the occurrence of salt springs, salt deposits, and brackish waters between St. Louis and the Mandans (e.g., June 6–7, July 21, September 10 and 20, October 3 in the monthly weather diary, and October 19, 1804) and they often documented the origin of the salt, usually from a spring, the taste of the water, its degree of brackishness, and effect on the individual drinking it as compared to the laxative Glauber's salt.

Once past the Mandans, the captains were also very diligent in noting the occurrence of salts that were derived from evaporating groundwater discharge (mentioned in eight daily journal entries in April 1805 and fourteen daily journal entries in May 1805):

> the salts which have been before mentioned as common on the Missouri, appears in great quantities along the banks of this river, which are in many so thickly covered with it that they appear perfectly white. (Lewis, April 22, 1805)

On April 28, 1805, Lewis correctly noted the increasing amounts of salts as the expedition advanced into a more arid climate. Throughout the month of May 1805, the captains expressed amazement at both the amount of salts they were encountering and the lack of fresh water:

> great appearance of quarts and mineral salts, the latter appears both on the hills and bottoms, in the bottoms of the gullies which make down from the hills it lies incrusting the earth to the debth of 2 or 3 inches, and may be with a fether be swept up and collected in large quantities, I preserved several specimines of this salts. (Lewis, May 11, 1805)

> I have not seen a bould fountain of pure water except one since I left the Mandans; there [NB: *are*] a number of small ones but all without exception are impregnated with the salts which abound in this country, and with which I believe the Missoury itself considerably impregnated but to us in the habit of useing it not perceptible. (Lewis, May 20, 1805)

The reporting of salt occurrences in this region ended at the Great Falls (see journal entries for June 4 and 20, 1805), but Lewis and Clark, always comparing and contrasting what they were observing to what they had previously encountered, correctly noted the recurrence of salts in the area of the Big Hole (Wisdom) River on August 3, 1805, and along the Marias River on July 20, 1806:

> the mineral salts also frequently mentioned on the Missouri we saw this evening in these uneven bottoms. (Lewis, August 3, 1805)

> the mineral salts common to the plains of the missouri has been more abundant today than usual. (Lewis, July 20, 1806)

As was the case with coal, it is unlikely that Lewis or Clark needed instruction on how to recognize salt. The numerous citations of salt in the journals was probably a fortuitous result of the captains examining every important stream confluence that entered the Missouri River, which gave them the opportunity to sample the waters and note its saline character. Lewis and Clark often evaluated these saline waters by simply comparing a sample to their standard of acceptable drinking water. (Clark even noted the salt line on the waters of the Columbia River as they approached the Pacific coast; see November 27, 1805, journal entry.) In addition to following Jefferson's instructions, which listed salt as a mineral worthy of note, the use of salt licks by native wildlife and the need to locate potable drinking water facilitated the consistent documentation of this essential mineral.

NITER AND SULFUR

Niter is a very soluble crystalline salt and forms as a result of nitrification, one of the processes of soil formation.[67] Lewis and Clark were familiar with the term "niter" because it was synonymous with saltpeter, a naturally occurring potassium nitrate that had many uses in this era as an ingredient in fertilizer, soap, and gunpowder:

> the earth and sand which form the bars of the river are so fully impregnated with salt that it shoots and adhers to the little sticks which appear on the serface it is pleasent & seems niterous. (Lewis and Clark, weather journal for October 3, 1804)

The other readily identifiable compound the captains noted frequently was sulfur (often spelled as "sulphur" in the journals), which is a nonmetallic chemical element:

> I burnt some of this coal but found it indifferent, nor could I discover while it was berning that it emitted any sulphurious smell. (Lewis, November 22, 1803)

> the bluff is now on fire and throws out considerable quantities of smoke which has a strong sulphurious smell. (Lewis, April 10, 1805)

> the water is as transparent as possible strongly impregnated with sulpher. (Lewis, June 16, 1805, regarding Sulphur Springs opposite the mouth of Belt Creek near Great Falls)

> this water boils up through some loose hard gritty Stone. a little sulferish. (Clark, July 7, 1806)

Sulfur is one of the most recognizable elements in nature; when it is in the form of hydrogen sulfide, it has a very characteristic odor that the captains could immediately identify; thus, it's likely they needed no training in this regard.

Alum, Argil, Arsenic, Cobalt, Copperas, Magnesia, Marcasite, Pyrite, "Silver," Silex, Talc, Quartz, and Isinglass

Alum is a colorless or white aluminum sulfate mineral that has a sweet-sour, astringent (harsh) taste. Lewis clearly could recognize this taste:

> this water partakes of the taste of glauber salts and slighty of allumn. (Lewis, April 14, 1805)

> it possessed less of the glauber salt, or alum, than those little streams from hills usually do. (Lewis, April 15, 1805)

Argil is essentially clay, typically white-colored. Lewis used the term correctly on January 10, 1806, when describing a mineralogical specimen that Clark had collected during his crossing of Tillamook Head. Lewis also used the term "argillaceous" to describe a rock or sediment that contained an appreciable amount of clay:

> the earth of which this mud is composed is white or bluish white and appears to be argillacious. (Lewis, August 9, 1805)

Cobalt is an element, typically a lustrous bluish-gray, that has been used for centuries to color ceramics (e.g., tile and pottery) and glass:

> An emence quantity of *Cabalt* or a Cristolised Substance which answers its discription is on the face of the Bluff. (Clark, August 24, 1804)

> at 7 miles passed a white Clay marl or Chalk Bluff under this Bluff is extensive I discovered large Stone much like lime incrusted with a Clear Substance which I believe to be *Cabalt*, also ore is imbeded in the Dark earth, resembling Slate much Softer. (Clark, August 27, 1804)

In addition to cobalt, there were several other metals and minerals that Lewis and Clark attempted, but mostly failed, to identify accurately. Arsenic is a steel-gray metallic element that commonly occurs in granular or kidney-shaped masses. Copperas is another name for the mineral melanterite,[68] a sulfate that results from the weathering of pyrite and marcasite, although the name is occasionally applied to other sulfate minerals. Magnesia is magnesium oxide, which possesses an earthy white color. Marcasite and pyrite are dimorphous; pyrite is a common sulfide mineral that generally ranges in color from bronze to yellow and is called fool's gold because of its resemblance to genuine gold. Pyrites occur in sedimentary rocks and coal seams in the form of nodules or concretions. Silex is essentially silica:

> This Bluff contain Pyrites alum, Copperass & a Kind Markesites also a clear Soft Substance which <will mold and become pliant like wax> Capt lewis was near being Poisoned by the Smell in pounding this Substance I belv to be *arsenic* or Cabalt. (Clark, August 22, 1804)

> there is a stra of white earth (see specimen No. [blank]) which the neighbouring Indians use to paint themselves, and which appears to me to resemble the earth of which the French Porcelain is made; I am confident this earth contains Argill, but wether it also contains Silex or magnesia, or either of those earths in a proper proportion I am unable to determine. (Lewis, January 10, 1806)

The captains' "silver" in the May 16, 1804, entry was actually a pyrite or marcasite:[69]

> this hill appears to Contain great quantytes of Coal, and also ore of a rich appearance haveing greatly the resemblance of Silver. (Clark, May 16, 1804)

Speaking of silver, there is a definitive absence in the journals about precious metals such as silver and gold, but I don't think this was an accidental oversight. The lack of emphasis on such pursuits must have come directly from Jefferson, as evidenced by a correspondence to William Dunbar during this same time period that indicated how little Jefferson cared about the search for precious metals. In his April 15, 1804, letter to Dunbar, Jefferson was referring to a Dr. George Hunter, who would subsequently accompany Dunbar up the Ouachita River in October 1804–January 1805 to the hot springs in present-day Hot Springs, Arkansas:

> The thing to beguarded against is that an indulgence to his principal qualification [chemistry] may not lead to a hazarding of our mission to search for gold and silver mines. These are but an incidental object, to be noted if found in their way, as salt, or coal, or lime would but not to be sought after.[70]

Lewis tried in vain to identify the mineral talc on two occasions and quartz at least six different times along the Missouri River between the

Milk River and the Marias River confluences. In all fairness to Lewis, there are many minerals that have a quartzlike appearance, but it's clear that Lewis was not trained to recognize the external characteristics of these minerals in the field.

There is, however, an astute mineral identification that was only mentioned in Clark's journal of May 31, 1805, in reference to a specimen of the natural stone walls near the White Cliffs of the Missouri River:

> Capt Lewis ... Collected Some of the Stone off one of the walls which appears to be a Sement of Isin glass black earth. (Clark, May 31, 1805)

The term "isinglass" is a synonym for muscovite, a specific variety of mica that is a prominent constituent of igneous rocks. Mica is defined as a widely distributed rock-forming group of minerals that have a recognizable flaky and sheetlike form; when present in thin, transparent sheets, this mineral does, in fact, resemble glass. Mica minerals are present in the shonkinite igneous rock that comprises these natural stone walls. It's intriguing that Clark, but not Lewis, would record the presence of this mineral—perhaps another indication that Clark was capable of his own independent mineralogical analyses.

Granite, "Lava," and "Pumice"

As compared to their achievements in correctly identifying limestone and coal, Lewis and Clark had less success with other common rock lithologies. The captains only identified granite correctly twice (April 22 and May 8, 1805) when it was part of a surficial glacial deposit; however, they misidentified granite whenever it was part of a rock exposure along the river (e.g., May 25, July 16–17, 19, 31, and August 1, 1805). It doesn't appear that Lewis and Clark knew how to recognize granite even when a close inspection of the rock was possible. Two obvious occurrences of granite along the expedition route were along the Salmon River that Clark reconnoitered in August 1805 and the rocks surrounding the (Lolo) hot springs along the Nez Perce Trail, but neither captain identified it as such, calling these rocks either stone "of a grey colour" or a "grey freestone rock," respectively.

Similarly, the captains' observations of lava were never correct (e.g., September 20, 1804; April 9, 11, 17, and 22, 1805) nor were the nearly twenty "pumice" or "pumicestone" outcrop observations actually related to a volcanic rock. However, in Clark's March 21, 1805, journal entry that describes an experiment in which various earths and clays were placed in a makeshift furnace, he records that "the hard Clay became a pumice Stone Glazed." This suggests that the captains' definition of pumice was not the now technically restricted, volcanically derived vesicular glassy rock but rather any fused or baked rock (termed "clinker"), which explains why they most consistently noted its occurrence in the regions where coal beds had burned and slightly metamorphosed the adjacent rock strata. Further evidence of the captains' understanding of this causal relationship is found in Codex T:

> The Pumies Stone which is found as low as the Illinois Country is formd by the banks or Stratums of Coal taking fire and burning the earth imedeately above it into either pumies Stone or Lavia. (Clark, Codex T, undated, ca. 1806)[71]

This is a good example of why it is important not to dismiss outright the captains' lithologic observations as simply wrong in those instances when they did not have the most technically correct terminology at their disposal.

Flint

Although the term "flint" is technically synonymous with chert, an extremely dense and hard quartz crystalline sedimentary rock, the word itself has ancient history dating back to A.D. 700 and meaning "anything hard."[72] Review of the captains' use of the term "flint" in the journals indicates that they often correctly associated it with occurrences of chert (e.g., November 24–26, 1803; June 7, 1804) but also used it to describe any massive, very hard rock that yielded a spark when struck:

> The sides of these mountains present generally one barren surface of confused and broken masses of stone. above these are white or brown and towards the base of a grey colour and so hard that when struck with a steel, yeald fire like flint. (Lewis, August 23, 1805, reporting Clark's reconnaissance of the Salmon River)

Identifying flint in general terms played to the captains' practical strength because they could literally test the rocks along the route for such characteristics as opposed to relying solely on a rock's physical appearance for identification, which had the tendency to introduce error. Lewis and Clark also generically applied the word "flint" to describe any stone that the natives fashioned into knives and arrowheads (e.g., August 22–23, September 27, and October 17, 1805). Although some of this flint was probably chert, or perhaps a variety of quartz called chalcedony,[73] the captains' descriptions suggest that their definition of flint could have included other commonly used rocks such as obsidian (e.g., like the specimen Lewis describes on August 22, 1805, as "transparent as the common black glass and much of the same colour").

Springs and Mineral Waters

Lewis and Clark noted the occurrence of salt and mineral springs throughout the expedition, particularly along the lower (e.g., June 6–7 and September 5 and 10, 1804) and upper sections of the Missouri River (e.g., April 11 and June 16, 1805):

> a large Salt Spring of remarkable Salt water much frequented by Buffalow, Some Smaller Springs on the Side of the hill above less Salt, the water excesiv Salt. (Clark, September 10, 1804)

> the water is as transparent as possible strongly impregnated with sulpher, and I suspect Iron also. (Lewis, June 16, 1805, regarding Sulphur Springs near Great Falls)

Given the essential need for fresh water, Lewis and Clark made a point in the journals to differentiate between mineral springs, such as the aforementioned salt springs and sulfur springs, and those springs that yielded fresh water, such as the Giant Springs near the Great Falls:

> the largest fountain or Spring I ever Saw, and doubt if it is not the largest in America Known, this water boils up from under th rocks near the edge of the river and falls imediately into the river 8 feet and keeps its Colour for ½ a mile which is emencely Clear and of a bluish Cast. (Clark, June 18, 1805)

> the water of this fountain is extreemly tranparent and cold; nor is it impregnated with lime or any other extranious matter which I can discover, but is very pure and pleasent. (Lewis, June 29, 1805)

The location of springs was judged to be of such importance that Lewis made a point of consistently mentioning them in Codex O, and he often characterized their quality on an improvised, but readily understandable, graduated scale of usability (e.g., "springs of excellent water," "fine bould springs of limestone water," "said to be brackish," "springs of salt water," "water of this creek is excessively salt").[74]

The only true hot springs that Lewis and Clark recorded in the journals were the hot springs along the Nez Perce trail (now referred to as Lolo Hot Springs) and the springs Clark encountered in the Big Hole (Wisdom) Valley (now referred to as Jackson Hot Springs). Per Jefferson's instructions, they remembered to note the temperature of these springs, but unfortunately their last working thermometer had been broken less than two weeks before they encountered Lolo Hot Springs. Nevertheless, the ever-resourceful William Clark attempted to assess the temperature of these springs in cleverly indirect ways:

> in further examonation I found this water nearly boiling hot at the places it Spouted from the rocks (which a hard Corse Grit, and of great size the rocks on the Side of the Mountain of the Same texture[)] I put my finger in the water, at first could not bare it in a Second. (Clark, September 13, 1805)

> the principal Spring is about the temperature of the Warmest baths used at the Hot Springs in Virginia. (Clark, June 29, 1806)

> we arived at a Boiling Spring.... this Spring contains a very considerable quantity of water, and actually blubbers with heat for 20 paces below where it rises. it has every appearance of boiling, too hot for a man to endure his hand in it 3 seconds. I directt Sergt. Pryor and John Shields to put each a peice of meat in the water of different Sises. the one about the Size of my 3 fingers Cooked dun in 25 minits the other much thicker was 32 minits before it became Sufficiently dun. (Clark, July 7, 1806)

"Broken by Some Convulsion"—The Forces of Erosion

Once the expedition moved beyond the Mandan village, the Lewis and Clark journals reveal major changes in the geomorphological landscape and the principal erosional processes operating on that landscape. There are a couple of journal entries below the Mandans where Lewis and Clark noted entire hillsides had "Sliped into the river" (e.g., July 16 and 18–19 and August 24, 1804), but throughout 1805 and 1806, the captains would observe more extraordinary geological forces at work. Nowhere in their instructions were they tasked with evaluating the stability of the rock strata or the mechanisms that would cause such mass wasting. Yet, their journals are rich with enticing vignettes of complex geological history. Lewis and Clark easily recognized the erosive forces of water, and they accurately described this in many of their journal entries after departing Fort Mandan (e.g., April 9, May 25–27 and 30–31, June 13 and 29, July 17 and 19, and November 11, 1805, among others). A typical observation is their description of the erosional processes occurring in the Missouri Breaks and White Cliffs region:

> great quantities of stone also lye in the river and garnish it's borders, which appears to have tumbled from the bluffs where the rains had washed away the sand and clay in which they were imbeded. (Lewis, May 27, 1805)

Certainly, William Clark never forgot the day he was nearly killed, along with Sacagawea and Charbonneau, in a terrifying flash flood:

> the rain appeared to decend in a body and instantly collected in the rivene and came down in a roling torrent with irrisistable force driving rocks mud and everything before it which opposed it's passage.... he could scarcely ascend faster than it arrose till it had obtained the debth of 15 feet with a current tremendious to behold. (Lewis, June 29, 1805, describing Clark's close call in a ravine near the Great Falls)

As Clark reported the next day, "the place I Sheltered under filled up with hugh Rocks."[75] Clark made a similar observation along the Salmon River on August 23, 1805 when he reported that "The Torrents of water which come down aftr a rain carries with it emence numbers of those Stone into the river."[76] Several months later, Clark's observations of erosion along the Pacific Ocean coastline provided a riveting account of the power of these forces:

> The Coast in the neighbourhood of this old village is slipping from the Sides of the high hills, in emence masses; fifty or a hundred acres at a time give way and a great proportion of an instant precipitated into the Ocean. those hills and mountains are principally composed of a yellow Clay; their Slipping off or Spliting assunder at this time is no doubt Caused by the incessant rains which has fallen within the last two months. (Clark, January 8, 1806)

Lewis and Clark observed several other erosional phenomena as they proceeded on up the Missouri:

> the broken hills of the Missouri about this place exhibit large irregular and broken masses of rocks and stones; some of which tho' 200 feet above the level of the water seem at some former period to have felt it's influence, for they appear smoth as if woarn by the agetation of the water. this collection consists of white & grey gannite, a brittle black rock, flint, limestone, freestone, some small specimens of an excellent pebble and occasionally broken stratas of a stone which appears to be petrefyed wood. (Lewis, April 22, 1805)

> I could observe no regular stratas of it [limestone], tho' it lies on the sides of the river hills in large irregular masses, in considerable quantities. (Lewis, April 26, 1805)

> Capt Clark also met with limestone on the surface of the earth in the course of his walk. (Lewis, May 3, 1805)

> The country on the Lard. side of the river is generally high broken hills,

with much broken, grey black and brown grannite scattered on the surface of the earth in a confused manner. (Lewis, May 8, 1805)

Lewis had just accurately described the occurrence of glacial erratics[77] and the cornucopia of different rock types that can be transported by glacial action. Glaciers pick up rock debris, transport it long distances during their advance, and abruptly release it when they recede. Lewis's choice of the words "irregular" and "confused" and the list of unrelated rock types and their shapes accurately convey the surficial appearance of glacial drift deposits.

Lewis and Clark also had a keen eye for displaced rock masses and visually reconstructing the landscape:

the lard. shore on which I walked was very broken, and the hills in many places had the appearance of having sliped down in masses of several acres of land in surface. (Lewis, April 14, 1805)

on the Lard. Side emence piles of rocks appears as if Sliped from the Clifts under which they lay. (Clark, October 21, 1805)

passed Several places where the rocks projected into the river & have the appearance of haveing Seperated from the mountains and fallen promiscuisly into the river. (Clark, October 30, 1805)

Bluff on the Lard. Side which has Sliped into the river and filled up ⅓ of the river. (Clark, July 25, 1806)

high Bluff on the Lard. Side laterly Sliped into the river. (Clark, July 31, 1806)

Lewis and Clark were not familiar with mechanisms of faulting and mass wasting, two powerful geological processes that can move massive amounts of rock material.[78] Yet, their observations never failed to identify locations where subsequent geological mapping and investigation would indicate the presence of faults or locations vulnerable to massive collapses of strata:

no one Clift is Solid rock, all the rocks of everry description is in Small pices appears to have been broken by Some Convulsion. (Clark, July 19, 1805)

I observed that the rocks which form the clifts on this part of the river appear as if they had been undermined by the river and by their weight had seperated from the parent hill and tumbled on their sides, the stratas of rock of which they are composed lying with their edges up; others not seperated seem obliquely depressed on the side next the river as if they

FIGURE 5.3. William Clark's notes on his reconnaissance of the Salmon River in present-day Idaho on August 23, 1805, perfectly captured the rugged geology of this inaccessible region, now referred to as the River of No Return Wilderness: "Those Mountains which I passed were Steep Contain a white, a brown, & low down a Grey hard stone which would make fire, those Stone were of different Sises all Sharp and are continuly Slipping down, and in maney places one bed of those Stones inclined from the river bottom to the top of the mountains." As Lewis reported on this day after conferring with Clark, "the rocks approach the river so near in most places that there is no possibility of passing between them and the water. . . . The sides of these mountains present generally one barren surface of confused and broken masses of stone." Photograph by John W. Jengo. (See Color Plate 16.)

had sunk down to fill the cavity which had been formed by the washing and wearing of the river. (Lewis, July 25, 1805)

the river was again closely hemned in by high Clifts of a solid limestone rock which appear to have tumbled or sunk in the same manner of those discribed yesterday.... the country to the right of the S. W. fork like that to the left of the S. E. fork is high broken and mountainous as is that also down the missouri behind us, through which, these three rivers after assembling their united force at this point seem to have forced a passage. (Lewis, July 27, 1805)

the difficulty of his road which lay along the steep side of a mountain over large irregular and broken masses of rocks which had tumbled from the upper part of the mountain.... The sides of these mountains present generally one barren surface of confused and broken masses of stone. (Lewis, August 23, 1805, describing Clark's reconnaissance of the Salmon River)

The descriptive and insightful observations of erosional forces made by Lewis and Clark, principally the action of rivers in the Missouri and Columbia River watersheds and mass wasting in the Rocky Mountains, are another representative example of how the captains surpassed Jefferson's original instructions by expanding their natural history notations to include exceptional, and very often unanticipated, phenomena.

Sedimentological Processes

FALLING BANKS AND ROLLING SANDS

One of the most memorable aspects of the Lewis and Clark expedition was the ever-constant battle against the crumbling riverbanks and erosive currents of the Missouri River. There are numerous nail-biting journal entries that document the explorers' turbulent struggle up the Missouri, especially those events that played havoc with navigating the keelboat:

we attempted to pass up under the Lbd. Bank which was falling in So fast that the evident danger obliged us to Cross between the Starbd. Side and a Sand bar in the middle of the river, we *hove* up near the head of the Sand bar, the Sand moveing & banking caused us to run on the Sand. The Swiftness of the Current wheeled the boat, Broke our *Toe* rope, and was nearly over Setting the boat ... untill the Sand washed from under the boat. (Clark, May 24, 1804)

passed between two Islands, a verry bad place, Moveing Sands, we were nearly being Swallowed up by the roleing Sands ... we were Compelled to pass under a bank which was falling in. (Clark, June 15, 1804)

> at half past one oClock this morning the Sand bar on which we Camped began to under mind and give way ... the land had given away both above and below our Camp & was falling in fast. ... the bank under which the Boat & perogus lay give way, which would Certainly have Sunk both Perogues, by the time we made the opsd. Shore our camp fell in. (Clark, September 21, 1804)

Between Camp Dubois and the Mandans, the captains continued to note the effects of the erosive power of the river along the banks:

> passed a part of the River that the banks are falling in takeing with them large trees of Cotton woods. (Clark, June 10, 1804)

> the Banks washing away & trees falling in constantly for 1 mile. (Clark, August 4, 1804)

> In every bend the banks are falling in from the Current being thrown against those bends by the Sand points. (Clark, August 5, 1804)

> The base of the river banks being composed of a fine light sand, is easily removed by the water, it happens that when this capricious and violent current, sets against it's banks, which are usually covered with heavy timber, it quickly undermines them, sometimes to the debth of 40 or 50 paces, and several miles in length. The banks being unable to support themselves longer, tumble into the river with tremendous force, distroying every thing within their reach. (Lewis, March 31, 1805)[79]

and they occasionally would make very perceptive comparative analyses of the relative instability of the banks to erosion:

> worthey of remark as we approach this great River Plate the Sand bars much more numerous and the quick or moveing Sands much worst than they were below at the places where Praries approach the river it is verry wide those places being much easier to wash & under Mine than the wood Land's. (Clark, July 19, 1804)

From a geological perspective, the actions that Lewis and Clark witnessed are part of a significant sedimentological process involving bank erosion and point bar deposition termed "cut and fill," which describes how a river can erode and subsequently redeposit vast quantities of sediment within its channel. There may be no better layman description of this process than Lewis's study of the interaction between the Platte and Missouri Rivers:

> by a boiling motion or ebolition of it's [the Platte's] waters occasioned no doubt by the roling and irregular motion of the sand of which its bed

is entirely composed. the particles of this sand being remarkably small and light it is easily boi[l]ed up and is hurried by this impetuous torrent in large masses from place to place in with irristable forse, collecting and forming sandbars in the course of a few hours which as suddingly disapated to form others and give place perhaps to the deepest channel of the river. (Lewis, July 21, 1804)

And Clark's characteristically descriptive remarks about the Missouri and Bighorn Rivers:

the Soil of the entire bottom between the high land, being the mud or *Ooze* of the river of Some former period mixed with Sand & Clay easely melts and Slips, or washies into the river the mud mixes with the water & the Sand collects on the points. (Clark, August 5, 1804, describing the Missouri River)

it's Current is regularly Swift, like the Missouri, it washes away its banks on one Side while it forms extensive Sand bars on the other. (Clark, July 26, 1806, describing the Bighorn River)

Lewis and Clark were especially attentive throughout the expedition in noting the quantity and type of suspended sediment being carried by the rivers they were encountering:

The Mississippi when full throws large quantitys of mud into the mouths of these rivers whose courents not being equal to contend with it's power become still or eddy for many miles up them. (Lewis, November 25, 1803)

this [Niobrara] River is 152 yards wide at the mouth & 4 feet Deep Throwing out Sands like the Platt (only Corser) forming bars in its mouth. (Clark, September 4, 1804)

Capt Lewis and my Self went up this river [White River] a Short distance and Crossed, found that this differed verry much from the Plat [Platte River] or que Courre [Niobrara River], threw out but little Sand. (Clark, September 15, 1804)

the Current [of the Cheyenne River] appears gentle, throwing out but little Sands. (Clark, October 1, 1804)

this river [Grand River] is 120 yards wide, the water of which at this time is Confined within 20 yards, dischargeing but a Small quantity, throwing out mud with Small propotion of Sand. (Clark, October 8, 1804)

the bed [of the Columbia River] is principally rock except at the entrance of Labuish's river [Hood River] which heads in Mount hood and like the quicksand river [Sandy River] brings down from thence vast bodies of sand. (Lewis, April 14, 1806) it [the Tongue River] is Shallow and throws out great quantities of mud and Some cors gravel. (Clark, July 29, 1806)

But Lewis and Clark did more than just assess the relative quantity and grain size of bedload material being deposited by the Missouri River and its tributaries. After departing the Mandans, the captains began to speculate on the source of the river deposits they were encountering:

it's appearance [Little Missouri River] in every respect, resembles the Missouri; I am therefore induced to believe that the texture of the soil of the country in which it takes it's rise, and that through which it passes, is similar to the country through which the Missouri passes after leaving the woody country. (Lewis, April 12, 1805)

the Sides of the river is bordered with coars gravel, which in maney places have washed either together or down Small brooks and forms bars at Some distance in the water, around which the current passes with great valocity. (Clark, May 25, 1805, describing the Missouri River in the vicinity of the Missouri Breaks)

The sides of the mountains are very steep, and the torrents of water which roll down their sides at certain seasons appear to carry with them vast quantities of the loose stone into the river. (Lewis, August 23, 1805, describing Clark's reconnaissance of the Salmon River)

a verry Considerable Stream Dischargeing its waters through 2 Chanels which forms an Island . . . composed of Corse Sand which is thrown out of this quick Sand river Compressing the waters of the Columbia and throwing the whole Current of its waters against its Northern banks . . . This Stream has much the appearance of the *River Platt:* roleing its quick Sands into the bottoms with great velocity. (Clark, November 3, 1805, describing the Sandy River)

The November 3, 1805, journal entry is a fine example of the current utility of the geological observations of Lewis and Clark. The Sandy River today differs markedly from sediment-laden river described by Clark, and therein lies an interesting geological story. Geologists have determined that the captains were witnessing the aftermath of a circa 1781 eruption of Mount Hood, located some thirty-five miles to the southeast, that generated a mudflow (technically termed a "lahar") that temporarily choked the Sandy River watershed with volcanic ash and volcaniclastic fragments.[80] Clark's description of the Sandy River's shallow channel, its displacement into the Columbia River, and the quicksand consistency of the sediment perfectly captured the nature of this volcanically induced deposition and, until the advent of radiocarbon and lichenometric dating, was the best source in deducing the timing of this volcanic event.

By the time the expedition was winding down, Lewis and Clark could draw on their experience to make comparisons between the rivers they had investigated and conclude that the grain size of riverbed material steadily decreased the farther they traveled away from the source of the rock. This is particularly evident in Clark's evaluation of the Yellowstone River at various points along his descent of this waterway:

> this river below the big horn river resembles the Missouri in almost every perticular except that it's islands are more noumerous & Current more rapid, it's banks are generally low and falling in the bottoms.... the younded stone [NB: *round stones*] which is mixed with the Sand and formes bars is much Smaller than they appeared from above the bighorn, and may here be termed Gravel. (Clark, July 27, 1806)

> The lower portion of the river ... Contains more islands and bars; of corse gravel sand and Mud.... The Colour of the Water differs from that of the Missouri it being of a yellowish brown, whilst that of the Missouri is of a deep drab Colour containing a greater portion of mud than the Rochejhone.... the bed of this river is almost entirely composed of loose pebble.... as you decend with the river from the mountain the pebble becomes smaller and the quantity of mud increased untill you reah Tongue river where the pebble ceases and the sand then increases and predominates near it's mouth. (Clark, August 3, 1806)

Lastly, an entire paper could be written about the literally hundreds upon hundreds of channel-scale geomorphic features such as rapids, point bars, and sandbars noted by Lewis and Clark, each occurrence indicative of some type of depositional river process. Suffice to say that:

> Sand bars are So noumerous, that it is impossible to discribe them, & think it unnecessary to mention them. (Clark, October 1, 1804)

"SUBJECT TO OVERFLOW"

Among the many hydrology observations made by the captains, including notations on channel width, current velocities, and water temperature and color, there are at least forty daily journal entries where Lewis and Clark noted the potential for a river or stream to overflow. Although interesting to geologists because it reveals information about the hydraulic geometry relationship between a watercourse and its flood plain, Lewis and Clark probably had several other objectives in mind, principally the vulnerability of the adjacent lands to both constructive and destructive flooding. They could have also been evaluating the frequency of such overbank flows as it related to the enhancement of the fertility of the adjacent lands, particularly the bottomlands along the Missouri River.

Lewis and Clark made a total of seven observations about flooding in the Mississippi River valley (e.g., November 17, 22, 24–25, and December 5, 11–12, 1803), with an emphasis on its impact on settlements:

> I yesterday measured the bank on the W. side of the Mississipi and found it 52 feet 8 Inches and the bank at this hight is sometimes overflown so that allowing the water to be on a level a dike in the point to be on a level with the opposite bank must be raised 16 feet and to render it completely safe a few feet higher. (Lewis, November 17, 1803)

> I took the hight of this bank above the present state of the water which was considered as very low and found it's elevation 32 feet 6 inches; this bottom seldom overflows at least not since the present settlement has been formed which has been about 4 years. (Lewis, November 22, 1803)

> at the lower point is a Settlement on land which does not appear to have been over flown latterly. (Clark, December 12, 1803)

Once on the Missouri River, Lewis and Clark were very consistent in noting the flooding potential of the river and its tributaries below the confluence of the Missouri and Little Sioux Rivers (e.g., June 13, 21, 27, 30, July 8, 11, 13–14, and August 5, 1804). They resumed these types of observations west of the confluence of the Missouri and Milk Rivers (e.g., May 9, 20, 29, June 14, 23, July 22, 26–27, and August 2, 5–6, 1805) until they reached the Big Hole (Wisdom) River. Many of their remarks were in conjunction with an assessment of soil quality and fertility; additionally, the captains often estimated the distance inland that appeared to be subject to such overflows, the total acreage that was vulnerable to flooding, and the river or creek bank height that would have to be breached for the flooding to occur.

On his return trip through this region, Lewis not only noted the potential of flooding on those rivers he was encountering for the first time, such as the Blackfoot and Clark's Fork (July 4, 1806), the Teton River (July 17, 1806), Cut Bank Creek (July 22, 1806), and Badger Creek (July 26, 1806), he also evaluated those waterways that were being revisited in their previously unexplored upper reaches, such as the Dearborn (July 8, 1806) and Sun Rivers (July 9, 1806). Meanwhile,

Clark documented flooding on the new river he was exploring, the Yellowstone (e.g., July 15, 26, and August 3, 1806).

Although there were only a few observations about flooding on the Columbia River and its tributaries (e.g., October 18 and November 4, 1805; March 31 and April 1 and 29, 1806), Lewis and Clark took special note of a significant river obstruction on the Columbia River between the Dalles and the Great Shute that is worthy of our consideration:

> It may be proper here to remark that from Some obstruction below, the cause of which we have not yet learned, the water in high fluds (which are in the Spring) rise below these falls nearly to a leavel with the water above the falls; the marks of which can be plainly trac'd around the falls.... at 2½ miles the river widened into a large bason.... [H]ere a tremendious black rock Presented itself high and Steep appearing to choke up the river.... This obstruction in the river accounts for the water in high floods riseing to Such a hite at the last falls. (Clark, October 24, 1805)

> a remarkable circumstance in this part of the river is, the Stumps of pine trees are in maney places are at Some distance in the river, and gives every appearance of the rivers being damed up below from Some cause which I am not at this time acquainted with. (Clark, October 30, 1805)

> Several rocks above in the river & 4 large rocks in the head of the Shute; those obstructions together with the high Stones which are continually brakeing loose from the mountain on the Stard Side and roleing down into the Shute aded to those which brake loose from those Islands above and lodge in the Shute, must be the Cause of the rivers daming up to Such a distance above, where it Shows Such evidant marks of the Common current of the river being much lower than at the present day. (Clark, October 31, 1805)

> we find the trunks of many large pine trees s[t]anding erect as they grew at present in 30 feet water; they are much doated and none of them vegetating; at the lowest tide of the river many of these trees are in ten feet water. certain it is that those large pine trees never grew in that position, nor can I account for this phenomenon except it be that the passage of the river through the narrow pass at the rapids has been obstructed by the rocks which have fallen from the hills into that channel within the last 20 years; the appearance of the hills at that place justify this opinion; they appear constantly to be falling in, and the apparent state of the decayed trees would seem to fix the era of their decline about the time mentioned. (Lewis, April 14, 1806)

This is truly some inspired deduction. Lewis and Clark took the time to note the high-water marks on the canyon walls, and then they attempted to deduce the timing of the events by questioning the presence of the dead trees and their rate of decay. Lewis and Clark correctly identified the true cause and effect of what is now referred to as the Bonneville rock slide-debris avalanche, a catastrophic landslide off the slopes of Table Mountain and Red Bluffs. As the captains surmised, the landslide did indeed cause a major damming effect of the river channel and created a temporary lake that flooded the adjacent woodlands, which produced the ghost forest they so diligently noted.[81] This is one of those examples of Lewis and Clark transcending their instructions; there were no comments here about the possible effect on a future settlement or on bottomland fertility, but rather two inquisitive minds, presented with a natural history mystery, coming to an impressively logical conclusion based on their finely honed observations and their collective experience.

"ANCIENT BEDS OF THE RIVER"

The examples presented above have illustrated how Lewis and Clark could readily recognize the erosive force and depositional nature of rivers and how they attempted to assess its potential to flood. As the following journal entries indicate, both Lewis and Clark already had an excellent grasp on the larger-scale geomorphic changes that resulted from these active erosive and depositional processes even before the expedition arrived at Camp Dubois:

> There is a sand bar that extends about ¾ of a mile from the lower extremity of this Island, and reaches below the junction of the Ohio & Mississippi. . . . it's greater diameter with the course of the stream; and from the present appearance of the land on the Starbord wif [will?] soon form a part of the main land of that shore tho' at this moment it is devided from it. (Lewis, November 20, 1803)

> The chanel which forms the Island next to the fort is intirely dry, and appears to be filling up with Sand and mud. (Clark, December 4, 1803)

Lewis and Clark proved to be particularly adept in discerning how the river could quickly switch channels or cut through its broad, meandering bends. As such, they did a superlative job in documenting where the river had shortened its course and the degree to which open river channels could quickly become silted in:

> from the Camp of last night to this Creek, the river has latterly Changed its bed incroaching on the L. Side. (Clark, August 4, 1804)

> the high water passes thro this Peninsulia; and agreeable to the Customary Changes of the river I Concld. that in two years the main Current of the river will pass through. (Clark, August 5, 1804)

> the Channel formerly run on the right <but that side is now nearly filled up> with Sand. (Clark, August 8, 1804)

> a place where the river cut through and shortend the River Sevl. mls. (Clark, August 10, 1804)

> we Camped at the lower point of the Mock Island.... this now Connected with the main land, it has the appearance of once being an Island detached from the main land. (Clark, September 21, 1804)

> passed a Island on the S.S. made by the river Cutting through a point, by which the river is Shortened Several miles. (Clark, October 24, 1804)

In addition to documenting the contemporary locations and geometry of river channels and various confluences, Lewis and Clark also were able to recognize "ancient beds" of the river, including the presence of oxbow lakes and their origin as abandoned river channels:

> a large Lake on the S.S. which has the apperance of being once the bed of the river. (Clark, July 4, 1804)

> a place where the river formerly run leaving Ponds in its old Channel. (Clark, August 6, 1804)

> I have observed a number of places where the River has onced run and now filled or filling up & growing with willows & cottonwood. (Clark, August 11, 1804)

> some high banks 24 fee[t] abov the water, with bows & clare eviden[ce] of the land being made. (Clark, September 1, 1804)

> traces of the ancient beds of the river are visible in many places through the whole extent of this valley. (Lewis, May 3, 1805)

By the time the expedition passed the Mandans, Lewis and Clark had seen enough of the river's unbridled power to conclude that no low-lying area adjacent to the river would be safe from its erosive force:

> for so capricious, and versatile are these rivers, that it is difficult to say how long it will be, untill they direct the force of their currents against this narrow part of the low plain, which when they do, must shortly yeald to their influence. (Lewis, April 27, 1805, describing the Missouri and Yellowstone Rivers)

As every Lewis and Clark aficionado knows, it has long been assumed that both the Camp Dubois and Fort Mandan sites have been lost to shifting riverbanks of the "capricious" and "versatile" meandering Mississippi and Missouri Rivers, respectively (although both these assumptions have been called in question recently and, thus, await archaeological confirmation). Speaking of "meandering," Lewis and Clark often used that very term to accurately describe the wanderings of the Missouri and its tributaries (e.g., July 2, 4, 12, 30, August 11, and September 16, 1804; April 25, May 19, July 22–23, 26–27, and August 2 and 4, 1805; August 9 and September 5, 1806). On occasion, the captains would simply mention how a river was "verry Crooked" (July 15, 1805) or "emencly Crooked" (July 11, 1806), how it seemed to be "running in different directions thro the Bottom" (August 11, 1805), or how it was "devided in many places in a great number of Chanels" (October 6, 1804), a fine way to describe a braided river channel.

Lewis and Clark did not note such features during their descent of the Snake and Columbia Rivers because those rivers are generally confined between incised canyon walls, whereas the Missouri River and its tributaries meander through a low-lying flood plain. Once back on the Missouri River, however, the captains diligently followed up with a series of perceptive observations documenting major changes in the river channel that occurred since their outbound trip, and they effectively drew comparisons to their earlier observations:

> we passed the entrance of Marthy's river [Big Muddy Creek] which has changed it's entrance since we passed it last year, falling in at present about a quarter of a mile lower down. (Lewis, August 7, 1806)

> I observe a great alteration in the Corrent course and appearance of this pt. of the Missouri. in places where there was Sand bars in the fall 1804 at this time the main Current passes, and where the current then passed is now a Sand bar- Sand bars which were then naked are now covered with willow Several feet high. the enteranc of Some of the Rivers & Creeks Changed owing to the mud thrown into them. (Clark, August 20, 1806)

> the river much crowded with Sand bars, which are very differently Situated from what they were when we went up. (Clark, September 3, 1806)

By the time the expedition returned to St. Louis on September 23, 1806, Lewis and Clark had accurately documented such an array of sedimentological observations that it can be argued that this may be their most useful contribution to the geological sciences, as this information is now serving as invaluable baseline data for numerous scientific studies today.

"By Way of Experiment"

To conclude the review of the captains' mineralogical and geological observations, it is worthwhile to appraise Lewis and Clark as experimental scientists. The journals indicate that Lewis and Clark did indeed dabble in the realm of pure science a few times during the expedition when they conducted simple experiments to test specimens or ascertain the mineral content of springs. Although the captains knew that careful observation and experiment were part of Jefferson's Enlightenment philosophy, Lewis and Clark were obviously limited by the lack of equipment to conduct true experiments. As a result, they had to keep their experiments brilliantly simple. For instance, fire was employed on several occasions to assess the reaction of various geological materials to intense heat:

> I have frequently observed among the sand and pebble of the river a substance that resembled *pit-coal* but which evedently is wood that has remained a great length of time berried in the mud of the mois[t] banks of the river, & when these banks are again washed away becomes exposed to view the g[r]ain of the wood is easily persieved as was also the bark of some spesimines I met with which had not so perfectly assumed the coal state; I burnt some of this coal but found it indifferent, nor could I discover while it was berning that it emitted any sulphurious smell. (Lewis, November 22, 1803)

> I collected some Pumice Stone, burnt Stone & hard earth and put them into a furnace, the hard earth melted and glazed the other two a part of which i,e, the Hard Clay became a Pumice-Stone. (Clark, March 21, 1805)

> Stratums of bituminious Substance which resembles *Coal;* thoug Some of the pieces appear to be excellent Coal it resists the fire for Some[time], and consumes without emiting much flaim. (Clark, April 11, 1805)

> the coal appears to be of better quality; I exposed a specimen of it to the fire and found it birnt tolerably well, it afforded but little flame or smoke, but produced a hot and lasting fire. (Lewis, April 22, 1805)

There is also the well-known instance when Lewis conducted an experiment to determine the mineralogical content of a specimen:

> examonation of this (1) Bluff Contained alum, Copperas, Cobalt, Pyrites; a alum rock Soft & Sand Stone. Capt. Lewis in proveing the quality

"Mineral Productions of Every Kind"

of those minerals was near poisoning himself by the fumes & tast of the *Cabalt* which had the appearance of Soft Isonglass- Copperass & alum is verry pure.... Capt Lewis took a Dost of Salts to work off the effects of the Arsenic. (Clark, August 22, 1804)

Lewis and Clark also seemed to have employed their sense of taste to ascertain mineral content, particularly when judging the virtues of mineral waters:

Seveal Mineral Springs broke out of the water of which had a taste like *Salts*. (Clark, September 5, 1804)

a bittuminus matter resembling molasses in consistance, colour and taste. (Lewis, September 9, 1804)

there is a white substance t[h]at appears in considerable quantities on the surface of the earth, which tastes like a mixture of common salt and glauber salts. many of the springs which flow from the base of the river hills are so strongly impregnated with this substance that the water is extreemly unpleasant to the taste and has a purgative effect. (Lewis, April 11, 1805)

this [bituminous] water partakes of the taste of glauber salts and slighty of allumn. (Lewis, April 14, 1805)

the water of this creek as well as all those creeks and rivulets which we have passed since we left Fort Mandan was so strongly impregnated with salts and other miniral substances that I was incapable of drinking it. (Lewis, reporting on Clark's ramble through the countryside, April 15, 1805)

the water ... is so strongly impregnated with these salts that it is unfit for uce; all the wild anamals appear fond of this water; I have tryed it by way of experiment & find it moderately pergative, but painfull to the intestens in it's operation. (Lewis, May 23, 1805)

This is the last recorded instance in the journals of Lewis and Clark tasting strongly impregnated water solely for the sake of experiment, understandable given the documented side effects on their digestive tracts. Nevertheless, the captains made use of the spring in the vicinity of Great Falls in an attempt to restore Sagacawea's failing health, drank out of necessity from streams and rivers along the expedition route, occasionally commented on the "illy tasted" waters they were encountering (e.g., June 28, 1805), and partook of the hot spring waters encountered along the Lolo Trail and in the Big Hole (Wisdom) Valley. Overall, the pragmatic experiments conducted by Lewis and Clark yielded informative details that helped characterize the geological resources the captains encountered on the expedition.

"Ethnogeology"—Native and Expedition Uses of Geological Materials

One of the most intriguing aspects of evaluating the geological and mineralogical observations in the Lewis and Clark journals is their documentation of the native uses of geological materials, which went well beyond the use of flint. This was no doubt what Jefferson meant in his instructions when he required Lewis to note the native "ordinary occupations in agriculture, fishing, hunting, war, arts, & the implements for these."[82]

The universality of using heated stones to prepare food among the native cultures encountered by Lewis and Clark is fascinating (Mandans, December 23, 1804; Nez Perce, September 20, 1805, May 14, 1806, and June 11, 1806; Yakimas/Wanapams, October 17, 1805; Wishram, October 28, 1805; Tillamooks, January 8, 1806; Clatsop/Chinook, January 17, 1806, and March 4, 1806). Hot stones were also used to heat water for bathing (Nez Perce, October 10, 1805), to generate steam for sweat baths (Nez Perce, October 11, 1805), to cure snow blindness (Mandans, February 15, 1805), and to prepare skins to make shields (Shoshones, August 23, 1805).

Lewis and Clark also noted how stones were used to construct fish weirs and traps (Shoshone, August 21, 1805; Nez Perce, May 8, 1806) and to crush seeds in food preparation (Shoshone, August 26, 1805). Stones and rocks were also used to construct tombs (Nez Perce, May 6, 1806 and June 2, 1806), create bathing areas at hot springs (June 29, 1806), and serve as important markers on the Nez Perce Trail (June 27, 1806) and atop Pompey's Pillar (July 25, 1806). The captains also observed the utility of stones as mallets (Yakimas/Wanapams, October 17, 1805), knives (Shoshone, August 23, 1805), and arrow barbs or points (Shoshone, August 22–23, 1805; Yakimas/Wanapams, October 17, 1805; Chinooks, Clatsops, Cathlamets, and Tillamooks, January 15, 1806) and to create and decorate important ceremonial objects such as pipes (August 21, 1804, August 13, 1805, and June 6, 1806). Lewis also noted in his precise description of bead manufacture in the Mandan villages (March 16, 1805) the native uses of sand and clay in this process and the use of earth, clays, or limestone for making Shoshone pottery (August 23, 1805). Lastly, Lewis and Clark also recorded the role of stones in native mythology and beliefs, ranging from people turning into stone (Arikaras, October 13, 1804), an oracle stone (Arikaras, October 17 and 21, 1804; Mandans, February 21, 1805), or simply where the nearly departed wished to be placed to begin their journey into the afterlife (Mandans, February 20, 1805).

Lewis and Clark also availed themselves of available geological materials for an eclectic range of uses. The captains used stones as a replacement anchor during the confrontation with the Teton Sioux (September 28, 1804), as an essential building material for their Fort Mandan chimneys (November 21, 1804), and as weights to intentionally sink their canoes (August 23 and November 12, 1805). They also heated stones in an attempt to release the keelboat from the frozen waters of the Missouri at Fort Mandan (January 29 and February 3, 1805) and for their own medicinal uses, including an attempt to cure Clark's neck pains (October 22, 1804). Lewis and Clark also noted the occurrence of rocks that could serve as whetstones to sharpen knives and axes (June 10, 1804; April 22, 1805; July 18 and 23, 1806) and those suitable as grindstones (November 26 and December 5, 1803; October 18, 1804; July 16, 18, and 26, 1806).

Evaluation of Meriwether Lewis's Geological Mentors and the Source of the Geological Nomenclature Used by Lewis and Clark

The following evaluation attempts to identify the mentor or reference material that likely served as the source for both Lewis's geological education and the captains' use of the appropriate scientific terminology on the expedition with regard to "mineral productions of every kind."

Thomas Jefferson and *Notes on the State of Virginia*

It comes as no surprise that the types of mineralogical features in *Notes on the State of Virginia* would be nearly identical to the subsequent observations of Lewis and Clark. In *Notes*, Thomas Jefferson methodically cataloged the mining and production of gold, lead, copper, iron, pit coal, precious stones, marble, limestone, schist, slate, stone (particularly flint and isinglass or mica), earths (marls, chalk, ocher, and clay for brick), niter, and salt;[83] remarked on the veins of limestone and coal that were present in the mountain ranges of Virginia;[84] and wrote that "We hear of lime-stone on the Missisipi and Ohio, and in all the mountainous country between the eastern and western waters."[85] Although Lewis and Clark would not note any occurrences of gold, precious stones, or schist on the expedition, they would record observations of every other mineral production that Jefferson deemed noteworthy in Virginia.

Jefferson's geological remarks in *Notes* were also extensive in their scope and herald to a large degree the wide-ranging observations that would be recorded on the expedition. In *Notes*, reports of "pumice" floating on the Mississippi and the occurrence of fossil shells were given a prominent discussion.[86] Navigability was important to Jefferson dating back to his efforts to clear the Rivanna River of loose rock to improve its navigability; in *Notes*, Jefferson makes a point to mention the bed composition of the Ohio River and its effect on boat passage.[87] Perhaps mindful of the agriculture and settlement prospects of the West, Jefferson declared that the Missouri River's "over-flowings are considerable."[88] He engaged in geological conjecture, as evidenced by his speculation on how the Potomac River managed to cut a gap through the mountains at Harper's Ferry, when he stated that the rocks showed "evident marks of their disrupture and avulsion from their beds."[89] He speculated that the upturned beds of limestone he observed were "always attended with signs of convulsion, or other circumstances of singularity, which admitted a possibility of removal from their original position."[90] Thus, it's easy to imagine Jefferson instructing Lewis to investigate all these geologically related phenomena: the origin of the "pumice" observed floating down the Missouri, the rocky obstructions on the waterways of the West, the magnitude and extent that the rivers were subject to overflow, and the inclination of disrupted strata. Lewis and Clark would dutifully note all of these features on the expedition.

In the same Query IV response in *Notes* that contained the aforementioned discussion of mineral occurrences, Jefferson cataloged medicinal springs, including warm and hot springs. He used the term "sulphureous"[91] and paid particular attention to the temperature of the springs and the presence of minerals in the waters. In these particular instances, there are a few tantalizing connections between *Notes* and the captains' journal entries. For example, when describing the characteristics of the sulfur spring near Great Falls, Lewis noted that

> the water to all appearance is precisely similar to that of Bowyer's Sulphur spring in Virginia. (Lewis, June 16, 1805)[92]

Although Bowyer's Sulphur Springs is not identified by name in *Notes*, Jefferson indirectly made reference to it when he noted that

"We are told of a Sulphur spring on Howard's Creek of Greenbriar."[93] The absence of a formal name for this spring may be because Michael Bowyer did not receive clear title of land surrounding the spring until 1784—the same year that Jefferson sailed to France—so it's likely that Jefferson didn't know the new name of the spring when *Notes* was published. However, by the end of the eighteenth century, there was a rudimentary resort at Bowyer's Sulphur Springs and the name was well established locally.[94] Thus, either Jefferson was able to inform Lewis of this during Lewis's tenure as secretary to the president (although whether Jefferson actually knew of the name is not known since he did not add the new name of the spring to his personal copy of the Stockdale edition of *Notes*) or Lewis was familiar with this spring (which is located one hundred miles west of Charlottesville) of his own accord. The captains also referred in the journals to two caves that were specifically mentioned in *Notes:* Blowing Cave in Bath County, Virginia (June 20, 1805), and Madison Cave in Augusta County (February 27, 1806).[95]

In summary, it's likely that Lewis was familiar with both the concept and focus of *Notes*, either from an extensive review of it or from many one-on-one discussions with its author. Perhaps both men envisioned that Lewis's publication of the expedition journals upon his return, essentially a "Notes on Louisiana," would have mirrored the sweeping, eclectic scope of the original.

The Library of Thomas Jefferson

During Lewis's tenure as the president's secretary, he not only had Jefferson as a scientific mentor but also had ready access to Jefferson's expansive library. It probably cannot be truly discerned whether Lewis learned some of his geological concepts through Jefferson or directly from the books in the library, but it's reasonable to assume that any book Jefferson obtained prior to 1803 was a potential source of valuable information. Assessing the more than two dozen books in Jefferson's library that contained useful mineralogical and geological insights and information, I believe the most influential works were Comte de Buffon's *Histoire Naturelle, Époques de la nature,* and *Histoire naturelle des minéraux;* John Whitehurst's *An Inquiry into the Original State and Formation of the Earth;* Pliny the Elder's *Historia Naturalis;* John Woodward's *Essay Toward a Natural History of the Earth;* Antoine-Simon Le Page du Pratz's *History of Louisiana;* and William Bartram's *Travels.*[96]

APS Mentors Benjamin Smith Barton, Caspar Wistar, and Andrew Ellicott

When Jefferson wrote to the APS mentors in February 1803, particularly Benjamin Smith Barton, professor of materia medica, natural history, and botany at the University of Pennsylvania, and Caspar Wistar, professor of anatomy at the University of Pennsylvania, he acknowledged that it "was impossible to find a character who to a compleat science in botany, natural history, mineralogy & astronomy" was also a courageous, strong, expert woodsman who could be skillful when dealing with Indians.[97] While he praised Meriwether Lewis, whom he stated already "possesses a remarkable store of accurate observations" on the scientific topics, he requested that these mentors advise Lewis and prepare notes of what they thought "was most worthy of inquiry & observation."[98] It's readily apparent from these correspondences that Jefferson's preferences are botany and zoology; in neither letter does Jefferson specifically instruct these mentors to emphasize mineralogy, but he also suggested that Barton and Wistar include any information "which occur to you as most desireable for him to attend to."[99] Jefferson subsequently wrote Lewis that "These gentlemen will suggest any additions they will think useful."[100] Once in Philadelphia, Lewis replied on May 29, 1803, that "Drs. Barton and Wister have each promised to contribute in like manner any thing, which may suggest itself to them as being of any importance in furthering the objects of this expedition."[101]

Benjamin Smith Barton's principal exposure to geology and mineralogy was a result of the intricate connection these disciplines had with botany and, to a certain extent, medicine, but it appears Barton also had a genuine interest in geological studies. As early as May 1788, while attending Edinburgh University, Barton began to keep notes on geological and mineralogical features.[102] After returning to America in the fall of 1789, Barton continued to make notations of geological features during his travels. His notes indicate a bright and insightful mind, whether it was engaged in piecing together disparate outcrops of rocks seen while riding through the countryside—"we did see a good deal of limestone: but, if I do not mistake, it is not continued uninterrupted all the way to Frederick-town"[103]—or by dedicating considerable time in close study of sulfur springs: "During my residence in my brother's neighbourhood, I paid several visits to the 'Sulphur Spring.' . . . The water of the spring is pretty transparent, but tastes and smells of sulphur. . . . There is a good deal of slate-stone in the vicinity of the spring."[104]

Barton also kept a mineralogy notebook, perhaps as a teaching aid, in which he summarized the history of mineralogical advancement from the time of Aristotle through the mid-eighteenth century; Barton's erudite critique of the pioneering work of Pliny the Elder, John Woodward, Carl Linnaeus, and Axel Fredrik Crondstedt reveal that he was exceptionally well read in mineralogical history and had a fundamental understanding of the various proposed systems for mineralogical identification and classification.[105] Barton was also including geology in his academic courses by at least 1805, if not earlier, as evidenced by the contents of a student notebook.[106] Barton would go on to publish many papers on mineralogy and geology in his *Philadelphia Medical and Physical Journal* beginning in 1804, so there is no question that he was well informed about geology during the time of Lewis's mentoring visit in 1803.

Barton's published works clearly indicate that he was the most qualified in the geological sciences of the APS mentors who tutored Lewis. For example, the Barton papers in the 1804, part 1, volume 1, edition of the *Philadelphia Medical and Physical Journal* began with a discussion on whether earthquakes played a role in the "strata of limestone, slate, freestone, coal, iron-ore, &c." that were "generally disposed in a *horizontal* direction" in certain areas of the country.[107] Barton demonstrated his command of the science in these writings, using technically correct chemical and mineralogical terminology. He compared analytical results of salt with the material found "in certain calcareous caverns, in the western parts of Virginia";[108] tried to determine the source of "bituminous matter" of a rock specimen collected near Lake Erie;[109] and in an observation very reminiscent of Lewis and Clark, evaluated the chemistry of a sulfur spring in a report directed to Jefferson's attention, commenting that the spring "tastes and smells, very sensibly, of sulphur."[110] When discussing the mineral resource potential of the United States, Barton noted where "limestone, marble, and other forms of calcareous earth, and pyrites abound";[111] he observed that the "calcareous strata" in New York is "almost entirely made up of shells" with "almost every part of which is impressed with the images of sea-shells, and other animals";[112] and he reported that "Inexhaustible beds and quarries of coal have already been discovered in the United States, particularly in the western parts."[113]

The broad scope of Barton's geological thinking was illustrated in his 1807 *A Discourse on Some of the Principal Desiderata in Natural History,* which was read before the Philadelphia Linnean Society on June 10, 1807.[114] Throughout this oration, Barton revisited his previous writings on volcanics and the formation of walls composed of basalt. Barton was an early proponent of a natural origin of these stone walls, and his unwavering belief that such formations were not the artificial creation of man is reflected in Lewis's perceptive analyses of the shonkinite dike walls near the White Cliffs of the Missouri River (see Lewis's May 31, 1805, journal entry). Barton also confidently discussed the arrangement of strata and remarked that although the mechanisms for these arrangements was currently unknown, "I doubt if such a theory be beyond the reach or grasp of science. We shall, at some future period, possess a correct theory of the earth."[115] Barton may have had the expedition in mind when he railed against studying such phenomena by only using the information gleaned from "a cabinet of little fragments of stones, of earths, and of metals." "Nature disdains to be courted in this way," Barton asserted. "She will not answer us unless we interrogate her, in all the wild and majestic scenery of her works: on mountains, in vallies, in caverns, and in mines."[116]

In terms of mineral resources, Barton was perfectly aligned with Jefferson when he stated, "There cannot be a doubt, that the United-States possess within their limits, many important minerals, which might be applied to various useful purposes."[117] The realm of Barton's exposure to minerals is evident when he discussed the occurrences and usage of coal, pyrites, limestone, granite, chalk, cinnabar, iron, copper, lead, gold, tin, antimony, mineral springs, and bituminous or naphtha springs.[118] There are also fascinating glimpses in Barton's unpublished papers regarding his use of minerals in his medical practice. Barton would scribble notes on small scraps of paper describing the application of various minerals to effect cures. For example, regarding arsenic, Barton noted, "As arsenic is so well suited to the cure of intermittents and of rheuma[t]isms, a disease very nearly allied to intermittent, we should also expect our medicine useful in [curing] those violent . . . headaches."[119] Perhaps the attention that the captains paid to certain minerals on the expedition was due, in part, to the perceived medicinal value of these deposits.

Despite Barton's knowledge of geology and mineralogy, it is apparent that his ability to identify minerals correctly was not nearly as refined as that of Adam Seybert, Philadelphia's leading mineralogy expert, or James Woodhouse, chemical chair at the School of Medicine. Arguably, these two scientists would have been more qualified to teach Lewis the fundamentals of mineral identification, but they were apparently not in Jefferson's innermost circle, despite their membership in the APS (Seybert was elected to the APS in 1797, Woodhouse in 1796). Seybert would have been a particularly good choice, because by 1803 he was actively collecting minerals and was reaping the benefits of nearly four years of study in Edinburgh, London, Paris, and Göttingen.[120] It is assured that Jefferson was aware of Seybert's singular expertise because they both served on the Historical and Literary Committee that issued the circular letter in 1798 that encouraged the scientific community to contribute information to APS regarding the "Natural History of the Earth."[121]

It has been well established that Caspar Wistar was a leading authority of vertebrate fossils in America in 1803, and it is believed that Wistar, along with Jefferson, asked Lewis to make a stop at Big Bone Lick.[122] In a letter written to Jefferson from Cincinnati, Lewis's description of various fossil specimens collected at Big Bone Lick were precise, and he often used the word "lamina" to describe the fine layers of circular rings of the teeth.[123] In this same letter, Lewis referenced the time he spent with Wistar in Philadelphia examining type specimens of mammoth teeth, and he compared those observations to the specimens he was gathering at Big Bone Lick. Use of the term "lamina" probably came directly from Wistar, and Lewis may have assumed that it was not applicable for use in describing finely bedded geological strata because he never uses the term again. Overall, there were only a few paleontological observations in the Lewis and Clark journals.[124] Certainly, the nature of fossil deposits in the West were one of the principal reasons more specimens were not collected. For the most part, fossils in the West are deeply imbedded in solid rock, often disarticulated, and rarely exposed in their entirety; thus, they require a considerable amount of time to locate and remove for study, a luxury that Lewis and Clark could simply not have afforded (a fine example of this would be Clark's attempt on July 25, 1806, to extract a fossil bone that was "Semented within the face of the rock").

Andrew Ellicott, scientist and member of APS, had a talent for mathematics and astronomy that would lead to a highly successful career in surveying. Students of the expedition associate Ellicott with mentoring Lewis in celestial observations, yet Ellicott was also an astute geological observer. In 1796, Ellicott was chosen to lead a team of surveyors in the arduous task of surveying the boundary of Florida. Prefiguring the initial part of the expedition's route, Ellicott traveled down the Ohio River by boat, then down the Mississippi to the Gulf of Mexico. After being delayed for more than a year by Spanish authorities, Ellicott began the surveying effort of Florida in May 1798, finally returning to Philadelphia two years later.[125]

Ellicott's sharp observations and strong deductive reasoning were evident in his journal of the survey, which was published in 1803.[126] Included among Ellicott's geological observations were the method of manufacture of salt at salt works, the stratigraphy of limestone along the Ohio River, the extent of inundation evident in the Ohio's floodplain, the correlation of strata throughout the region, the formation of meanders in the broad floodplain of the Mississippi River, and the lithology and organic composition of the reefs and limestone deposits of Florida.[127]

It is easy to imagine Ellicott discussing his firsthand experiences on the Ohio and Mississippi Rivers with Lewis, knowing it was to be the very same route the expedition would take just a few months later (Ellicott, like Lewis, departed Pittsburgh in a keelboat). Ellicott's manner of describing the formation of meanders and the process by which the Mississippi River then shortens its course to form oxbow lakes—"in time a loop will be formed . . . which will increase in magnitude till the river, aided by an inundation, breaks through a shorter way. . . . and a lake will be formed. These lakes . . . bear evident marks of having been at some former period, a portion of the main bed of the river"[128]—was repeatedly echoed in the captains' description of these same types of features along the Missouri River. It is also possible that some of what Lewis knew about river hydrology and sedimentological processes may have come from Ellicott, because it is clear from Ellicott's *Journal* that he had an acute understanding of the unrelenting cut and fill hydraulics of rivers, including the sage advice that "In consequence of the banks of the river constantly giving way, no map or chart of it can be expected to be tolerably correct for more than a century to come."[129]

Richard Kirwan's *Elements of Mineralogy*

It may seem a bit odd that the only book on geology and mineralogy (that we know for certain) brought on the Lewis and Clark expedition was authored by the Irish chemist and natural philosopher Richard Kirwan. Lewis acquired *Elements of Mineralogy* in Philadelphia when he was purchasing supplies for the expedition, probably on the recommendation of either Jefferson or Barton.[130] *Elements of Mineralogy* was originally published as a single volume in 1784 but was followed by a significantly revised second edition in two volumes (1794, 1796), which was the edition that Lewis obtained. *Elements of Mineralogy* was a very well-known book and "was in the knapsacks of the majority of American field mineralogists in the early nineteenth century."[131] Because geology was just emerging as a separate science in the late 1700s, it was actually the European chemists, particularly those in the Jardin du Roi and its successors in France and the Royal Society in Britain, who led the effort in advancing the science of mineralogy. These chemists, Richard Kirwan among them, sought to understand the composition of the earth, the history of its formation, and the qualitative difference between the three realms of nature (vegetable, animal, and mineral) long before mineralogy was to fall under the domain of geologists.

In this time period, chemists were attempting to quantify the percentage of various constituents in minerals.[132] Kirwan was one of the strongest proponents of performing chemical analyses to achieve this goal, and his first edition of the *Elements of Mineralogy* was a veritable cookbook of chemical experimentation; specimens were crushed, mixed with acids or other reagents (e.g., vinegar), shaken, washed, dried, heated, dissolved, evaporated, and crystallized before determining their approximate composition. The outcomes of these experiments were compromised for a number of reasons, not the least of which was the indiscriminate grouping of minerals and rocks together based on the erroneous assumption that minerals were "all fossils that do not belong either to the vegetable or animal kingdoms."[133] Additionally, the residues generated by these experiments could only be identified in the most general terms, since it would be more than a century later before all the essential mineral elements were identified and the most complex chemical compositions of rocks fully understood. Thus, in this era, the "precise identification of minerals . . . and the determination of the mineral composition of most rocks, was a matter of great difficulty."[134] Although Jefferson believed chemistry to be "among the most useful of sciences," perhaps he summed up the confused nature of the science best in his July 19, 1788, letter to the Reverend James Madison: "The contradictory experiments of Chemists leave us at liberty to conclude what we please . . . It is yet indeed a mere embryon. It's principles are contested. Experiments seem contradictory: their subjects are so minute as to escape our senses; and their result too fallacious to satisfy the mind."[135]

In the first edition of *Elements of Mineralogy*, Kirwan did include descriptions of the external characteristics of minerals, but his dislike of the practice of using these physical properties of minerals as the sole device for identification was so strong that he dedicated most of the preface of the book to refuting its usefulness.[136] By singling out each of the external physical features one could readily observe in a mineral specimen (e.g., color, streak, luster, hardness, cleavage, parting, fracture, and specific gravity), Kirwan presented painfully obvious examples of how many minerals share each of these individual characteristics. Kirwan's purpose was to ensure that the chemical composition of a mineral was used as the primary means for its definitive identification, but he was blind at this time to the usefulness of the progressive manner in which the cumulative external physical properties of a specimen can work to narrow the possibilities of its identification.

To his credit, Kirwan modified this harsh view in the second edition of *Elements of Mineralogy*, the volumes that I believe Lewis purchased, based on my comparative review with the captains' journals. Kirwan stated, "In the Treatise I formerly compiled on this subject I considered the *internal* properties of minerals as the only that were sufficiently characteristic of the substances to which they belonged. A more mature consideration has undeceived me."[137] Throughout the second edition of *Elements of Mineralogy*, Kirwan methodically listed readily observable external characteristics to assist in mineral identification, including color, shape, luster, transparency, texture or fracture, cohesion, density, adhesion to the tongue or fingers, smell, and taste. Despite this concession, Kirwan remained an advocate of chemical testing, "It must be remarked, however, that, in distinguishing earths and stones which have never been analyzed, or which, independently of any analysis, have received their denomination from *mere external* characters, ambiguities frequently arise; and doubts may remain, which can be removed only by the application of chemical tests."[138]

Comparison of the mineralogical vernacular in the Lewis and Clark journals with the second edition of *Elements of Mineralogy* reveals that it was the primary reference source for specific mineral nomenclature, such as alum, argillaceous, bituminous, carbonated wood, calcareous, calx, magnesia, silex, and specific metals such as arsenic and cobalt. Additionally, Lewis's use in Codex O of technical terms for various limestone characteristics—"this stone . . . fracture imperfect conchoidal"[139]—closely mirrors Kirwan's description of limestone: "their fracture tends to the conchoidal."[140] It is also evident that Lewis and Clark occasionally used *Elements of Mineralogy* as a handbook in conducting rudimentary chemical tests of various mineral specimens. For example, Lewis's observation on November 22, 1803—"I burnt some of this coal but found it indifferent, nor could I discover while it was berning that it emitted any sulphurious smell"[141]—can be correlated back to Kirwan's diagnostic tests for bituminous shale: "Placed on burning coals, it burns with a weak flame, and sulphureous smell."[142] Clark's experimentation on March 21, 1805—"I collected . . . Stone Pumice Stone & a hard earth and put them into a furnace the hard earth melted and glazed the others two and the hard Clay became a pumice Stone Glazed"[143]—is reminiscent of several aspects in Kirwan's discussion "Of Clays in General" in which the fusibility of clays and earths are detailed.[144]

The most obvious example of the application of the quantitative experiments in *Elements of Mineralogy* on the expedition occurred on August 22, 1804, when Lewis debilitated himself during an experiment to ascertain the mineral content of a specimen. Without question, the idea of burning minerals to determine their identity was prompted by the procedures described in *Elements of Mineralogy;* in particular, the use of hot coals for roasting specimens was the universal method for testing various arsenical compounds.[145] Every arsenic diagnostic test in *Elements of Mineralogy* required smelling the fumes, whether it was indurated arsenic ("this Calx is often found in Clays and blue Marles and may be distinguished by its smell when thrown on burning Coals"[146]) or arsenic ores ("In the dry way, it is discovered by its evaporation, in the form of a white Smoke on burning Coals or red hot Iron, with its peculiar smell").[147] Nor was testing for cobalt any less hazardous, because that also required assessing the odor of the fumes: "When Arsenical it [cobalt] gives out that smell on burning coals."[148]

Later at Fort Clatsop, the winter 1805–1806 encampment on the Pacific Coast, it appears that Lewis was unable to conduct a wet chemical analysis when he reported on the mineralogical content of a "white earth" specimen collected by Clark: "I am confident this earth contains Argill, but wether it also contains Silex or magnesia, or either of those earths in a proper proportion I am unable to determine."[149] It's not difficult to imagine why Lewis couldn't perform diagnostic tests. A typical *Elements of Mineralogy* procedure for the chemical analysis of stones and earth had dozens of individual and complex steps involving numerous cycles of pulverization, evaporation, filtration, dilution, agitation, heating, drying, precipitation, washing, and the additions of reagents throughout the process.[150] Lewis and Clark must have realized that the experiments laid out in *Elements of Mineralogy* were an entirely impractical method of mineral identification. It is also likely that Lewis realized that he did not have the commonly used acids—nitrous (nitric), marine (hydrochloric), and vitriolic (sulfuric)—or typical laboratory equipment of the period such as distilled water and glass vessels to perform many of the tests specified in *Elements of Mineralogy*. As Kirwan himself had specified, "Before any analysis is attempted, the following substances should be procured in sufficient quantity, and in the greatest purity: concentrated vitriolic acid of the specific gravity of 1, 8, spirit of nitre 1, 400. 1, 250. 1, 110. spirit of salt 1, 12, distilled vinegar, pure vegetable alkali, crystallized soda, Prussian alkali, caustic and mild volatile alkalis, common lime-water, stronthian lime-water, barytic lime-water, acetated and nitrated barytes, solutions of nitrated calx, nitrated mercury and nitrated silver, sugar of lead, purified chalk, and spirit of wine, with plenty of distilled water."[151] This is most certainly not what one would consider a very portable chemistry kit to bring along on an eight thousand-mile expedition.

In summary, although *Elements of Mineralogy* was probably the most logical choice as a mineralogical reference book, it was also representative of the state of the mineralogical art at the end of the eighteenth century. At this time, the study of mineralogy was still in the throes of discovering and integrating the external descriptive, chemical composition, and newly discovered crystallographic structural properties of minerals into a valid classification scheme, a process that would take many more decades to achieve. A further handicap was that this cutting-edge research was being conducted in Europe, and contemporary sources attest to the fact that American mineralogical research in the year Lewis and Clark departed for the West was in its infancy.[152] Perhaps realizing their own limitations in this regard, Lewis and Clark made the wise choice to treat mineral specimens no differently than their botanical and zoological specimens by diligently collecting representative samples for shipment back East where a proper description and chemical analyses could take place.

ELEMENTS

OF

MINERALOGY.

BY
RICHARD KIRWAN, Efq. F.R.S. & M.R.I.A.
OF THE ACADEMIES OF STOCKHOLM, UPSAL,
BERLIN, MANCHESTER, PHILADELPHIA, &c.

SECOND EDITION,
WITH
CONSIDERABLE IMPROVEMENTS AND
ADDITIONS.

VOL. I.
EARTHS AND STONES.

LONDON:
PRINTED BY J. NICHOLS,
FOR P. ELMSLY, IN THE STRAND.

M DCC XCIV.

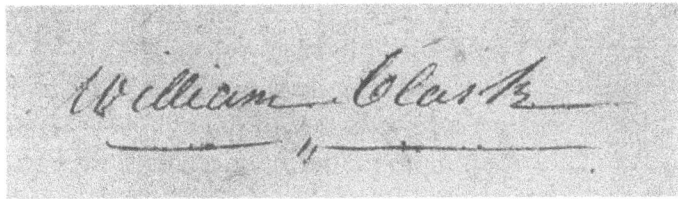

FIGURE 5.4. Irish chemist Richard Kirwan's *Elements of Mineralogy* (1794, 1796) was the principal geology reference book that Lewis and Clark brought with them on the expedition. It was their primary source of specific mineralogical nomenclature, lithologic descriptions, and suggested experimentation. This copy of the *Elements of Mineralogy* that I found in a University archive contained a signature of "William Clark" on the flyleaf. Although some striking similarities exist, both Dr. Gary Moulton (University of Nebraska-Lincoln) and Jim Holmberg (Filson Historical Society) believe that this inscription differs in some respects from signatures known to be in Clark's hand. The book was owned by Albert Huntington Chester, professor of chemistry and mineralogy at Rutgers College, and was donated to the university in 1903. Photographs by John W. Jengo, PG. Courtesy of the Rutgers University Special Collections and University Archives. (See Color Plate 17.)

Conclusions
The Perceived Geology "Blank Spot" of Thomas Jefferson and Meriwether Lewis

There have been several stinging indictments of the quality and quantity of geological and mineralogical observations made by Lewis and Clark, which have then been related back to Jefferson's perceived indifference to the science. It has also been suggested that Jefferson's lack of affection for geology was reflected in his instructions to Lewis and, as a result, the captains would "pay little attention to the vast eruptions, upheavals, and subsidences that formed the face of the West."[153] It has also been stated that Lewis and Clark had little to say about the "forbidding mountains, what forces made them, how the great canyons were cut, what ingredients were fused to make the craggy skyline," and that the dearth of geological observations "was a blank spot in Lewis's thinking that he almost surely had acquired from Jefferson."[154] I believe these opinions to be presentism simplifications that require analyses and correction.

When historians comment that Lewis and Clark made uninspired geological notations, what is not accounted for in this view is the true state of the geological science in 1803. Geology, as we know it today, was only just emerging as a separate physical science in Europe at the close of the eighteenth century; in fact, it was at that time "at best but an admixture of cosmogony and erroneous deduction."[155] Modern scholarly opinion has softened somewhat about the quality of physical facts and observations gathered by eighteenth-century naturalists and explorers, but nearly all geological historians agree that the science of geology during this time period lacked a unifying theory to explain the vast array of extraordinary phenomena from angular unconformities to volcanoes.

The modern science of geology arguably began with the publication of James Hutton's *Theory of the Earth, with Proof and Illustration* in 1795, which presented radical, paradigm-shattering geological theories, including that infinitely long periods of time were needed for rock formation, that erosion of the land surface produced sediments that were carried to the ocean to form sedimentary rocks, that the internal heat of the earth converted these sediments into lithified rocks, that rocks such as granite were formed by igneous processes, and that it was conceivable that geological forces could raise rocks from the bottom of the sea to form mountains.[156] Despite this significant breakthrough in geological thinking, it would be several decades after the Lewis and Clark expedition returned home before geology would materialize in America as a distinguishable science, set apart from mineralogy, chemistry, and geography.[157] When Lewis was under the tutelage of the APS mentors in the spring of 1803, the battle between the Neptunists and Plutonists had only just begun, the enormity of geological time was only being discretely recognized by a select few because it was in direct conflict with the Mosaic chronology of the Bible,[158] the organic origin of fossils (that they were remains of once-living creatures) was still being hotly debated, the idea that vertebrate fossils represented extinct species of animals was too fanciful to be believed, there was widespread disagreement about how fossil shells could end up on mountaintops far from the sea, the true source of volcanic action was unknown, correlation of rock strata between disparate locations was just beginning, chemists were hotly debating the chemical combinations that comprised minerals and rocks, and geology was not being taught as a true science in colleges or other institutions of learning in America nor were there any textbooks of the science.

What restrained geology from being fully understood in 1803? First, although natural science in the early nineteenth century was dominated by a zeal for describing natural phenomena, whether it was zoology, botany, or mineralogy, there was little progress in this time period to ascertain the processes behind the formation of the natural world. In other words, while scientists were actively recording "the phenomena of springs, mineral ore deposits, earthquakes, volcanoes, and the like," all of these observable facts were viewed as "fixed aspects of an essentially static world."[159] Geology only came of age after such phenomena and the formation of the earth were analyzed as "data to be understood through the processes that caused them," which would occur long after the expedition returned.[160] Second, it would be many years later that American mineralogy began to emerge as a science within a geological context, rather than an adjunct of chemistry, and by extension, medicine. As Benjamin Smith Barton stated in 1807, "Of all the branches of natural history, there is not one which has been cultivated with so little attention, zeal, or success, in the United-States, as Geology, or Mineralogy."[161] Thus, it was the nascent state of the science in 1803 (particularly the lack of proven theories of geological processes), rather than deficiencies in the captains' dedication or attention, that precluded a comprehensive reporting and evaluation about the forces that caused the "vast eruptions, upheavals, and subsidences that formed the face of the West."

The Facts Behind the Perceived Gaps in the Captains' Geological Observations

Historians have also stated that "As Lewis and Clark moved on up the Missouri they had less and less to say about minerals," and when the captains began to encounter "new and extraordinary plants and animals and stirring experiences with Indians," this "diverted their attention from such lackluster objects as coal, limestone, and lead ore."[162] Their mineralogical and geological journal entries have also been characterized as "routine and unexciting."[163] Perhaps the most severe assessment of all was that "From the Great Divide to the Pacific their journal entries contain virtually no geological descriptions. Those which do appear are worthless."[164]

Such harsh opinions are based upon a failure to recognize or acknowledge the extent of geological observations contained in the Lewis and Clark journals, particularly the sedimentological insights, and thus do not accurately represent the captains' efforts. It should be evident from the numerous examples cited above that the captains' journal entries were, in fact, full of fascinating geological detail and that their mineralogical collections and observations actually intensified as they approached the Mandans and were equally as strong as they traveled to the headwaters of the Missouri River the following year. In addition, Clark's journal of his return trip down the Yellowstone River and Lewis's observations of the geology of the Marias River watershed were both exceptionally thorough as the captains explored new territory, a testament to their efforts to apply what they had learned on the outbound journey. Overall, Lewis and Clark brought a level of diligence and dedication in recording the occurrence of "mineral productions" throughout the expedition. When a mineral such as coal or salt could be recognized readily, either visually or by taste, the captains consistently noted its presence and relative absence, which belies the opinion that Lewis and Clark were not paying attention to geological phenomena as the expedition progressed westward. To a large degree, the absence of more esoteric mineralogical and geological observations in the journals was not due to a loss of interest by the captains in complying with Jefferson's instructions, but were a result of the relative difficulty of making expeditious rock and mineral identifications.

However, the nature of the captains' geological observations west of the Continental Divide does bear some examination and discussion.

Superficially, it would appear that Lewis and Clark had indeed completely forgotten, or did not care, to make geological or mineralogical observations as they pushed their way to the Pacific Ocean. Setting aside the absence of a Lewis journal for the better part of the outbound journey, which has robbed us of his keen observations. In all probability, the paucity of geological and mineralogical notations in the journals has nothing to do with the captains having a diminishing interest. Yes, these were heady times, the expedition proceeded on with much urgency, and there were daily interactions with the native tribes, but the reasons lie elsewhere. Upon reaching the Weippe Prairie and subsequently working their way down the Clearwater, Snake, and Columbia Rivers, Lewis and Clark were passing through a geological regime—the Columbia Plateau—that is strikingly and unusually uniform.

Lewis and Clark always excelled in recording what changed day to day in their travels, whether it was the movement of the river, the flora and fauna, the topography, or the composition of the riverbed, but passing through the Columbia Plateau, virtually nothing changes geologically. The Columbia Plateau is one of the most extensive accumulations of basaltic lava on earth, so when the expedition passed through this region, all the rocks the captains were encountering were volcanic basalts, which require a modern expertise to distinguish from one another. The mineralogical nature of basalt was unknown—it had only just been tentatively associated with volcanic action—and so Lewis and Clark could do little better than to repeatedly mention all the "black rock" they were encountering.[165] Thus, the captains recorded "less" about their geological surroundings because there was less to record. But here, less is more. The absence in the journals of the once familiar Missouri River lithologies such as limestone and coal were not oversights because the captains' attention was diverted elsewhere, but rather a result of these features not being present in the Columbia Plateau. So rather than "worthless," the captains' observations reflect the absence of geological variability, which was perhaps what Patrick Gass had in mind when he noted on October 15, 1805, that "there is so much uniformity in the appearance of the country."[166] Furthermore, the mineralogical specimens documented in the Adam Seybert mineral collection definitively prove that Lewis continued his mineral collecting west of the Continental Divide and all the way to the Pacific Ocean; as such, this should put to rest any notion that Lewis and Clark neglected this essential duty.[167]

The Lasting Contribution of Thomas Jefferson and the APS Mentors

From Thomas Jefferson, Lewis learned his goals and objectives for the expedition, particularly the types of mineral resources to be noted and the geological questions to be answered. Lewis no doubt also gained a significant grounding in stratigraphic fundamentals and earth history from discussions with Jefferson and perhaps learned an effective method of scientific writing through his review of Jefferson's *Notes on the State of Virginia*. From Benjamin Smith Barton came the knowledge that freestanding stone walls were a natural, not man-made, phenomenon; the importance of noting stratigraphic inclinations; basic mineralogical identifications; the economic and medicinal importance of minerals; and the chemistry of mineral springs. From Caspar Wistar came the descriptive terminology for describing vertebrate fossils. From Andrew Ellicott came some insider knowledge of the limestone stratigraphy of the Ohio River valley and insight into recognizing the landforms that result from an actively meandering river channel.

In addition to specific technical knowledge, what Thomas Jefferson and the APS mentors provided to Lewis through their writings and conversations were enviable models of expressive scientific language. As mentioned previously, the natural sciences in 1803 were characterized by a zeal for describing natural phenomena, in part because the underlying processes were still hidden from view. As such, Lewis was primed when he departed for the West to effectively describe, to the best of his ability, the geological features and landscape that he was to encounter. There should be no question that Lewis fully embodied Jefferson's vision of the ideal explorer, as defined by Jefferson himself in a February 11, 1806, letter to Constantin-François de Chasseboeuf Volney: "These expeditions are so laborious, & hazardous, that men of science, used to the temperature & inactivity of their closet, cannot be induced to undertake them. They are headed therefore by persons qualified expressly to give us the geography of the rivers with perfect accuracy, and of good common knoledge and observation in the animal, vegetable & mineral departments."[168] The lucid and articulate journals Lewis and Clark left behind, by which modern-day readers can readily identify exactly what the captains were describing and where these observations took place, are the best evidence of the successful completion of their mission.

The Geological Record in the Journals of Lewis and Clark

Despite Jefferson's implicit instructions, it is remarkable how much geological information was recorded by Lewis and Clark, given the magnitude of their other important priorities during the expedition. For example, the captains were responsible for documenting the discoveries in botany, zoology, and ethnology; recording meteorological information; tending to the men's injuries and illnesses; tribal diplomacy; critical-decision making; survey/map making; and of course guiding the expedition across the continent and back. So, how much geology and mineralogy was recorded throughout the expedition? While determining the number of plants or animals that Lewis and Clark described is fairly straightforward, quantifying the amount of geological observations requires a careful appraisal of the captains' journals. Nevertheless, it is a revealing exercise to quantify the degree to which Lewis and Clark included geological and mineralogical observations in their daily journals, which I have attempted to do through a meticulous interpretative review.

From the day the explorers left Camp Dubois on May 14, 1804, to their arrival at the site of Fort Clatsop on December 7, 1805, and excluding times of (1) extended encampments throughout the journey to hold councils, obtain astronomical data, make repairs, or gather provisions, (2) the winter 1804–1805 layover at Fort Mandan, and (3) the month-long Great Falls portage in late June and early July 1805, the expedition was on the move through new and unexplored country on the outbound trip for almost 320 days. Even taking into account Lewis' well-documented lapses in keeping a journal, the captains made some kind of geological notation (e.g., notes on stratigraphic relationships, types of mineral resources, observations on erosion or mass wasting, etc.) in greater than 45 percent of their daily journal entries over this time period. If the myriad of sedimentological observations (e.g., notes on "ancient beds of the river," the cut and fill deposition occurring in the river channels, the type of sediments carried by various rivers, creeks, and streams, etc.) are included in this calculation, the percentage of the captains' daily geological notations exceeds 60 percent.[169] This is a remarkably complete and relatively continuous account of the geological terrain of the expedition route and one that is simple to follow and understand two hundred years later.

I believe that Lewis and Clark would have been able to fulfill the mineralogical promises made in the Conrad and Company prospectus for the publication of the journals, providing essential answers to long-standing questions about "the cause of the muddiness of the Missouri, of volcanic appearances, and other natural phenomena which were met with in the course of this interesting tour."[170] Perhaps the narrative would have been in an informational style similar to the letters the captains issued from Fort Mandan, such as Clark's description of the area around the mouth of the James River, which he summarized as containing "great quantities of mineral, cobalt, cinnebar, alum, copperas, and several other things; the stone coal which is on the Missouri is very indifferent."[171] Perhaps this information would have been presented in a more formalized scientific publication similar to the geological writings of Benjamin Smith Barton[172] covering the broad range of memorable observations the captains made through their journey.[173] Thus, it can be argued that the Lewis and Clark expedition should rightly be considered the forerunner of the four great federal geological/topographical surveys of the West that were conducted in the second half of the eighteenth century by Ferdinand V. Hayden, John Wesley Powell, Clarence King, and Lieutenant George Wheeler,[174] which was exactly what Jefferson had envisioned when he declared, "When the route shall be once open and known, scientific men will undertake, & verify & class it's subjects."[175]

In the end, the principal geological value in the journals of Lewis and Clark should not rest upon their rock or mineral identifications. The captains often misidentified rocks such as granite and minerals such as quartz because they did not have at their disposal the tools necessary to complete a comprehensive lithological evaluation of all the rocks they encountered. Had the science of mineralogy been more advanced and had a more pragmatic reference book on mineralogy been available to Lewis and Clark, I have no doubt that they would have done a superlative job in mineral identification during the expedition, especially in light of their demonstrated skill in recording coal, limestone, and salt occurrences.

Rather, the true value of the Lewis and Clark journals from a geological perspective lay in their geomorphic, sedimentological, erosional, and economic geology observations. From these journals, an explorer would know where to find sources of salt, fresh water and mineral springs, fertile soils, building materials (e.g., clay for brick, limestone for buildings), economic geology resources (e.g., coal) in addition to untillable terrain, overflowing rivers and streams, saline soils, and rocky rivers that resisted navigation. The captains' geological observations also serve as irrefutable geographic landmarks throughout the expedition route. In summary, Lewis and Clark revealed in their journals a tantalizing geological preview, including:

- sequences of generally undeformed, horizontal strata, principally clays, "slates," sandstone, and limestone (some fossil-bearing), in the Missouri River valley;
- the presence of interbedded, thin layers of coal and "carbonated wood," which were particularly prevalent west of the Mandans in the Missouri and Yellowstone River valleys;
- the absence of volcanoes and an explanation of the true origin of the "pumice" and "lava" seen floating down the Missouri River;
- an accurate mapping of salt and mineral springs;
- indications of massive geological upheavals throughout the Rocky Mountains, as evidenced by shattered "irregular and broken masses of rocks," upturned strata, and displaced hillsides;
- the unrelenting "cut and fill" and overbank flooding of a meandering and braided Missouri River and its tributaries and the accurate identification and mapping of a profusion of abandoned river channels and oxbow lakes;
- an exhaustive inventory of the type of suspended sediment carried by the rivers and tributaries of the expedition route, a direct indicator of the surficial geology of the watersheds they drain; and,
- the uniform geological terrain of the Columbia River valley, of a hard "black rock" that lacked discernable strata and contained in an incised canyon that was prone to cataclysmic flooding and sedimentation.

This is as applicable a descriptive sketch of the stratigraphy, geomorphology, and geological setting of the expedition route today as it was two hundred years ago—yet another testament to the foresight and vision of Thomas Jefferson, the insights and sage advice conveyed by the APS mentors, and exceptional observational, descriptive, and cognitive abilities of Meriwether Lewis and William Clark.

Notes

This paper is dedicated to the memory of the brilliant Stephen Jay Gould, the late, great paleontologist and evolutionary theorist, whose unsurpassed insightful writings and innate ability to coax new truths from old books served as a constant inspiration to look beyond my particular technical specialty to discover the fascinating interconnections in the captains' scientific endeavors, and to Robert J. Peterson, my American history teacher at Colonia High School nearly thirty years ago, the most challenging and memorable educator I ever knew, for igniting my undiminished interest in early American history, particularly the era of Jefferson. My appreciation to the hard-working staffs at the Library of Congress, the Firestone Library of Princeton University—Rare Books Collection, the

Alexander Library and the Library of Science and Medicine of Rutgers University, and the Rutgers University Special Collections and University Archives. Many thanks to Rob Cox and the American Philosophical Society for access to the unpublished works of Benjamin Smith Barton and to the Missouri Historical Society for copies of selected references. Recognition to Patrick Pringle of the Division of Geology, Washington Deptartment of Natural Resources, for providing me with his research and essential articles on the Bonneville landslide and the Mount Hood lahar. Warm thanks to Nancy Davis, Tom Davis, Bob Weir, and Frank Muhly of the Philadelphia Chapter for their encouragement and the opportunity to present this research at the Lewis and Clark Trail Heritage Foundation Annual Meeting in Philadelphia on August 11, 2003. My appreciation to editor Terry Fagan, geologist Andy Hersey, and reviewer Geoff Back for their diligent grammatical reviews of the manuscript. I'm also indebted to Larry and Bonnie Cook of Missouri River Outfitters and especially to river guide extraordinaire Dave "Parch" Parchen for those unforgettable canoe trips down the Missouri River through the White Cliffs and Missouri River Breaks, which greatly facilitated my research. Thanks also to Stephen E. Ambrose and Dayton Duncan for their many exceptional and inspirational books on Lewis and Clark. And lastly, I'm grateful to my fellow Lewis and Clark Trail traveling companions, "The Corps of Rediscovery"—Jon Bloom, Brian Byrd, Chuck Coblentz, Sean Fagan, Terry Fagan, Charles Lutz, Tom Scull, Phillip Weaver, Lovey Williams, Ken Varga, and Larry Zarra, who have accompanied me along the trail for many years, for their saintlike tolerance of my fireside journal readings and single-minded obsession to retrace every footfall and paddle-wake of the expedition in order to experience firsthand the geological wonders described in the captains' journals.

1. Silvio A. Bedini, *Thomas Jefferson Statesman of Science* (New York: MacMillan Publishing Company, 1990), 1, 346, 486, 488, 490, and passim.

2. Julian P. Boyd, ed., *The Papers of Thomas Jefferson*, Vol. 6 (Princeton, N.J.: Princeton University Press, 1952), 204.

3. Barbara B. Oberg, ed., *The Papers of Thomas Jefferson*, Vol. 29 (Princeton, N.J.: Princeton University Press, 2002), 389–91.

4. Bedini, *Statesman of Science*, 437.

5. Thomas Jefferson, *Notes on the State of Virginia* (Chapel Hill, N.C.: University of North Carolina Press, [1787] 1955).

6. Boyd, *Papers of Thomas Jefferson*, 6:163.

7. Charles Thomson also provided Jefferson with erudite commentaries to *Notes on the State of Virginia* relating to sedimentology and geology. He mentions how the Delaware River "overflowed to the distance of from ten to fifteen miles back from the river, and to have acquired a new soil by the earth and clay brought down," and he reviewed the effects of geological upheavals in "other parts of this country which bear evident traces of a like convulsion"; see Jefferson, *Notes*, 198. A charming passage in Thomson's commentaries involved his self-proclaimed "visions of fancy" where he ruminates on the effects of a "convulsion or shock of nature" to form land masses, erode mountains, and flood vast areas of country; see Jefferson, *Notes*, 199. Because of Thomson's correspondence and his insightful commentaries, Jefferson remained engaged in geological observations and theories.

8. Julian P. Boyd, ed., *The Papers of Thomas Jefferson*, Vol. 10 (Princeton, N.J.: Princeton University Press, 1954), 104.

9. Ibid., 10:608.

10. Julian P. Boyd, ed., *The Papers of Thomas Jefferson*, Vol. 11 (Princeton, N.J.: Princeton University Press, 1955), 323.

11. Ibid.
12. Julian P. Boyd, ed., *The Papers of Thomas Jefferson*, Vol. 12 (Princeton, N.J.: Princeton University Press, 1955), 160.
13. Ibid.
14. Jefferson, *Notes*, 98–100.
15. Thomas Jefferson to Thomas Mann Randolph, June 5, 1791, *The Papers of Thomas Jefferson*, Library of Congress, Manuscripts Division.
16. John Catanzariti, ed., *The Papers of Thomas Jefferson*, Vol. 24 (Princeton, N.J.: Princeton University Press, 1990), 109.
17. John Catanzariti, ed., *The Papers of Thomas Jefferson*, Vol. 25 (Princeton, N.J.: Princeton University Press, 1992), 81.
18. Ibid., 25:625.
19. Ibid., 25:79–81.
20. John Catanzariti, ed., *The Papers of Thomas Jefferson*, Vol. 28 (Princeton, N.J.: Princeton University Press, 2000), 240.
21. Ibid., 28:505. Jefferson made a similar remark in a March 24, 1789, letter to Joseph Willard: "What a feild have we at our doors to signalize ourselves in! . . . it's [America's] Mineralogy is untouched." See Julian P. Boyd, ed., *The Papers of Thomas Jefferson*, Vol. 14 (Princeton, N.J.: Princeton University Press, 1958), 699.
22. Catanzariti, *Papers of Thomas Jefferson*, 28:425.
23. Gilbert Chinard, "Jefferson and the American Philosophical Society," *Proceedings of the American Philosophical Society* 87(3) (July 1943): 270.
24. Donald Jackson, ed., *Letters of the Lewis and Clark Expedition, with Related Documents: 1783–1854*, Vol. 1 (Urbana: University of Illinois Press, 1978), 63.
25. Thomas Jefferson to Samuel or Thomas Freeman, April 14, 1804, *The Papers of Thomas Jefferson*, Library of Congress, Manuscripts Division.
26. Thomas Jefferson to William Dunbar, March 13, 1804, and William Dunbar to Thomas Jefferson, May 13, 1804, *The Papers of Thomas Jefferson*, Library of Congress, Manuscripts Division.
27. Julian P. Boyd, ed., *The Papers of Thomas Jefferson*, Vol. 7 (Princeton, N.J.: Princeton University Press, 1953), 602.
28. Julian P. Boyd, ed. *The Papers of Thomas Jefferson*, Vol. 9 (Princeton, N.J.: Princeton University Press, 1954), 400–401; Boyd, *The Papers of Thomas Jefferson*, 10:609–10.
29. Two excellent references describing colonial and early American uses of metals are John C. Greene and John G. Burke, "The Science of Minerals in the Age of Jefferson," *Transactions of the American Philosophical Society*, Vol. 68, pt. 4 (July 1978): 109 pp.; James A. Mulholland, *A History of Metals in Colonial America* (University: University of Alabama Press, 1981), 215 pp., especially 74–98 and passim.
30. Jackson, *Letters*, 1:69–99.
31. In the final months of the expedition, when their stock of provisions was at its lowest ebb, Lewis no doubt came to appreciate how incredibly valuable a trading commodity some of the utilitarian items he purchased turned out to be. The captains traded scraps of various metals for essential items during their return journey (see journal entries for April 20 and 22, May 20, and June 7, 1806) after they had exhausted their store of Indian presents. They took the time to extract every last iron nail from their abandoned canoes (July 11–12, 1806) and the red pirogue (July 28, 1806) and to excavate (and possibly retrieve) the frame of the iron boat (July 14, 1806). In addition, the captains documented the use of copper and brass kettles, brass teakettles and coffee pots, brass wire, and sheet copper and brass as common trade items while at Fort Clatsop (see January 9 and 14, 1806, journal

entries) and the presence of "Brass kittles & frying pans" in native burial vaults (October 31, 1805), the wearing of copper, brass, and iron bracelets by native Americans (March 19 and May 13, 1806), and the use of brass as ad hoc currency (April 18, 1806).

32. Jackson, *Letters*, 1:162.

33. For a detailed discussion that unravels the complicated collection history and ultimate fate of all the captains' mineralogical specimens, see John W. Jengo, "Specimine of the Stone: The Collection History and Fate of the Lewis and Clark Mineralogical Specimens," *We Proceeded On* 31 (in press).

34. All quotations or references to Lewis and Clark journal entries in the text are by date and, thus, can be found in Gary E. Moulton, ed., *The Journals of the Lewis and Clark Expedition*, Vols. 2–8 (Lincoln: University of Nebraska Press, 1986–93): Vol. 2, *August 30, 1803–August 24, 1804*; Vol. 3, *August 25, 1804–April 6, 1805*; Vol. 4, *April 7–July 27, 1805*; Vol. 5, *July 28–November 1, 1805*; Vol. 6, *November 2, 1805–March 22, 1806*; Vol. 7, *March 23–June 9, 1806*; Vol. 8, *June 10–September 26, 1806*.

35. Jackson, *Letters*, 1:60.

36. That being said, there are occasional hints in Clark's 1804 journal writings of Lewis's distinctive "voice," such as this entry from July 4, 1804: "nature appears to have exerted herself to butify the Senery by the variety of flours Delicately and highly flavered raised above the Grass, which Strikes & profumes the Sensation, and amuses the mind throws it into Conjectering the cause of So magnificent a Senerey in a Country thus Situated far removed from the Sivilised world." This suggests that some of the more flowery observations that Clark made were a collaboration between the captains. See Moulton, *Journals*, 2:346, for this journal entry.

37. Moulton, *Journals*, 3:477. The Fort Mandan mineralogical specimen numbers used in this discussion follow those that were recorded in the APS Donation Book; see Moulton, *Journals*, 3:473–78. Any reference to a mineral specimen in the text that is prefaced by "Fort Mandan mineralogical specimen" refers to those minerals sent back East from Fort Mandan in April 1805.

38. Jackson, *Letters*, 1:126–31.

39. For an in-depth analysis of Lewis's geological descriptions on this extraordinary day, see John W. Jengo, "'High Broken and Rocky': Lewis and Clark as Geological Observers," *We Proceeded On* 28(2) (May 2002): 22–27. See also John W. Jengo, "'Broken Masses of Rock and Stones': Lewis and Clark as Geological Trailblazers," *The Professional Geologist* 39(10) (November 2002): 2–6.

40. Moulton, *Journals*, 4:225.

41. Lewis's description reads like a veritable definition of a dike, including its uniform thickness, its scale relative to other igneous features, and its characteristic steeply inclined to vertical nature. I have also run across passages in early geological books that are strikingly similar to Lewis's lyrical phrasing. For example, W. O. Crosby's *Geological Collections* book, published by the Museum of the Boston Society of Natural History in 1892, contains this phrase: "The sides of dikes are often as parallel and straight as those of built walls, the resemblance to human workmanship being heightened by the numerous joints which, intersecting each other along the face of a dike, remind us of well-fitted masonry" (213).

42. In fact, Ferdinand Vandiveer Hayden, trailblazing American geologist, specifically refers to the captains' description of this region in his 1860 paper "Geological Sketch of the Estuary and Fresh-water Deposit of the Bad Lands of the Judith, with Some Remarks Upon Surrounding Formations," published in the *Transactions of the American Philosophical Society*, New series, 11:123–38. Hayden remarked that the captains gave an

"accurate description of the physical features of this remarkable region," particularly in the region of the "Stone Walls."

43. The brick analogy Lewis used to describe the characteristic jointing pattern of the stone walls can scarcely be refined. Furthermore, the jointing of the rock must have been a memorable feature as most of the "walls" depicted on the expedition maps of this region were drawn as rectangles subdivided by numerous lines, resembling how one might depict a row of bricks. See Gary E. Moulton, ed., *The Journals of the Lewis and Clark Expedition*, Vol. 1: *Atlas of the Lewis and Clark Expedition* (Lincoln: University of Nebraska Press, 1983), maps 53 (Clark's finished map) and 60 (Clark-Maximilian Sheet 24).

44. See mineralogical descriptions for Fort Mandan mineralogical specimens Nos. 6, 13, and 43 in Moulton, *Journals*, 3:473–74, 476.

45. Robert L. Bates and Julia A. Jackson, eds., *Glossary of Geology* (Falls Church, Va.: American Geological Institute, 1980), 69.

46. Moulton, *Journals*, 3:476.

47. Ibid., 3:96.

48. Bates and Jackson, *Glossary*, 86.

49. Moulton, *Journals*, 3:477–78.

50. Lewis did well to comment on both the white sandstone and the iron concretions, because they are intrinsically related. Long before the Eagle Sandstone was exposed at the surface, reducing groundwater migrated through this permeable rock, dissolving hematite (Fe_2O_3) and literally bleaching the color out of this formation. The hematite was then reprecipitated upon contact with oxidizing waters into the array of iron concretions that can be seen today eroding out from the surrounding rock.

51. See the undated entry in Moulton, *Journals*, 2:147.

52. Moulton, *Journals*, 3:358.

53. Ibid., 3:341.

54. Ibid., 3:342.

55. Clark's interest in lead mines grew after his move to St. Louis in 1808, as evidenced by numerous letters to his brother Jonathan in which he touted the prospects and economical opportunities of lead mining in Missouri. See James J. Holmberg, *Dear Brother: Letters of William Clark to Jonathan Clark* (New Haven, Conn.: Yale University Press in association with The Filson Historical Society, 2002), 153, 161, and 167.

56. Moulton, *Journals*, 4:405.

57. Moulton, *Journals*, 3:339.

58. Perhaps because writing slates were so common; Lewis had them included on his list of items needed to outfit the expedition. See Jackson, *Letters*, 1:69.

59. As reported in Moulton, *Journals*, 2:114, whiting is a pigment made from powered chalk or limestone.

60. Moulton, *Journals*, 3:354.

61. So-called pit coal refers to firm, unweathered coal that was normally encountered in man-made pits that have penetrated below the softer, weathered coal exposed at the surface.

62. Coal is now ranked or classified based on the degree of transformation of the original plant material to carbon. The four general coal ranks range from lignite through subbituminous and bituminous to anthracite, reflecting the progressive increase in the amounts of carbon and the maturity of the coal deposit.

63. Moulton, *Journals*, 3:478. Lewis also commented under Fort Mandan mineralogical specimen No. 62 that "I can hear of no burning mountain in the neighborhood of the Missouri or its Branches, but the bluffs of the River are now on fire at Several places. . . .

The plains in many places, throughout this great extent of open country, exhibit abundant proofs of having been once on fire."

64. Jefferson had been skeptical that these floating rocks were actually pumice. See Jefferson, *Notes*, 20. He didn't think that volcanoes could exist in midcontinent areas far from the ocean. He also apparently did not consider that ancient beds of pumice could have been eroding out somewhere within the Missouri River watershed.

65. Jackson, *Letters*, 1:180–82.

66. Moulton, *Journals*, 3:349–50. Lewis goes on to state, "I am therefore disposed to believe, that those travellers who have reported it's exhistance, must have mistaken this massive salt, formed by concretion, for that substance." Lewis may be addressing the myth of the salt mountain, such as the one described by Thomas T. Davis in a letter to Jefferson: "Tomorrow I set out for Saint Louis to see a French man named Shoto [Chouteau] who it is said has just returned from Santa Fee & reports that he has found a Salt Rock of immense size." Thomas T. Davis to Thomas Jefferson, October 5, 1803, *The Papers of Thomas Jefferson*, Library of Congress, Manuscripts Division.

67. Bates and Jackson, *Glossary*, 424.

68. Moulton, *Journals*, 2:502.

69. Ibid., 2:232.

70. Thomas Jefferson to William Dunbar, April 15, 1804, *The Papers of Thomas Jefferson*, Library of Congress, Manuscripts Division.

71. Moulton, *Journals*, 8:414. Dr. Robert N. Bergantino, a major contributor of the geology footnotes in the Moulton *Journals*, has suggested that the captains may have used Owen's *Dictionary of the Arts and Sciences* for their definition of pumice, listed therein as "a flag or cinder of some fossil, originally bearing another form, and only reduced to this state by the action of the fire"; Society of Gentlemen, *A New and Complete Dictionary of Arts and Sciences; Comprehending all The Branches of Useful Knowledge, With Accurate Descriptions as well of the various Machines, Instruments, Tools, Figures, and Schemes necessary for illustrating them, As Of The Classes, Kinds, Preparations, and Uses of Natural Productions, whether Animals, Vegetables, Minerals, Fossils, or Fluids; Together with the Kingdoms, Provinces, Cities, Towns, and other Remarkable Places throughout the World. Illustrated with above Three Hundred Copper-plates, curiously engraved by Mr. Jeffreys, Geographer and Engraver to his Royal Highness the Prince of Wales. The Whole extracted from the Best Authors in all Languages, By a Society of Gentlemen* (London: Printed for W. Owen, at Homer's Head, in Fleet-street, 1754, 1755).

72. Bates and Jackson, *Glossary*, 234.

73. Chalcedony is a cryptocrystalline variety of quartz with a white, pale-blue, gray, brown, or black color and "is the material of much chert," according to Bates and Jackson, *Glossary*, 104.

74. Moulton, *Journals*, 3:339–41 and 345.

75. Moulton, *Journals*, 4:346.

76. Moulton, *Journals*, 5:156.

77. Glacial erratics are rock fragments carried by glacial processes and deposited a noticeable distance from their area of origin. The sizes of these rocks can vary from pebbles, as Lewis noted on April 22, 1805, to immense blocks, as recorded on April 26, 1805.

78. Faults are zones of fractures where there has been displacement of rock strata, often accompanied by the crushing, shattering, and shearing of rock. Mass wasting is defined as the displacement of soil and rock under direct application of gravity. It includes slow displacement of soil and rock but is most often used to describe rockfalls, rock slides, and debris flows, all of which the captains observed in their travels.

79. Jackson, *Letters*, 1:223.

80. The latest research can be found in Patrick T. Pringle, Thomas C. Pierson, and Kenneth A. Cameron, "A Circa A.D. 1781 Eruption and Lahar's at Mount Hood, Oregon—Evidence from Tree-Ring Dating and From Observations of Lewis and Clark in 1805–6 [Abstract]," *Geological Society of America Abstracts with Programs* 34(6) (October 2002): 511.

81. Work on dating the timing of this landslide continues, but it is now estimated that the slide occurred approximately 350 years prior to the expedition's arrival (ca. a.d. 1450) as opposed to the twenty years that Lewis estimated. For the latest estimates on dating the landslide, see Robert Schuster and Patrick T. Pringle, "Engineering History and Impacts of the Bonneville Landslide, Columbia River Gorge, Washington-Oregon, USA," in *Landslides*, ed. J. Rybiṇ, Josef Stemberk, and Peter Wagner, 689–99 (Netherlands: A. A. Balkema Publishers/Swets & Zeitlinger Publishers, 2002). The latest research can be found in Patrick T. Pringle, Jim E. O'Connor, Robert L. Schuster, Nathaniel D. Reynolds, and Alex C. Bourdeau, "Tree-Ring Analysis of Subfossil Trees from the Bonneville Landslide Deposit and the 'Submerged Forest of the Columbia River Gorge' Described by Lewis and Clark [Abstract]," *Geological Society of America* Abstracts with Programs 34(5) (May 2002): A-34. For fascinating photographs of the now-inundated ghost forest, see the seminal work of Donald B. Lawrence and Elizabeth G. Lawrence, "Bridge of the Gods Legend, Its Origin, History and Dating," *Mazama* 40(13) (1958): 33–41.

82. Jackson, *Letters*, 1:62.
83. Jefferson, *Notes*, 26–34.
84. Ibid., 18–19, 29.
85. Ibid., 30.
86. Ibid., 20 and 31–33.
87. Ibid., 11.
88. Ibid., 8.
89. Ibid., 19.
90. Ibid., 30.
91. Ibid., 35.
92. Moulton, *Journals*, 4:300.
93. Jefferson, *Notes*, 36.
94. John W. Lund, "White Sulphur Springs, West Virginia," *Geo-Heat Center Quarterly Bulletin* 17(2) (May 1996): 11–16. The spring was subsequently renamed White Sulphur Springs and is now part of the Greenbrier Resort in White Sulphur Springs, West Virginia.

95. Jefferson, *Notes*, 21–24; Moulton, *Journals*, 4:320; Moulton, *Journals*, 6:356. It is possible that Lewis was aware of these caves independent of Jefferson. For example, Lewis appears to have personally visited Madison Cave, which is located twenty-five miles northwest of Charlottesville, as he refers to seeing a particular species of rat there.

96. See E. Millicent Sowerby, *Catalogue of the Library of Thomas Jefferson*, Vol. 1 (Washington, D.C.: Library of Congress, 1955), for details on when Jefferson obtained the books by Buffon (300 and 466–67), Whitehurst (303), Pliny (458–59), and Woodward (301). I believe Lewis diligently reviewed Le Page du Pratz's *History of Louisiana* because during the time Lewis was in St. Louis in the winter of 1803–1804, he inquired locally about the production of lead mining in some of the same areas discussed in *History of Louisiana*. Lewis carried the 1774 edition of the book on the expedition: Antoine-Simon Page du Pratz, *The History of Louisiana or of the Western Parts of Virginia and Carolina: Containing a description of the Countries that lie on both Sides of the*

River Missisipi: With an Account of the Settlements, Inhabitants, Soil, Climate, and Products, Translated from the French of M. Le Page du Pratz; with some Notes and Observations relating to our Colonies (London: Printed for T. Becket, Corner of the Adelphi, in the Strand, 1774), 387. The full title of William Bartram's *Travels* is *Travels through North and South Carolina, Georgia, East and West Florida, the Cherokee Country, the Extensive Territories of the Muscogulges or Creek Confederacy, and the Country of the Chactaws; containing an account of the Soil and Natural Productions of those regions, together with observations on the Manners of the Indians* (Philadelphia: James and Johnson (printers), 1791).

97. Jackson, *Letters*, 1:16–18.
98. Ibid., 1:17.
99. Ibid., 1:18.
100. Ibid., 1:44.
101. Ibid., 1:52.
102. An unpublished geology note in the Barton collection at APS includes this passage: "The ... *Whin Rock* is neither of a regular nor of a prysmatical figure; nor does it form any vertical strata such as as [*sic*] the Basaltes, but is found heaped together in large irregular masses. This species of Rock is very fertile in metals, and does not contain any Petrefactions or other extraneous fossils. The Castle of Edinburgh is built on this stone*_ The above note is transcribed, but not verbatim, from Mr. Wm Jameson's copy of Dr Walker's Mineralogical Notes_ Benjamin Smith Barton, Brickfield, May 10th, 1788." Benjamin Smith Barton Papers (Series II, Subject Files: Geology), American Philosophical Society, transcribed by the author. This may be the origin of Barton's knowledge on the characteristics of igneous rocks and the formation of natural walls, learned during a period of significant breakthroughs of geological thinking in Scotland at this time.
103. Benjamin Smith Barton Papers (Series II, Subject Files: Geology), American Philosophical Society, unpublished, transcribed by the author.
104. Benjamin Smith Barton Papers (Series III, Bound Volumes: 4. Sulphur Springs), American Philosophical Society, unpublished, transcribed by the author.
105. Benjamin Smith Barton Papers (Series III, Bound Volumes: 18. Notebook on mineralogy), American Philosophical Society, unpublished.
106. Carol Faul, "A History of Geology at the University of Pennsylvania: Benjamin Franklin and the Rest," in *Geologists and Ideas: A History of North American Geology*, ed. Ellen T. Drake and William M. Jordan, 378 (Boulder: Geological Society of America, 1985).
107. Benjamin Smith Barton, "Memorandums Concerning the Earthquakes of North-America," *Philadelphia Medical and Physical Journal*, Vol. 1, Pt. 1 (1804): 62.
108. Benjamin Smith Barton, "Miscellaneous Facts and Observations," *Philadelphia Medical and Physical Journal*, Vol. 1, Pt. 1 (1804): 152.
109. Ibid., 162.
110. Benjamin Smith Barton, "Notice of the Sulphur-Springs, in the County of Ontario, and State of New-York," *Philadelphia Medical and Physical Journal*, Vol. 1, Pt. 1 (1804): 166.
111. Barton, "Miscellaneous Facts and Observations," 160.
112. Ibid., 160–61.
113. Ibid., 164. It's easy to gain a respect for Barton and his foresight in the latter portion of this paragraph when he stated that "Notwithstanding this [the discovery of coal deposits], however, it is to be hoped, that the inhabitants of the United-States will, in future, be more careful of the preservation of forest-timber, than they have, hitherto, been. It will hardly be denied, that much of our timber is daily cut down, with scarcely any regard to the future."

114. Benjamin Smith Barton, *A Discourse on Some of the Principal Desiderata in Natural History and on the Best Means of Promoting the Study of this Science in the United-States* (Philadelphia: Denham & Town, 1807).
115. Ibid., 55.
116. Ibid.
117. Ibid., 56.
118. Ibid., 55–59.
119. Benjamin Smith Barton Papers (Series II, Subject Files: Alkali and Minerals), American Philosophical Society, unpublished, transcribed by the author. Another note in this file indicates some uncertainty about the universal effectiveness of arsenic: "In the Summer and autumn of 1808, I also gave the arsenic ... in several cases of intermittents, in the Penn. Hospital. In several of these cases, likewise, the medicine seemed less efficacious than I had generally found it."
120. Greene and Burke, "Science of Minerals," 28, and Faul, "History of Geology," 379.
121. Chinard, "Jefferson and the American Philosophical Society," 270.
122. Paul Russel Cutright, *Contributions of Philadelphia to Lewis and Clark History* (West Conshohocken, Pa.: James-Allan Printing and Design Group, [1982] 2001), 15–16.
123. Jackson, *Letters*, 1:126–31.
124. See Robert Moore, "Lewis & Clark and Dinosaurs," *We Proceeded On* 24(2) (May 1998): 26–29, for a review and discussion of the captains' paleontological observations.
125. George W. White, "Andrew Ellicott's Geological Observations in the Mississippi Valley and Florida, 1796–1800," in *The Geological Sciences in the Antebellum South*, ed. James X. Corgan, 11–17 (University: University of Alabama Press, 1982).
126. Andrew Ellicott, *The Journal of Andrew Ellicott, late Commissioner on behalf of the United States during part of the Year 1796, the Years 1797, 1798, 1799, and Part of the Year 1800: for Determining the Boundary between the United States and the Possessions of His Catholic Majesty in America, Containing Occasional Remarks on the Situation, Soil, Rivers, Natural Productions, and Diseases of the Different Countries of the Ohio, Mississippi and the Gulf of Mexico, with Six Maps Comprehending the Ohio, the Mississippi from the mouth of the Ohio to the Gulf of Mexico, the whole of West Florida, and part of East Florida. To which is Added An Appendix...* (Philadelphia, Pennsylvania: Printed by William Fry, [1803] 1814).
127. Ibid., 14, 19–23, 120–22, 234, 245, 252–53.
128. Ibid., 121–22.
129. Ibid., 137.
130. Jackson, *Letters*, 1:96.
131. Greene and Burke, "Science of Minerals," 14.
132. Ibid., 11.
133. Richard Kirwan, *Elements of Mineralogy* (London: P. Elmsly, 1784), 1. The current, restricted definition of a mineral is a homogenous, inorganic solid that possesses a fairly definitive chemical composition and a very characteristic crystalline structure, whereas rocks are aggregates of minerals.
134. V. A. Eyles, "The Extent of Geological Knowledge in the Eighteenth Century, and the Methods by Which It Was Diffused," in *Toward a History of Geology*, ed. Cecil J. Schneer, 175 (Cambridge, Mass.: MIT Press, 1969).
135. Julian P. Boyd, ed., *The Papers of Thomas Jefferson*, Vol. 13 (Princeton, N.J.: Princeton University Press, 1956), 381.
136. Kirwan, *Elements*, vi–xiv.
137. Richard Kirwan, *Elements of Mineralogy*, Vol. 1, *Earths and Stones* (London: Printed by J. Nichols for P. Elmsly, in the Strand, 1794), 23.

138. Ibid., 24–25.
139. Moulton, *Journals*, 3:339.
140. Kirwan, *Elements*, 1:373.
141. Moulton, *Journals*, 2:103.
142. Kirwan, *Elements*, 1:184.
143. Moulton, *Journals*, 3:318.
144. Kirwan, *Elements*, 1:177–78.
145. In fact, the heating of specimens was a critical diagnostic tool throughout *Elements of Mineralogy* when wet chemistry could not be performed. Kirwan often referred to this approach as "the dry way."
146. Richard Kirwan, *Elements of Mineralogy*, Vol. 2, *Salts, Inflammables, and Metallic Substances* (London: Printed for P. Elmsly, in the Strand, 1796), 259–60.
147. Ibid., 438.
148. Ibid., 273.
149. Moulton, *Journals*, 6:193–94. Investigating this area, I found that white clay strata can occasionally be seen along the ocean-facing, upper cliff faces in Ecola State Park (located between Cannon Beach and Seaside, Oregon). A recent small exposure of this "white earth" can be seen at the Old Military Bunker Viewpoint between Tillamook Head and Bird Point, accessible via the Oregon Coast Trail.
150. Kirwan, *Elements*, 1:459–507.
151. Ibid., 1:461.
152. Greene and Burke, "Science of Minerals," 21.
153. Donald Jackson, *Thomas Jefferson and the Stony Mountains* (Urbana: University of Illinois Press, 1981), 33.
154. Ibid., 197.
155. George P. Merrill, *The First One Hundred Years of American Geology* (New Haven, Conn.: Yale University Press, 1924), 1.
156. Hutton's geology was entirely at odds with the ideas advanced in Abraham Gottlob Werner's "Short Classification and description on the different rocks," published in 1786. Werner believed that all rocks had been formed as a result of aqueous crystallization precipitation from waters of global deluge, thus the followers of this theory were called "Neptunists," while Hutton recognized the possibility that rocks formed as a result of igneous action deep within the earth's crust, thus the followers in this camp were nicknamed "Plutonists."
157. It was none other than Richard Kirwan who vehemently challenged Hutton's theories when they were first presented in text form in the first volume of the Royal Society of Edinburgh's *Transactions* in 1788, motivating Hutton to reinforce his theory with hundreds upon hundreds of pages of additional proofs and illustrations when he published the seminal *Theory of the Earth* in 1795. Thus, the very same man whose own geological theories were incorrectly Neptunist played a significant role in helping the true geological story of the earth emerge.
158. Mosaic geology is a type of geology that seeks to reconcile observations of the earth's crust with the account of earth's origin and early history as described in the Old Testament, and allegedly by Moses. See David Oldroyd, *Thinking about the Earth: A History of Ideas in Geology* (Cambridge: Harvard University Press, 1996), xxi.
159. Kenneth L. Taylor, "Geology in 1776: Some Notes on the Character of an Incipient Science," in *Two Hundred Years of Geology in America*, ed. Cecil J. Schneer, 80 (Hanover, N.H.: University Press of New England, 1979).
160. Ibid., 84.

161. Barton, *Discourse*, 51–52.

162. Paul Russell Cutright, *Lewis and Clark: Pioneering Naturalists* (Urbana: University of Illinois Press, 1969), 57.

163. Donald Jackson, *Among the Sleeping Giants* (Urbana: University of Illinois Press, 1987), 15.

164. Donald Jackson, "Some Books Carried by Lewis and Clark," *Missouri Historical Society Bulletin* 16(1) (October 1959): 8.

165. One unresolved question is why the captains did not attempt to identify these rocks as basalts; there was a very good description of basalts and their characteristic columnar shapes in Kirwan, *Elements*, 1:231.

166. Gary E. Moulton, ed., *The Journals of the Lewis and Clark Expedition*, Vol. 10, *The Journal of Patrick Gass* (Lincoln: University of Nebraska Press, 1996), 155.

167. These specimens include "Pumice. Pacific ocean. Captn. Lewis.," "Green Clay. from the Kooskoosche River, west of the Rocky mountains. Captn. Lewis.," "Keffekill [impure clay]. found at the Wallenwaller [Walla Walla] nation on Columbia River. Captn. Lewis.," and "Magnetic Iron sand, borders of the Pacific ocean near the mouth of Columbia river. Captn. Lewis." See Seybert's "Catalogue of Minerals" as reported in Greene and Burke, "Science of Minerals," 29–30.

168. Paul Leicester Ford, *The Writings of Thomas Jefferson*, Vol. 8 (New York: Knickerbocker Press, G. P. Putnam's Sons, 1897), 420–21. Also be found in Merrill D. Peterson, ed., *Thomas Jefferson Writings* (New York: R. R. Donnelley & Sons Company, 1984), 1159–60.

169. John W. Jengo, "Geological Trailblazers: Observations of Western Geology in the Journals of Lewis and Clark," *Geological Society of America Abstracts* 35(6) (October 2003): 605. Presented at the Pardee Symposia, The Science of Lewis and Clark: Historical Observations and Modern Interpretations, at the Annual Meeting of the Geological Society of America, November 5, 2003, in Seattle, Washington.

170. Donald Jackson, ed., *Letters of the Lewis and Clark Expedition, with Related Documents: 1783–1854*, Vol. 2 (Urbana: University of Illinois Press, 1978), 395.

171. Jackson, *Letters*, 1:228.

172. If only Barton had been able to fulfill his promise to assist in the publication of the scientific volume. In a letter dated April 3, 1813, Jefferson was still beseeching Barton for news on the progress of the publication: "When shall we have your book on American botany, and when the 1st volume of Lewis & Clarke's travels? both of these works are of general expectation, and great interest, and to no one of more than to myself." Benjamin Smith Barton Papers (Series I, Correspondence: Thomas Jefferson to Benjamin Smith Barton, April 3, 1813), American Philosophical Society, transcribed by the author.

173. Review of the Nicholas Biddle notes provides a representative picture of the types of geological observations that were of sufficient interest for Biddle and William Clark to discuss circa April 1810 during the time Biddle was preparing the journals for publication, including the composition and source of the "muddiness of Missouri [River]"; saltpeter; lead mines; salt springs; the cut-and-fill deposition of the Missouri and Platte Rivers; occurrences of "lava" and "pumice" and the absence of volcanoes; and the landslides along the Columbia River. See Jackson, *Letters*, 2:504, 508, 530, and 539–40.

174. These surveys were called the "Great Surveys" because they were federally funded expeditions that explored huge areas of the American West, employed a large number of personnel including experts in many scientific disciplines (such as

naturalist Elliott Coues, future editor of the Lewis and Clark journals), and published an astonishing array of geological, ethnological, and natural history data along with extraordinarily detailed topographical maps and geomorphological panoramas.

175. Ford, *Writings of Thomas Jefferson*, 8:421.

6

Displaying the Expanding Nation to Itself

The Cultural Work of Public Exhibitions of Western Fauna in Lewis and Clark's Philadelphia

Brett Mizelle

IN HIS JUNE 1803 instructions to Meriwether Lewis, President Thomas Jefferson provided specific orders about the route, suggestions on how to deal with both the Europeans and the Native Americans they would meet along the way, and indications about what information and specimens they should collect. Jefferson's instructions to Lewis, like his confidential message to Congress from January 1803, reveal his major interests in western exploration, including both the "purposes of commerce" and "extending & strengthening the authority of reason & justice among the people around" the new nation. Only briefly in his letter to Lewis does Jefferson turn to "other object[s] worthy of notice," including the climate, mineral productions, soil and agriculture, and "the animals of the country generally, & especially those not known in the U.S."[1]

Jefferson's determination to explore and control the West, partly by using knowledge to advance national power, lay behind the mandate he bequeathed to Meriwether Lewis, William Clark, and the Corps of Discovery, who explored the trans-Mississippi West between 1803 and 1806. But as many scholars have pointed out, Lewis and Clark's expedition was largely seen as a failure in its own time. Many of their countrymen presumed them dead; others kept extending American commerce westward as if the expedition didn't exist. Upon their return, the expedition was seen, as James Ronda has recently noted, as "at best a disappointment and at worst an embarrassing failure."[2]

This sense of irrelevance and failure extended to the scientific work of the expedition. In his important study of Lewis and Clark as "pioneering naturalists," Paul Russell Cutright concluded that "it took time for the world to comprehend the magnitude of Lewis and Clark's achievements—if, indeed, it has to this day."[3] Writing in the late 1960s,

Cutright hoped to make a case for the scientific significance of the Lewis and Clark expedition by detailing the ethnological, botanical, and zoological specimens "discovered" and described by the Corps of Discovery. But Cutright's vigorous effort to rebut the accusation that Jefferson had made a mistake by not choosing a "trained naturalist" to accompany the expedition ironically reveals some of the limitations and failures of the expedition, as he frequently resorts to describing the expedition in terms of its lost potential: If only Lewis had lived to write an account of the expedition, including its natural history. If only more of the living animals and preserved specimens and skins had survived the long journey back East. If only the federal government would have endowed and supported Charles Willson Peale's Philadelphia Museum so that its "precious deposits" could be preserved for posterity.

Cutright's description of the journey of the Corps of Discovery as "the transcendent achievement of its kind in this hemisphere, if not in the entire world," was, of course, itself part of the larger rediscovery and reappraisal of the Lewis and Clark expedition. As Thomas Slaughter has recently reminded us, "The expedition's triumph had to be found. It got lost in words never read and stories not told for a century after the explorers' return." This process of recovery, one in which "the success of the Lewis and Clark Expedition became a fiction treated as a fact transformed into a history that created a myth," has been so successful that we often lack critical perspectives on the journey, especially those that situate it in its nineteenth-century contexts.[4]

It is ironic, of course, that we largely have the various editions of the *Journals of the Lewis and Clark Expedition* to blame for this predicament. Because they compellingly focus our attention on the day-to-day dynamics of the expedition and because they are, as Andrew Cayton has recently observed, "remarkably open to interpretation," the words of the explorers invite our vicarious participation in their trek. At their best, the journals also "facilitate democratic conversation" by enabling contemporary Americans from all walks of life to "engage both the past and the present."[5] I would like to suggest, however, that despite the widespread public interest in Lewis and Clark, one building in these bicentennial years, we still don't know enough about how the expedition was understood in its own time by the American people. While I won't go as far as some who assert that the journey of the Corps of Discovery was, frankly, a failure, an exploration largely irrelevant to the larger, inevitable process of American expansion, I hope to trace some of the connections among American explorers, political leaders, museum keepers, and audiences as they attempted to justify and interpret the process and meaning of America's westward expansion. While it is well known that Jefferson's vision of an expanding, agrarian nation lay behind both the Louisiana Purchase of 1803 and subsequent efforts to explore these newly acquired regions, I am more interested in the ways cultural entrepreneurs packaged this vision of transcontinental empire. Displays of western fauna proved central to this effort, although cultural entrepreneurs faced many challenges as they worked to create public interest in the natural history specimens, both those brought back by Lewis and Clark and other government-sponsored explorers and, more commonly, those collected by individuals hoping to make a living in the popular culture of the early American republic.

In short, I'd like to take a somewhat different approach to the study of Lewis and Clark as naturalists, focusing not on the ultimate scientific uses to which their discoveries were put or to the rich discourse of America's intellectual and cultural elites that surrounded their achievements (which should be read firsthand in both Cutright and in Donald Jackson's *Letters of the Lewis and Clark Expedition with Related Documents* [1978])[6] but on the place of exhibitions of and ideas about western nature in the larger popular culture of the early American republic. It is my contention that exhibitions of western fauna were intended, if often implicitly or unconsciously, to display the expanding nation to itself, to provide American audiences with both living and preserved specimens of the nature upon which they were building their nation. However, the intentions of museum keepers and political leaders did not always correspond to the public interest, leading many cultural elites to lament the fact that the American public was not particularly interested in their own "curiosities." Instead, American audiences consistently preferred to attend exhibitions of exotic foreign animals such as elephants and tigers or shows of performing animals, including animal acts featuring tightrope-walking monkeys and the feats of the "pig of knowledge." Accordingly, promoters of nationalism and proprietors of exhibitions of "American productions" had their work cut out for them as they sought to attract the public to their shows. Yet even in this effort to procure and display exotic animals from the American interior, private individuals—almost always unnamed and obscure men—were more successful than state-sanctioned explorers and museum keepers. For these men who were using nonhuman animals to pursue their "main chance" in the early nineteenth century, profit proved more important than nationalism, although they were not averse to using nationalist appeals to attract a paying crowd. It is in this less organized, less institutional milieu, then, that we can find the complicated and often incomplete conjunction of national expansion and public exhibitions in postrevolutionary America.

Before turning to some of the specific instances of this effort to create public interest in American natural history, however, I would like to provide the larger context for this inquiry, for without understanding the broad popularity of animal exhibitions in postrevolutionary America it will be difficult to see the challenges faced by those who hoped to exhibit American fauna. In the wake of the American Revolution, residents of America's cities and towns could view numerous exhibitions of lions, camels, bears, and apes in the streets, at taverns, and at museums or attend amusing and provocative animal acts featuring performing pigs, monkeys, and dogs in theaters and private homes. My current book project examines the cultural work of these exhibitions of exotic and performing animals in the early republic, demonstrating how diverse individuals used ideas about animals and animality both to construct and to contest the boundaries of their public and political culture and to make sense of their rapidly transforming postrevolutionary society.

My study suggests that the popularity of animal entertainments was tied to their postrevolutionary context, for the need for Americans to come to grips with the implications of their twinned revolutions—the political and market revolutions—made exhibitions of exotic and performing animals useful "sites" and "sights" for thinking about uncertain and shifting identities. For example, human ideas about animals were central to conceptions of race, gender, and hierarchy. Exhibitions of nonhuman primates reflected intense interest in the boundaries between the human and the animal while both reinscribing and undermining identities and social relationships thrown into question by the American Revolution. Similarly, the fledgling animal exhibition itself was caught up in larger struggles over the acceptable use of leisure time and the nature of spectatorship. Cultural entrepreneurs manipulated ideas about animals (and animals themselves) for their livelihood, audiences reinterpreted and mobilized these ideas to a wide range of purposes, and together they struggled to define the relationships between popular culture and public interest and between animals and human identity.

This exploration of the relationship between displays of western fauna and conceptions of American national identity is a subset of my larger examination of animals as national symbols during the revolution and in the new nation's contentious partisan politics. Exhibitions and representations of nonhuman animals played an important role in the effort to define the nation and the citizen in the early republic, because much of the often intense debate over the shape of the new nation involved, as Christopher Looby has argued, "a metaphorical exchange between images of natural order and ideas of social and political order." American cultural leaders used the "order that they represented nature as exhibiting" to represent their society "to itself in order to certify its existence and legitimacy."[7] As part of this mutual representation of American nature and culture, ideas about animals and animality were both positively appropriated and negatively mobilized to define the human, the citizen, and the nation itself.

Public exhibitions served as a crucial site for this cultural work. As Tony Bennett has argued, museums, art galleries, and world's fairs constituted an "exhibitionary complex" that provided "object lessons in power—the power to command and arrange things and bodies for public display."[8] Animals were frequently part of these displays of power. Harriet Ritvo has shown how exotic animals in Victorian Britain served as stand-ins for the "exotic peoples that Europeans subjugated in the course of the nineteenth century." Attentive to the roles played by ideas about animals in promulgating an "abstract process of domination" within British society, Ritvo persuasively demonstrates that the "maintenance and study of captive wild animals, simultaneously emblems of human mastery over the natural world and of English domination over remote territories, offered an especially vivid rhetorical means of reenacting and extending the work of empire."[9]

A similar but inchoate impulse can be found in the efforts of the painter Charles Willson Peale to have his Philadelphia Museum—which presented a combination of art and natural history from 1786 until after his death in 1827—represent the "world in miniature." In a recent study of Peale's museum as "a cultural production, rather than the expression of one man's ideas," the art historian David Brigham has traced "the impulse toward order in the museum, ... [one] suggestive of a broader need to establish economic, social, and political structures within a country recently independent of monarchical rule and colonial status."[10] Brigham's study, along with the pioneering work of Charles Coleman Sellers and the scholars working with the Peale Family Papers project, has shown how Peale's museum was intended to promote both Enlightenment science and American nationalism. In fact, throughout his career Peale constantly appealed for government support for his museum to formalize this connection.

The interplay among classification, display, and nationalism can also be seen in the preparations for the journey of the Corps of Discovery undertaken in Philadelphia. Meriwether Lewis almost certainly visited Peale's museum during his April 1803 visit to Philadelphia to consult with members of the American Philosophical Society about what observations to make and specimens to collect on their expedition.[11] While we will never know enough about their personal relationship, Peale clearly respected Lewis and later frequently described himself as in Lewis's debt for expanding the collection of his museum. In 1807 Peale even manufactured and displayed a wax figure of the explorer "dressed in an Indian dress presented to Capt. Lewis by Comeawahait, Chief of [the] Shoshone Nation," that celebrated the accomplishments of the Corps of Discovery. Peale also included the now-familiar portraits of both Lewis and Clark in his gallery and poignantly described Lewis's eventual suicide in a letter to his son Rembrandt.[12]

Peale clearly viewed the items brought back by Lewis and Clark as what Cutright calls "a prize haul" that "provided increased prestige and a stimulus to Peale to improve the quality of his exhibits."[13] But while "Indian artifacts, minerals, and animal and plant life" obtained by the Lewis and Clark expedition were to make up one of the major gifts to Peale's Philadelphia Museum, even before the Corps of Discovery returned from its three-year expedition into the trans-Mississippi West (and before Americans had an opportunity to read about its journey), a large consignment of articles collected during the explorers' travels had been shipped to President Thomas Jefferson. Jefferson kept most of the ethnographic artifacts for his "Indian Hall" at Monticello but sent most of the natural history items, including a living magpie and prairie dog, to Charles Willson Peale in Philadelphia.[14]

Jefferson's October 6, 1805, letter to Peale describing the articles he was sending to Philadelphia noted that the skeletons of the white hare, badger, antelopes, and "burrowing wolf" were "in great disorder as they came here, having been unpacked in several places on the road, & unpacked again here before I returned, so that they have probably got mixed." Jefferson hoped that Peale could make sense of the skeletons to decide whether Lewis "has not mistaken the Roe for the Antelope" before adding a comment about what he (incorrectly) called the marmot: "I am much afraid of the season of torpidity coming on him before you get him. he is a most harmless & tame creature."[15]

FIGURE 6.1. *American Antelope.* Titian Ramsay Peale, ca. 1819–1820. Pencil and watercolor on paper, 11 × 13⁷⁄₁₆" (28 × 34.1 cm). American Philosophical Society, Philadelphia. (See Color Plate 18.)

Peale's November reply to Jefferson failed to discuss the prairie dog but did begin by describing the "Magpye" as arriving in "good health." Peale was surprised by how much it resembled the European species, leading him to "inquire whether this breed of the Magpye has not origionally been from Europe." Peale continued to compare the Lewis and Clark specimens in his possession with the accounts of European naturalists, although he noted that he faced some difficulty in this task due to the damage to the skins and skeletons that occurred on their long journey to the East. Before turning to a description of the repairs he was making to Jefferson's polygraph, Peale noted: "I am very much obleged

FIGURE 6.2. Peale, Titian Ramsey. *Prairie Dog* (1820). Titan Ramsey Peal Sketches, American Philosophical Society.

to Captn. Lewis for his endeavors to encrease our knowledge of the Animals of that newly acquired Territory." He added, "It is more important to have this Museum supplied with the American Animals than those of other country'es, yet for a comparative view it ought to possess those of every part of the Globe!" While this comment reflected Peale's belief that his museum could be a "world in miniature," that it could embody the full range of natural and artificial productions from around the globe, it also helped make a nationalist case for public funding for his enterprise, which could become "a lasting benefit to our Country."[16]

In a subsequent letter to Jefferson that included his analyses of the Lewis and Clark specimens (in it Peale finally noted that although the prairie dog "stirs but little, It is a pleasing little Animal, and not in the least dangerous to handle like our Ground Hog"), Peale mentioned that he was beginning work on a museum catalog. Using the language of "instructive amusement" shared by other cultural entrepreneurs, Peale wrote: "I shall endeavor to make it combine the pleasing with the useful, giving a general view of all the subjects in the several departments of the Museum, and, it will at least have the merit of correcting some mistakes of Authors who have wrote on American subjects."[17]

Peale's correspondence with Jefferson concerning the specimens returned from the Lewis and Clark expedition, however, tells us more about their interests in American natural history and their efforts to correct or improve upon the observations and assertions of European naturalists than it does about their ideas about the American West. Although Peale describes how he assembled and mounted the skeletons and skins for observation and study by naturalists who used them as type specimens or created engravings of many of these animals, this correspondence is surprisingly silent about how this fauna from the trans-Mississippi West was packaged for consumption by the broader public.[18] In other words, did these exhibitions of both living and preserved animals in Peale's museum help create a publicly accessible vision of the national interior, and if so, how? Unfortunately, despite his assertion that "everything that comes from Louisiana must be interesting to the Public,"[19] a comment itself more of a wish than a statement of fact, Peale's letters tell us more about his attempts to turn his museum into both a national asset and "a world in miniature" than they do about the public reception of these artifacts.

I have found no indication, however, that these two living natural history specimens from the Lewis and Clark expedition attracted much public notice. I would suggest that this is partly because these creatures, while not familiar to Easterners, were similar enough to other small animals and birds to not appear all that spectacular. Both the prairie dog and the magpie lacked the appeal of the charismatic megafauna (such as lions, tigers, bears, etc.) that attracted audiences to public exhibitions in the early nineteenth century and attract visitors to zoos and wildlife parks today. Perhaps more importantly, these animals didn't possess the "thinkability" often necessary to ensure the success of an exhibition. Yes, naturalists were interested in whether the prairie dog would hibernate and whether the magpie was truly distinct from the European species, but neither creature had much to offer the general public, especially in contrast to the exotic and performing animals (not to mention the other attractions in early national popular culture) that did grab a share of their attention.

Although it is extremely difficult to trace how the public attended and understood animal exhibitions, undoubtedly many Philadelphians saw Lewis and Clark's prairie dog and magpie (at least while they remained alive) in Peale's museum, for there were many other natural and artificial curiosities there to attract the curious. Both local residents and visitors to Philadelphia marveled at the museum's natural history specimens; historical portrait collection; wax figures of Native American, Asian, and African types; and other valuable objects. The tremendous breadth of Peale's collections produced a concomitant variety of audience reactions, ranging from praise for the natural history collections (which were "arranged with the greatest order and judgment, agreeably to the mode prescribed by Linnaeus") to disdain for Peale's "pretended portraits of worthies, born only to be forgotten." Many viewers likely shared the conclusion of the traveler John M. Duncan, who observed that Peale's museum contained "a good deal that is worth seeing, mingled with many miscellaneous monstrosities which are not worth house-room."[20]

The most famous exhibit in Peale's museum at the time of the arrival of the Lewis and Clark specimens was the assembled fossil skeleton of the mastodon, which Peale had installed in the museum in 1801. The size of the skeleton of this "enormous antediluvian," along with fanciful descriptions of its ferocity, awed viewers and prompted both scientific and popular speculation about the possible extinction of species as well as the relationship of the new American nation to its prehistoric past. Peale's exhibition of the mastodon in Philadelphia, along with the subsequent tours of the skeleton, ignited a "mammoth fever" that swept the nation. President Jefferson was particularly interested in this "mammoth" and hoped that Lewis and Clark would not only find further fossil bones of this creature but perhaps encounter living specimens in the western wilderness.[21]

Lewis and Clark did not, of course, discover any living mastodons in the trans-Mississippi West. They did, however, describe numerous terrifying encounters with the grizzly bears they hunted, which Lewis noted as "being so hard to die [that they] reather intimedates us all."[22] Peale finally received some of these truly compelling living creatures from the American West in 1807 when Jefferson offered Peale "two cubs of the Grisly bear." These animals were captured by Captain Zebulon Pike during his bold venture into the southern Rocky Mountains. Although the president told Peale that these "perfectly gentle" and "good humored" bear cubs would profitably educate the public in the Philadelphia Museum, Jefferson privately told his granddaughter that the grizzlies were becoming "too dangerous and troublesome for me to keep." Peale exhibited these bears (described as specimens of "the most formidable wild beasts of the continent of America") to his Philadelphia audience beginning in January 1808. Unfortunately, the bear

FIGURE 6.3. *Missouri Bear.* Titian Ramsay Peale, ca. 1819–1822. Watercolor drawing from museum mounting; published as lithograph in *Doughty's Cabinet of Natural History and American Rural Sports*, 1830. American Philosophical Society, Philadelphia. (See Color Plate 19.)

cubs did not remain docile or playful for long. As Peale noted in his *Autobiography*, "when full grown they thirsted for blood and any animals coming within their reach were sure to suffer." A monkey on display in an adjacent cage was dismembered by one of the bears, and eventually one of the cubs escaped its enclosure and rampaged through Peale's residence below the museum. Peale barricaded the grizzly in the kitchen overnight, then shot it in the morning. He then killed the other bear in its cage so he could later stuff and mount both of them in a less dangerous display of wild American nature.[23]

The grizzly bear cubs in the Philadelphia Museum were perhaps the most exceptional of many exhibitions of western fauna in the early American republic. In an advertisement in *Poulson's American Daily Advertiser*, Peale described them as "shaggy tyrants of the woods," noting their "tremendous paws" and a disposition that made them "fierce combatants." Exhibitions of living and preserved animals such as these bears in Peale's museum were intended to create a vision of a national interior while celebrating territorial expansion, including the bravery of men such as Pike who captured these grizzlies. But Peale ultimately had to take these bears off display, "as the Museum does not conveniently admit of the exhibition of live animals." In short, although the display of specimens from the trans-Mississippi West undoubtedly helped display the expanding nation to itself, this exhibition of the nation's nature was often fraught with difficulties.[24]

Yet while these exhibitions of American creatures spread awareness of the new nation's fauna, proprietors faced another more significant difficulty in drawing audiences to see these "natural curiosities." As the Reverend William Bentley of Salem, Massachusetts, noted, "this taste for our own productions has not been much known among us," for audiences generally continued to prefer the exotic over the local.[25] In an 1803 letter to Jefferson, Peale noted that even the grizzly bear didn't necessarily draw large audiences. Peale sent Jefferson one of handbills used by "a French-man; an Indian trader from new Orleans," to advertise his exhibition of a "Grisley-bear," adding that "he expected to make a fortune by the Animal, but he was disappointed, altho' it differed considerably from the common, yet nevertheless it was a Bear, & as such did not excite much curiosity."[26]

This somewhat blasé reaction of many Philadelphians to a living exhibition of American natural history was not just a problem for operators of institutions that promised "instructive amusement" to their patrons. Indeed, many ordinary Americans had to work extremely hard to attract the public to their displays of American nature. Unlike Peale, who had much more to offer at his Philadelphia Museum than just local fauna, these men depended on the animals they exhibited and traveled with for their livelihood. One of the more interesting examples of this dependence on an exotic American animal and the challenge involved in getting people interested in it involves Samuel Dean, a veteran who brought a bison with him when he returned from fighting Indians in present-day Ohio.

At Mr. Tyler's Tavern in Providence, in 1795, Dean exhibited a bison brought "from the Miame Indian village." After describing this curious animal, Dean added that he was "totally disabled from bodily Labour, by Reason of the Wounds he received at Gen. S. Clair's Defeat, Nov. 4. 1791," and that "having no other Means of Subsistence, humbly hopes for the Assistance and Encouragement of the Public."[27] Prior to leaving Providence, Dean again advertised his bison, this time referring to it as "One of those surprizing Beasts, by Nature placed in the vast Forests of our Continent," whose "Strength and savage Aspect . . . must be pleasing to the curious." Perhaps indicating the difficulty of getting people to see an animal that resembled their own livestock, Dean ultimately informed the gentlemen of Providence that if they would "subscribe such sums as they may think proper," he would "turn the Bison loose . . . that the Gentlemen may take the Diversion of pursuing her on Horse Back." While the newspapers did not describe the resulting "Bison Chace," Dean's advertisement explicitly connected animal exhibitions and national expansion, bringing America's exotic western nature back to the East.[28] It also reveals how one entrepreneur sought to make his exhibition of American wildlife more exciting and appealing.

Other western animals also grabbed the public's attention, but only, it seems, if they could be described as wild and dangerous. In 1798 the Columbian Museum in Boston featured "A monstrous SERPENT, 25 feet in length, lately brought from the Spanish Main." This creature was "fixed on large trees in the Museum Hall, in fine preservation, and appears natural as life."[29] Sometime between 1799 and 1805, an illustrated broadside was printed and distributed describing Jacob Berriman's 1794 encounter with a snake in the Ohio Valley said to measure thirty-six feet in length and three feet in diameter. The identical illustration was used to call viewers' attention to another broadside in 1815 that described the tracking and killing of "a monstrous serpent" in Kentucky. This serpent had been terrorizing the residents of Versailles by destroying "great numbers of their Calves, Lambs, Swine, &c." Because most of the male inhabitants of the area were in New Orleans with General Andrew Jackson, three American prisoners tracked the monster, which was twenty-two feet in length and as big around as the thigh of a large man. While skinning this serpent, the men discovered "a young lamb entire, beside many detached limbs of other young animals," within its body. Interestingly, they promised at the end of the letter reprinted as this broadside to send the skin to Peale's museum in Philadelphia "for the satisfaction of the curious."[30]

While it is impossible to ascertain the veracity of these stories, this sensationalism undoubtedly created spectacular interest in the American interior and perhaps prefigured the wild stories about the dangers of the frontier (accompanied by wonderful woodcuts) that graced the

FIGURE 6.4. *A Monstrous Serpent.* "Discovered and killed in January last (1815.) near the banks of the Ohio, in Kentucky, by *THREE AMERICAN PRISONERS.*" Printed with an extract of a letter, dated February 13, 1815, written by one of the soldiers to his brother in Philadelphia, and published by N. Coverly, Milk-Street, Boston, June 1815. American Antiquarian Society.

several editions of *Davy Crockett's Almanack* in the 1830s. The illustration of "A Narrow Escape from a Snake" from 1838, like the earlier story of a serpent terrorizing frontier residents, was, at least, compelling, especially in comparison to the exhibition of the placid living prairie dog at Peale's museum.[31] The great appeal of these sensational encounters with American wildlife can also be registered in early American periodicals, which were filled with accounts of other dangerous animals, especially the catamount, or American panther, a creature described as "in America, what the Lion and Tyger are in Africa and Asia, the tyrant of the wilderness." A natural history essay in the *New York Magazine* in 1795 contained an illustration of a catamount that was captured as a cub near the Ohio River. While this creature seemed fearsome, the account noted that

> Notwithstanding the strength, the agility, and the powers of this animal, he is not the object of dread to the hunter, or even the benighted bewildered pilgrim: for, except in the case of children, he carefully shuns the face of man. It is a singularity in the history of nature, that while the forests of Europe, Asia and Africa resound with the shrieks of the victims to the Lion, the Tyger, the Leopard, and the Hyena, the sojourner in America, with no other weapon than a staff of reed, may traverse its wilderness in perfect safety, from the unlimitted ocean of the west, to the shores of the Atlantic.[32]

While the journey of the Corps of Discovery validated this writer's hypothesis about transcontinental travel, not all magazine accounts emphasized the shyness of the catamount. In 1805 the *Boston Weekly Magazine* warned its readers about the presence of "that ferocious and dangerous animal, the Cat-o'-mount," in the Salem area. Accounts of close calls with wild animals proved a staple in early national newspapers and magazines. Stories such as these undoubtedly heightened readers' curiosity, encouraging them to see these creatures firsthand when they were exhibited to the public in the taverns, museums, and streets of the early republic.[33]

Printed accounts of exotic fauna thus existed in a symbiotic relationship with the physical venues where Americans could encounter and contemplate wild nature. In this sense, early national periodicals, which were frequently marketed as self-conscious efforts to create an American culture, are like museums in that they bring diverse contents together in the interests of both profit and nationalism. Menageries served a similar function and occasionally used nationalist sentiments to market creatures from wilderness areas within the boundaries of the nation. In 1799, an exhibitor displayed a menagerie of "Natural Curiosities" (including "a live Alligator, with two of her young," "a Gonnah, equally curious, nearly of the same specie," and "a beautiful white Doe . . . perfectly tame") in New England. Perhaps because these creatures failed to capture the popular imagination as had contemporaneous exhibitions of elephants, tigers, and polar bears, the proprietor noted that "As these animals are a natural production of our country, and have never been exhibited in the northern parts of it, the proprietor flatters himself that all who have the curiosity to see them will be highly gratified."[34] Such exhibitions as "Animals from the Forests of Maine" and "Blue Mountain Bears" from western Pennsylvania also shared in this effort to make "domestic specimens" appeal to audiences.[35]

These exhibitions of animals from the American periphery were frequently couched in nationalist terms, serving to link regions together while demonstrating their distinctiveness. Proprietors increasingly made appeals to nationalist sentiment to attract audiences to shows of what they referred to as "American Productions," creating public spaces where individuals could demonstrate national patriotism by observing a united regionalist nature. A common curiosity bound together audiences in different regions of the country in celebrating America's biological diversity. For example, a broadside advertisement for an exhibition titled "Animals from the Forests of Maine," which included a bear, raccoon, deer, caribou, and two moose, urged the attendance of "the naturalist and man of science, as well as the curious and lovers of novelty," all of whom "will find an ample satisfaction in viewing these animals, so intimately associated with our early history." Exhibition of these "handsomest tenants of the American forest" enabled Americans to vicariously encounter their past—already defined as a time when wild animals were a more tangible presence—and explore distant, frontier regions.[36] In another instance, the proprietor of a 1799 menagerie titled "Exhibition of Natural Curiosities" used a patriotic argument to attract audiences. Opening in Philadelphia in December 1799, the proprietor began his advertisement by noting how a "crowded company" had supported this exhibition of native fauna in New England. He then called for local residents to support this display with the same patriotic fervor as had the citizens of Boston.

The advertised highlight of this collection of natural curiosities was an exhibition in which "a fine little bird, a beautiful flying squirrel, a rattle snake and other animals are living in the most amicable terms in a neat strong cage."[37] This aggregation of generally incompatible animals—known as a "happy family"—brings us to a final way that proprietors sought to create interest in American nature, one used by both anonymous exhibitors and museum keepers such as Charles Willson Peale, who called readers' attention to a "Singular Association" in which an eagle and a chicken shared the same cage in 1797.[38] A "happy family" made ordinary animals, including domesticated ones, compelling. It also provided the popular equivalent of the "promise of social unanimity" that American cultural leaders such as Jefferson, William Bartram, and Peale found in the study of nature. As Christopher Looby has noted, "In the 1780s and '90s . . . classificatory natural science exemplified for Americans the ideal of scientific inquiry" while providing "a model for the organization of state and society."[39] This paradigm explains why American writers so strenuously refuted the claims of European naturalists that the New World environment was marked by shrunken and "degenerated" animals.[40] It also explains why the exhibition of a "happy family" may have resonated with contemporary audiences. For while these exhibitions of harmony required substantial human intervention—animals were constantly overfed to prevent them from attacking and devouring each other—proprietors clearly thought that this demonstration of tranquility among "naturally" hostile interests would appeal to the public, one perhaps weary of the fractious foreign and domestic politics of the 1790s.[41]

This conjunction of exhibitions of animals and the wish for political and social order brings us back, finally, to the Lewis and Clark expedition. For just as the "happy family" represented tranquility between competing interests, Peale's display of specimens returned by the Corps of Discovery depicted American expansion as just, orderly, and benevolent. Many displays in Peale's museum, such as portraits of Columbus, Vespucci, Magellan, and Cortez, celebrated European expansion.[42] The Native American artifacts shown at the museum collected by Lewis and Clark and donated by Jefferson were labeled and displayed in a manner that was designed both to advance human knowledge and to depict American dominion over these peoples and their lands. As the historian James Ronda has observed, this "knowledge was not to be gathered by the explorers for its own sake, however, but in the service of government and commerce."[43]

In short, these exhibitions displayed the expanding nation to itself in a manner similar to that of the animal exhibitions charted above. Like the "happy family," displays of ethnological artifacts were used to further a theme of harmony. For example, Peale displayed calumets and peace pipes that symbolized "peace and understanding" and included evidence of clothing and foodways that invited visitors to "find shared practices or measure the degree of difference between themselves and Native Americans." These displays of both Indian artifacts and living natural history specimens in effect "tamed" the West, packaging it as ready for peaceful settlement by an expanding nation. When artifacts indicated a history of conflict between Americans and Indians or between Americans and wild animals, they demonstrated that ultimately white men would prevail. Ferocious grizzly bears were, after all, captured, tamed, and eventually killed and mounted for display. Similarly, Indian weaponry on exhibition at the Philadelphia Museum was taken from the Blackfoot Indians "who attacked Capn. Lewis and were killed by himself and [the] party."[44]

Yet in depicting American dominance, these displays also represented a wild and potentially dangerous West, one that would continue to appeal to many Americans. What remains to be explained is why, given this broad interest in the trans-Mississippi West, so many Americans didn't seem particularly interested in attending public displays of western artifacts and specimens. Perhaps the presence of so much so-called virgin land kept people's attention focused on the actual West rather than on its display back East. Perhaps public interest in American natural history could only ultimately emerge as nostalgia for a lost frontier experience. Unfortunately, we will never really know what American audiences thought about most of these displays, which, I suggest, served as mechanisms that helped ordinary Americans make sense of their vast national domain. It is clear, however, that much of this work was done in the realm of popular culture, although not always in a manner that drew clear connections between the exploration of the trans-Mississippi West and an emerging belief in what John L. O'Sullivan would later refer to as America's manifest destiny.

Notes

1. Reprinted in Reuben Gold Thwaites, ed., *Original Journals of the Lewis and Clark Expedition, 1804–1806*, 8 vols. (New York: Dodd, Mead, 1994), 7:247–52.

2. James P. Ronda, "'A Darling Project of Mine': The Appeal of the Lewis and Clark Expedition," in *Voyages of Discovery: Essays on the Lewis and Clark Expedition*, ed. James P. Ronda (Helena: Montana Historical Society Press, 1998), 333.

3. Paul Russell Cutright, *Lewis and Clark: Pioneering Naturalists* (Urbana: University of Illinois Press, 1969), 393.

4. Cutright, *Lewis and Clark*, 397; Thomas P. Slaughter, *Exploring Lewis and Clark: Reflections on Men and Wilderness* (New York: Alfred A. Knopf, 2003), 204.

5. Andrew R. L. Cayton, "Looking for America with Lewis and Clark," *William and Mary Quarterly*, 3d ser., 59(3) (July 2002): 709.

6. Donald Dean Jackson, *Letters of the Lewis and Clark Expedition, with Related Documents, 1783–1854* (Urbana: University of Illinois Press, 1962).

7. Christopher Looby, "The Constitution of Nature: Taxonomy as Politics in Jefferson, Peale, and Bartram," *Early American Literature* 22(3) (1987): 253–55.

8. Tony Bennett, *The Birth of the Museum: History, Theory, Politics* (London & New York: Routledge, 1995), 59–88, quotation on 63.

9. Harriet Ritvo, *The Animal Estate: The English and Other Creatures in the Victorian Age* (Cambridge: Harvard University Press, 1987), 41, 11, 205.

10. David R. Brigham, *Public Culture in the Early Republic: Peale's Museum and Its Audience* (Washington, D.C.: Smithsonian Institution Press, 1995), 149.

11. Lillian B. Miller, ed., *The Selected Papers of Charles Willson Peale and His Family*: Vol. 2, *Charles Willson Peale: The Artist as Museum Keeper, 1791–1810*, 2 vols. (New Haven: Published for the National Portrait Gallery, Smithsonian Institution, by Yale University Press, 1988), 1:582n. Henceforth cited as AMK.

12. Cited in Cutright, *Lewis and Clark*, 354.

13. Ibid., 352. Cutright presents no specific evidence that these specimens actually increased the prestige of Peale's Philadelphia Museum.

14. AMK, 2:829n. This donation was recorded by Peale in 1809. A list of these items was published in *Poulson's American Daily Advertiser*, March 1, 1810.

15. Jefferson to Peale, October 6, 1805, AMK, 2:894–895.

16. Peale to Jefferson, November 3 and 4, 1805, AMK, 2:908–9.

17. Peale to Jefferson, April 5, 1806, AMK, 2:952.

18. See, for example, "The Prong-Horned Antelope," lithograph by A. Ryder drawn from museum mounting, in *The Cabinet of Natural History and American Rural Sports, with Illustrations*, ed. Gail Stewart, 136–37 (Barre, Mass.: Imprint Society, 1973; originally published 1830–1833).

19. Jefferson added that "I am much afraid of the season of torpidity coming on him [the prairie dog] before you got him. He is a most harmless and tame creature. You will do well to watch Cap't Cormack's arrival at the stage office, that no risks from curiosity may happen to him between his arrival and your getting him." Jefferson to Peale, October 6, 1805, AMK, 2:893–95; Peale to Jefferson, January 12, 1806, and October 22, 1805, AMK, 2:921, 2:900–901.

20. James Hardie, William Newnham Blane, and John M. Duncan, cited in Brigham, *Public Culture in the Early Republic*, 58, 60, 53.

21. See Paul Semonin, *American Monster: How the Nation's First Prehistoric Creature Became a Symbol of National Identity* (New York & London: New York University Press, 2000), esp. 315–61.

22. Gary E. Moulton, ed., *The Lewis and Clark Journals: An American Epic of Discovery: The Abridgment of the Definitive Nebraska Edition* (Lincoln and London: University of Nebraska Press, 2003), 109 (May 11, 1805).

23. Jefferson to Peale, November 5, 1807, AMK, 2:1041–43; Jefferson to Anne Randolph, November 1, 1807, AMK, 2:1055; Peale, *Autobiography*, AMK, 2:1065; Charles Coleman Sellers, *Mr. Peale's Museum: Charles Willson Peale and the First Popular Museum of Natural Science and Art* (New York: W. W. Norton & Co., 1980), 206–7.

24. *Poulson's American Daily Advertiser*, February 5, 1808. Peale exhibited the bears

to the public until February 13. Laura Rigal has explored how Peale's discovery, exhumation, and display of the mastodon was part of Jeffersonian-Republican self-production. See Laura Rigal, *The American Manufactory: Art, Labor, and the World of Things in the Early Republic* (Princeton: Princeton University Press, 1998), 91–113.

25. William Bentley, *The Diary of William Bentley, D.D., Pastor of the East Church, Salem, Massachusetts,* 4 vols. (Salem: Essex Institute, 1907), 3:498 (February 14, 1810).

26. Peale to Jefferson, March 18, 1804, cited in Jackson, *Letters of the Lewis and Clark Expedition,* 296. Always the entrepreneur, Peale bought this bear from the Frenchman but had to shoot it when it broke loose. Peale then sent "a hind quarter" of the animal to Jefferson.

27. *Providence Gazette,* June 20, 1795. Ellen Sacco has described how individuals with disabilities were occasionally able to make a living by appearing in museums. See Ellen Fernandez Sacco, "Spectacular Masculinities: The Museums of Peale, Baker, and Bowen in the Early Republic" (PhD diss., University of California, 1998).

28. [Providence] *United States Chronicle,* June 25, 1795.

29. *Massachusetts Mercury,* July 12, 1798.

30. "The Following Is Copied from the Journal Kept by Mr. Jacob M. Berriman, During His Tour to the Westward of Fort Recovery," Broadside (Suffield, Conn.: Printed by Edward Gray, [Between 1799 and 1805]); "A Monstrous Serpent. Discovered and Killed in January Last near the Banks of the Ohio, in Kentucky, by Three American Prisoners," Broadside (Boston: Printed by N. Coverly, 1815).

31. Illustration in Joshua C. Taylor, *America as Art* (New York: Harper & Row, 1976), 92.

32. "Of the Catamount, or Panther, [with an Engraving]," *The New-York Magazine; or, Literary Repository* (April 1795): 193–94.

33. "That Ferocious and Dangerous Animal, the Cat-O'-Mount, Now Exist...," *Boston Weekly Magazine* (January 5, 1805). I have found several instances where periodicals included accounts of animals that had recently been on display in their city of publication.

34. [Philadelphia] *Poulson's American Daily Advertiser,* February 5, 1808; [Boston] *Independent Chronicle,* June 20, 1799; *Newburyport Herald,* August 6, 1799.

35. "Animals from the Forests of Maine," undated broadside (Harvard Theatre Collection). The bears appeared as part of a "Grand Exhibition of Animals" in which several native animals were chased in a "pleasing and comic manner." The proprietor had begun soliciting animals in January 1798 and noted in his announcement that "he has taken great pains to train up the animals for the chace," which would present "only a picture of reality to which nothing will be introduced repugnant to humanity." *Claypoole's American Daily Advertiser,* January 29 and May 23 and 28, 1798.

36. "Animals from the Forests of Maine," undated broadside (Harvard Theatre Collection).

37. *Claypoole's American Daily Advertiser,* December 7, 1799.

38. Ibid., January 6, 1797. Rubens Peale exhibited together a rattlesnake, squirrel, and bird in 1810. *Poulson's American Daily Advertiser,* June 21, 1810.

39. Looby, "The Constitution of Nature," 260–61.

40. The editors of the *American Museum,* for example, encouraged citizens of the United States "to explode the European creed, that we are infantile in our acquisitions, and savage in our manners, because we are inhabitants of a new world, lately occupied by a race of savages." Cited in "The Literature of the New Republic, 1776–1836," in *The Harper American Literature,* ed. Donald McQuade et al., 310 (New York: HarperCollins College Publishers, 1996).

41. [Philadelphia] *Claypoole's American Daily Advertiser,* December 7, 1799. Firsthand observation of nature was also a major emphasis of this advertisement, for the proprietor provided "large magnifiers" so that people could view the recently shed skin of one of his snakes. For Peale's "Singular Association," see [Philadelphia] *Claypoole's American Daily Advertiser,* January 6, 1797. David Brigham (*Public Culture in the Early Republic,* 124) has observed of this exhibition that "If harmony were the natural state among lower animals, then surely humans could also be expected to live in peace."

42. Brigham, *Public Culture in the Early Republic,* 139.

43. James P. Ronda, *Lewis and Clark among the Indians* (Lincoln & London: University of Nebraska Press, 1984), 4.

44. *Memoranda of the Philadelphia Museum,* December 28, 1809, 43–45, cited in Brigham, *Public Culture in the Early Republic,* 140.

7

NINETEENTH-CENTURY SCIENTIFIC OPINION OF LEWIS AND CLARK

Andrew J. Lewis

To the People of the Great West:
Jefferson gave you the country. Lewis and Clark showed you the way. The rest is your own course of empire. Honor the statesman who foresaw the West. Honor the brave men who first saw your West. May the memory of their glorious achievement be your precious heritage! Accept from my heart this undying record of the beginning of all your greatness. E. C.
ELLIOT COUES, 1893

THE DEDICATORY PREFACE to Elliot Coues's 1893 edition of the Lewis and Clark journals[1] was written by an author in tune with the conclusions of Frederick Jackson Turner, the University of Wisconsin professor, who argued famously that same year that the frontier had closed and with it the first chapter in American history. Coues urged an appreciation of Lewis and Clark, those who "first saw" the land and began the American "course of empire." In Coues's edition of the journals, the first new version published since 1814, the editor emphasized the expedition's scientific achievements and credited the explorers with the discovery of new species of plants, trees, fish, insects, birds, and mammals. Coues—a distinguished ornithologist, naturalist, and surgeon—wished to award Lewis and Clark the first sightings and descriptions of these specimens in an attempt to wrestle from usurpers the title of discover. It would seem that Coues wanted a place for Lewis and Clark, as explorers and as scientists, in the founding generation of American heroes, a place reserved usually for politicians and military men.

But Coues's three-volume edition was more than an exercise in correcting the historical record and giving Lewis and Clark the fame associated with the label of scientific pioneer. Coues's edition was a reintroduction of Lewis and Clark to an American reading public who had largely forgotten the Corps of Discovery. Coues's rehabilitation of Lewis and Clark recast the expedition as a scientific errand conducted for Thomas Jefferson, not merely the adventure story it had become.

And, the edition was an effort to revive and to appreciate a dormant literary genre—natural history exploration literature—that blended natural history findings with a sense of awe and wonder. Natural history literature embodied the dominant ethic of the early republic, a scientific-spiritualist approach to the American landscape that employed natural history techniques of description and classification, not as ends in themselves, but as aids to contain the immensity and incomprehensibility of American nature, a subject Americans knew little about. This literature encouraged early republic Americans to celebrate the complexity of the natural world, and by extension God, through an intimate understanding of its products. This scientific-spiritualist approach crossed boundaries of class and education, jumped denominational lines, and assuaged guilty consciences over the racial genocide that accompanied expansion across the continent. Lastly, Coues's 1893 edition cast Lewis and Clark as part of a grand American imperial project and became part and parcel of an effort to whet the appetite of, and to prepare the American nation for, a new round of frontier conquest and empire-building, this time not in North America but overseas.

Of late, the Lewis and Clark expedition has captured the imagination of many Americans to a degree not seen since the early nineteenth century. The bicentennial celebration—accompanied by proclamations from federal, state, and local officials; the completion of scholarly editions of the journals; film and television documentaries; magazine and newspaper coverage; reenactments; and associated conferences—have made Lewis and Clark household names in ways that would likely have surprised the expedition members. Various reasons are given for their resurgence in the popular imagination, with no shortage of explanations. Still, a consensus has emerged even as appreciators, critics, and scholars argue over the expedition's importance and meaning: that Lewis and Clark are a part of an American history "filled with remarkable examples of heroism and adventure, and the voyage of Lewis and Clark is one of the most remarkable of them all. . . . Their expedition became an epic of endurance and discovery, and that epic became an American legend which all Americans should know about, and they should teach their children about it, as well."[2] These words are echoed by the conclusion of the popular media that Lewis and Clark are important because of the greatness of their story and the many threads that are woven into it.[3] Among these threads are moments of heroic adventure, encounters with nature red in tooth and claw, cultural contact and conflict, and a number of scientific firsts. Reading into this consensus, it is not difficult to surmise that, for most Americans, Lewis and Clark are originary symbols in celebratory historical narratives that form the bedrock of our national identity—the settling of the West, the spread of industrial capitalism, and the rise of a scientific society.

Yet, for all their visibility today and their role in versions of American identity, it might surprise many to learn of the nineteenth-century *unimportance* of Lewis and Clark. As twenty-first-century Americans, we know more about Lewis and Clark and their expedition than did those who lived during that time. In fact, by the 1830s and 1840s it is doubtful if many beyond a circle of naturalists and explorers would have known in great detail who Meriwether Lewis or William Clark were. After the excitement and celebrations surrounding their return in 1806–1807 and publication of the Allen/Biddle narrative in the 1810s, Lewis and Clark faded from public consciousness, their expedition and its accomplishments lost in the cacophony of early republic print culture, their fame superseded by other expeditions and more dramatic exploration figures.[4] Knowledge about Lewis and Clark languished through the nineteenth century but spiked at the turn of the twentieth century with the publication of the Elliot Coues and Reuben Gold Thwaites editions of the journals. Since Coues and Thwaites, interest in the expedition waxed and waned. After Donald Jackson published *Letters of the Lewis and Clark Expedition* in 1962, however, attention steadily increased, reaching its apogee with the bicentennial. The efflorescence in attention and scholarship devoted to Lewis and Clark—now some forty years long—is unprecedented.[5]

Two historiographical axioms explain why Lewis and Clark faded from memory during the nineteenth century. First, the delay in the publication of the "official" Biddle/Allen account doomed their deserved fame. The American attention span waned after only a few years, and by the time the Biddle narrative did appear, few Americans were interested in its story or its contents. Second, Lewis's death in 1809, coupled with Benjamin Smith Barton's failure to complete the natural historical material as promised and his death in 1815, compromised the genuine effort to include the "scientific" information in the narrative. The result of these missed opportunities was an expedition "stripped of its intellectual content" and "increasingly viewed by Americans as a great national adventure."[6] In short, Lewis and Clark faded into obscurity because nineteenth-century Americans did not appreciate what the expedition accomplished.

These interpretations—while plausible and not without some explanatory power—are then marshaled to defend Jefferson from latter-day criticisms for not having sent a "trained naturalist" on the expedition. To counter these attacks, early republic naturalists are depicted as having little or no university training, their "enthusiastic preoccupation" with animals described as "purely avocational." Lewis's crash course in medicine, geography, botany, zoology, ethnology, and natural history acquired in Philadelphia and under the tutelage of Benjamin Rush, Robert Patterson, Caspar Wistar, Benjamin Smith Barton, and Andrew Ellicott purportedly gave him an equal standing with this cluster of naturalists, his only disadvantage being their "added years of field experience and a greater command of Linnaean nomenclature." To wit, Lewis is depicted as self-deprecating, unaware of his own abilities—capabilities, we learn, "often missing in naturalists, particularly an outstanding, inherent observational competence, an all-inclusive interest, and an objective, systematic, philosophical approach to understanding the natural world." In the context of early republic America, Meriwether Lewis was an "unusually capable naturalist, one with attitudes more consistent with scientists of the twentieth century than with those of his own."[7]

These arguments are counterfactual and, more specifically, they expect nineteenth-century Americans to appreciate something that they did not. And the arguments are anachronistic: they expect nineteenth-century Americans to understand Lewis and Clark as we do—as scientific pioneers. Historians and appreciators conclude that the reason nineteenth-century Americans did not appreciate Lewis and Clark as they should have is that Americans of the era did not understand what Lewis and Clark accomplished. But, a stronger way to understand Lewis and Clark, and nineteenth-century America, would embrace these realities and not explain them away. Thus, Lewis and Clark—in particular, their natural history contributions—were forgotten because their natural history contributions were not particularly notable for the period and their writings were little different for dozens, perhaps hundreds of works, just like them. This is not to suggest, as some scholars have, that early republic natural history was insignificant or unimportant. Quite the opposite is true. Rather, we need to understand natural history in its early republic context to understand why Lewis and Clark were overlooked. In short, we need to understand how and why natural history itself was important in order to understand why Lewis and Clark were relatively unimportant.

Contrary to received opinion, natural history was alive and well in early republic America, especially in Philadelphia. In 1806, the year of Lewis and Clark's return, the new nation boasted societies dedicated to studying the natural world in Philadelphia, New York, New Haven, Albany, Princeton, Boston, and Charleston; four significant scientific journals were in publication; botanical gardens had been established in Cambridge, New York, and Charleston; mineralogical cabinets had been established in Cambridge, New Haven, and New York; and Philadelphia had Charles Willson Peale's famous museum, replete with the famous mastodon skeleton unearthed near Newburgh, New York. Interest in the natural world was widespread but particularly vibrant in Philadelphia. It is not surprising that Thomas Jefferson sent Lewis to study science there; Philadelphia was the early republic's scientific capital. Early republic newspapers and magazines regularly devoted their pages to natural history topics, and the archives of the American Philosophical Society are filled with letters of interest from ordinary farmers and mechanics asking questions about animals, plants, and natural phenomena. In short, Lewis and Clark were not exceptional figures—the most scientific of their age, possessed of superior powers of observation. Rather, they were part and parcel of culture genuinely interested in the natural world, a society determined to know about the peoples, plants, and animals of the new nation. A nuanced appreciation of the early American republic and its scientific interests should provide new insights into the importance and meaning of Lewis and Clark's journey and the expedition's place in nineteenth-century American culture.

But early national natural history is little regarded today for a number of reasons. First, early republic America natural history is compared to European science of the same period to gauge its progress, its successes, and its shortcomings. This comparative approach generally shows American natural history to be derivative or playing catch-up to the advances taking place in Europe. The result of the comparative approach and the way in which institutions and individuals are studied leads to a conclusion that early national America was largely uninterested in the natural world with a few outposts of light scattered across the continent.

Second is the negative impression derived from the emotional and devotional quality to much of the scientific writing of the period, and with that emotionalism is a seeming resistance to sober, secular empiricism on the part of nineteenth-century actors. As twenty-first-century Americans, we have an expectation that science equals precise measurements and the search for universal, natural laws. In short, we want science of the past to be like science of the present. Therefore, in tracing the rise of science in nineteenth-century America, we expect to see a rise in empirical research and empirical precision. Instead, when we read early nineteenth-century scientific texts, we confront descriptions of animals and plants followed immediately by devotional passages and how the reader can use science to understand God. Also, instead of the slow death of fantastic claims about the natural world in the face of empiricism—for example, snakes that charm their prey or rumors of sea serpents—readers encounter a persistence and sometimes even efflorescence of these stories. We expect to see early republic Americans becoming increasingly sober and empirical, but instead we find the opposite—people becoming more enamored with wonders and more interested in awe, all the while using the language and rhetoric of science.

This should tell us something important, even fundamental, about natural history in early republic America: that its purpose was not to put an end to mysteries and wonders but to enhance an appreciation for them. Natural history enthusiasts of early republic America, in fact, saw increased empirical precision and increased knowledge about natural matters increasing an individual's sense of awe and wonder at the mysteries of life and the universe. In early republic America, empirical precision, better observations and descriptions of the natural world, and more exacting measurements worked hand in hand, not at odds, with a sense of wonder; each new discovery, each new piece of evidence that the natural world and the universe was complex did not communicate a sense that humans were closer to the truth or the settling of the ultimate questions. Rather, these questioned were not settled at all. As historians, we expect empirical observation to settle mysterious questions, to resolve issues of dispute. However, there was no sense that resolution was what readers of early national natural history believed that empirical observation was designed to do.

These findings can also help us to understand why Lewis and Clark were forgotten in nineteenth-century America. If wonder and awe were what natural history exploration literature aimed at, it is little wonder that Lewis and Clark did not endure. Their narrative did not emphasize the devotional characteristics that made natural history literature popular and accessible. With this more nuanced appreciation of the early American republic and its scientific interests, we can better gauge the importance and meaning of Lewis and Clark's journey and the expedition's place in nineteenth-century American culture.

Thomas Jefferson's instructions to Meriwether Lewis are used often as the yardstick to measure the expedition's successes and failures. While Lewis did not find a "direct & practicable water communication across the continent for the purposes of commerce" (a failure), he and Clark fulfilled Jefferson's requests to gather natural historical information about Louisiana's climate, soils, inhabitants, flora, and fauna (a success).[8] Historians highlighting Jefferson's commitment to the expedition and his status as the enterprise's intellectual giant have noted how the instructions to Lewis are similar in content and form to those of André Michaux's aborted 1793 expedition. But a reluctance to examine Michaux's and Lewis's instructions in historical context gives them an exceptional quality that they do not deserve. Jefferson's instructions to Lewis are typical for the period and derivative of the queries sent him by François Marbois, secretary of the French legation at Philadelphia, in 1780; his responses to Marbois's statistical questions form his famous *Notes of the State of Virginia*.[9] These queries asked him to describe Virginia's boundaries, rivers, climate, population, animals, vegetables, and "aborigines"; Jefferson offered detailed answers in twenty-three responses, ranging in length from about fifty words when describing Virginia's sea-ports to several thousand when cataloging its flora and fauna.[10] Thomas Jefferson's instructions to Lewis were more tightly focused on the natural historical contents of Louisiana than the more rangy diplomatic directives that characterize Marbois's queries of Jefferson. Still, Jefferson's appropriation of this bureaucratic apparatus to inquire about natural history suggests that Jefferson did not break with literary protocol and saw his aims in Louisiana as scientific and diplomatic.

American natural historians of the late eighteenth and early nineteenth centuries asked questions, similar to Marbois's, of far-flung domestic and international correspondents to gather information about the contents and character of the new nation. Correspondence networks of American gentlemen with interest in natural historical matters were the easiest, cheapest, and most convenient method to acquire new knowledge—books were prohibitively expensive, and face-to-face contact was often impossible. More often than not, these questions asked statistical information about the region and requested descriptions of geographic and geologic features, numbers and varieties of region's flora and fauna, and the population and character of the inhabitants, Native or newcomer. Natural historical epistolary exchange formed the backbone of early republic science and the primary method of natural knowledge acquisition in the Western world, the practice pursued in the American Philosophical Society in Philadelphia and the more esteemed Royal Society of London and Académie Royale des Sciences in Paris. The exchanges provided the questioner with information about regions unfamiliar and bound together learned gentlemen interested in the natural world. These letters were published from time to time in American as well as foreign scientific publications. The narratives and information they contained were instantly recognizable to readers as "scientific" and worthy of careful scrutiny.[11]

The natural historical books and pamphlets that resulted from these exchanges—of which there were many—possess distinctly early republic characteristics.[12] They are, like Jefferson's *Notes of the State of Virginia*, principally natural histories of a place—as small as a city or as large as a state. Benjamin Smith Barton's *Fragments of the Natural History of Pennsylvania* is a catalog of the natural history of Philadelphia and the surrounding environs. Jeremy Belknap's *The History of New-Hampshire*, Samuel Williams's *The Natural and Civil History of Vermont*, and John Filson's *The Discovery, Settlement and Present State of Kentucke* describe the natural historical contents of their respective states. What unifies these works is their content and form, all strikingly similar to Jefferson's *Notes*. Each begins with a discussion of the area's boundaries, describes various geographic and geologic features, and then offers a census of the area's flora and fauna, including a description of Indians if available. Like Jefferson, who used the testimony of neighbors to corroborate findings, the authors of these accounts and the genre in general cement their authenticity by gathering the testimony of many individuals, not just one gentleman. The facts in these accounts are established through authorial eyewitness testimony and through a multiplicity of secondhand accounts.

Jefferson's instructions to Lewis guided him to gather information for what would have been an initial natural history of Louisiana, the first of many such accounts Jefferson likely imagined. Lewis's observations were to have been preliminary impressions forming catalogs of natural history that the expedition witnessed: animals, plants, and Indians. He asked Lewis to record the fluctuations in climate "as characterized by the thermometer"; to account for "the animals of the county generally"; to describe "the face of the country, it's growth & vegetable productions"; and to acquire a population count and description of the territories' Indians. Jefferson's requests asked Lewis to acquire a working knowledge of the region's flora and fauna but not a detailed understanding of individual animals and how they existed in their environment. That is what Lewis and Clark provided: impressions, short discussions, and a few samples. Even the expedition's extended botanical or zoological discussion, not published until the Coues edition in 1893, are woefully short and superficial in comparison to detailed descriptions of individual animals available in scientific books, journals, or public lectures of the period. The expedition's description of the prairie dog (*Cynomys ludovicianus*) is an archetypal example. In the Coues edition, Lewis describes the prairie dog and some of its habits and attempts to flood it out for capture. This episode is recounted in less than 250 words.[13] Extended zoological discussion in other works of the same period are lengthier and more detailed. Typical is Samuel Williams's six-page dissertation on the beaver—its behavior, its food, and its reproductive and domestic habits in Vermont. More illustrative is Thomas Pennant's two-volume *Arctic Zoology*, a Scottish zoologist whose 1784 natural history described some of the animals Lewis and Clark encountered. Most importantly, consider Alexander Wilson's magisterial nine-volume *American Ornithology; or The Natural History of Birds in the United States*.[14] Wilson's remarkable ornithology, replete with full-color plates of observed birds and extended descriptions of avian behavior, was the standard against which early republic Americans judged other works. Had Lewis and Clark published their natural history volume, it would have fallen short of Wilson's work.

This exercise in contextualization is not intended to discredit the natural historical observations of Lewis and Clark; rather, it is to suggest that their account likely would have been considered—even with the natural history material included—along a continuum, with travel writing containing natural history material at one end and systematic, taxonomically driven scientific texts at the other. Early national travel narratives lacked formal systematic analysis but provided valuable information about regions unknown to the more settled East, especially natural historical material, but they were viewed with cautious skepticism by readers. Still, for the project of writing a catalog of the new nation's nature, travel accounts by gentlemen proved invaluable.[15] Thaddeus Mason Harris's 1804 journal of his travels through the Ohio Valley was frequently consulted by naturalists looking for information about plants, animals, and Native Americans. Harris—a congregational minister, librarian at Harvard College, naturalist, and antiquarian—traveled west to recover his failing health. Harris, like Lewis and Clark, thrice daily recorded the temperature with a thermometer and described the weather conditions. He detailed the natural and civil boundaries of the region; the country and soil; vegetable, animal, and mineralogical productions; the rivers and fish; towns; navigation; exports; antiquities; curiosities; government; and history of Indian wars. Harris's was one of many early national travel accounts of the Ohio Valley and was joined by those Zadoc Cramer and French traveler Constantin François Chasseboeuf, Count de Volney. News of Louisiana supplemented Ohio travel accounts when Zebulon Pike returned from his travels and published a report in 1810 and Henry Marie Brackenridge issued a memoir of his travels up the Missouri River in 1811.[16] Travel narratives of the period followed a particular form and combined personal reflections and subjective impressions along with purportedly objective observations of civil and natural history.

Early republic readers of travel narratives—including federal government-sponsored expeditions—scrutinized texts closely for natural historical information, checking them against one another to determine the relative truth of the information. Where different texts agreed, in the case of population density or a description of a cataract, for example, the information was regarded by naturalists as true fact. The imprimatur of truth or of settled scientific fact was withheld, however, when discrepancies between texts occurred or when authors announced the discovery of previously unknown plants and animals. Natural history of the period was not determined through replicable experiment, an epistemology with which we moderns are familiar. Instead, early republic natural history was an observational practice in which truth and fact were determined through the senses—sight the most important—and by community agreement. Consequently, the highest regard a natural historical phenomena could be accorded— the closest to a settled fact—was based on multiple eyewitnesses, not a single individual testifying to the truth of an animal or a plant. If an individual testified to having witnessed an animal, plant, or phenomena that was new or seemingly beyond the realm of the possible, the testimony was either discredited by readers for prejudicial reasons or it was regarded as provisionally true and possible, awaiting further corroborating testimony. An early republic naturalists did not, and could not, expect to be believed based on his authority alone or on his standing within the community; he needed the testimony of others to agree with him.[17]

There were gradations of authority within the naturalist community, of course. The word of Benjamin Smith Barton or Samuel L. Mitchill, the New York physician naturalist, carried greater weight than did the testimony of a western Pennsylvania farmer. But contemporary evidence suggests that early republic naturalists policed the boundaries of their community vigorously. And it appears that some naturalists were suspicious of Lewis and Clark's status as scientists, at least one questioning outright their qualifications. William Paul Crillon Barton, nephew of Benjamin Smith Barton, cast doubt on the scientific accomplishments of their travels. "The travels of Lewis and Clarke," he wrote in his 1817 *Vegetable Materia Medica of the United States,* "have put us in possession of the Indian names of many native dietetic articles, and these names have occasionally been accompanied by imperfect description." But not much more "than conjectures," he continued, could be expected "to arise from such informal and unscientific account; and indeed, little else has resulted, on this subject, from the rich opportunities of that governmental expedition." Barton may be more condemnatory of Lewis than many of his contemporaries, but he is representative of at least a segment of the period's naturalists who harbored a belief that the expedition was an opportunity lost. Among some early republic naturalists, it appears, Lewis and Clark were considered amateurs. "It is well known, that no botanist or naturalist accompanied those travellers," Barton reminded, and while it was neither his "intention, nor my province, in this place, to make any animadversion on the direction of that undertaking . . . we are warranted in the belief, that a very splendid harvest might have been reaped, had any competent botanist accompanied the party."[18] As Barton summed up for the reader: "The travels of Lewis and Clarke led to high expectations in every branch of science. . . . Unfortunately however for science, this information is not communicated in such a way, as to enable the botanist, the physician, or the agricuturalist, to draw very efficiently upon the extensive sources of knowledge they present."[19]

Lewis and Clark made it to the Pacific and back, along the way cataloging new plants and animals that would be corroborated and clarified by others in time. But William Barton (and others, one suspects) thought that the information was incomplete and superficial and amounted to little more than a list of new plants and new animals, little different from other travel narratives of the period. Early republic naturalists had an abiding interest in "useful knowledge." They believed that natural history properly oriented toward utility would lead to an improved and efficient agriculture, generate new technologies of manufacture, and assist the expansion of commerce. Charles Willson Peale, in a lecture at the University of Pennsylvania, called natural history "the science comprehending all nature," and in sketching the history of humankind he argued that observation of the natural world was the key to "the progress of society from a rude to a civilized state." Peale considered the study of natural history an individual and national interest: "it ought to become a NATIONAL CONCERN, since it is a NATIONAL GOOD." Nationalizing the practice and methods of natural history, Peale promised that agriculturists, theologians, merchants, and mechanics would benefit from the pursuit, each profession learning something new about materials and the material world.[20] But what information Lewis and Clark did supply (or would have supplied had the scientific narrative been published) was not the useful knowledge that naturalists and the wider reading public demanded.

Lewis and Clark did not discover an abundance of new plants for cultivation, new animals that could be husbanded, or new mines to be exploited. Without a strong "useful knowledge" component, their discoveries were regarded as little more than lists. Had their natural history finds been published in a separate volume, it is unlikely that it would have made an extraordinary impression among naturalists; rather, it would have joined a growing number of reports about Louisiana and probably would have been considered a narrative to be consulted when determining a territory's natural character. The narrative would have been welcomed, but early republic natural history got along without it just fine.

The years following the Lewis and Clark expedition witnessed other expeditions to Louisiana and beyond, these more generously financed and accompanied by better equipped and more extensively trained naturalists. Upon their return, the expeditions completed detailed natural history accounts that were consulted by naturalists interested in the region. These new narratives and continued exploration caused Lewis and Clark to fade from memory, little regarded as anything other than old news. The American reading public of the nineteenth century also contributed to the marginalization of Lewis and Clark. Their demand for natural histories—of particular animals, plants, states, or regions—was insatiable but much different than what Lewis and Clark offered the reader. American readers became increasingly interested in the specialized disciplines formerly covered by the rubric of natural history. Readers could easily obtain books exclusively devoted to zoology, botany, Indians, geology, and especially antiquities. The rapid expansion of books as well as newspaper and magazine articles devoted to natural history in all its forms rarely mentioned Lewis and Clark.

The explorers and their work languished until the late nineteenth century when historical trends and new geopolitical roles for the United States offered different perspectives on Lewis and Clark. Elliot Coues published the first new edition of the journals since Allen/Biddle in 1893, the same year that Frederick Jackson Turner argued famously that the frontier had closed and "with its going has closed the first period of American history."[21] While Coues finished his new edition in Washington, D.C., an increasingly vocal chorus could be heard on Capitol Hill calling for the beginning of an American empire, which began in fact only five years later. There can be little doubt that Coues saw Lewis and Clark as part of the larger processes of scientific advancement and American progress; his call to "honor" Jefferson, Lewis, and Clark and by extension "your own course of empire" fused historical study and patriotism. But for Coues, honoring Lewis and Clark involved not just a new edition of their journals but a corrected one. Coues worked to give credit to Lewis and Clark for describing species then unknown to naturalists. In so doing, Coues's edition, and the historiography and commentary that followed, became exercises that emphasized firsts: Lewis and Clark as the first Americans to ascend the Missouri, first to see a prairie dog and a cutthroat trout, first Americans to see the Pacific and to return safely. Honorary projects such as Coues's often fail to consider historical nuance. Hopefully, with the bicentennial celebrations we can do better.

Notes

1. Elliot Coues, *History of the Expedition under the command of Lewis and Clark* (New York: Dover Publications, Inc.), iii. The epigraph at the start of the chapter is also contained here.

2. George W. Bush, Remarks by the President at the Bicentennial of Lewis and Clark's "Voyage of Discovery," July 3, 2002.

3. Walter Kirn, "The Journey That Changed America," *Time,* June 30, 2002, www.time.com/time/2002/lewis_clark/lessay.html.

4. A search of the American Periodical Series—the most comprehensive database of nineteenth-century periodicals—reveals that after the 1810s, Lewis and Clark nearly disappeared in print culture, save for the occasional credit given them as the first Americans to report an Indian tribe or geographical feature. Exceptions to this generalization can be found, of course, but on the whole Lewis and Clark faded from public consciousness. For an example, see Annonymous, "Manners and Customs of Several Indian Tribes," *The North American Review* 22 (January 1826): 53–120. James P. Ronda comes to the same conclusion in "'A Darling Project of Mine': The Appeal of the Lewis and Clark Story," in *Voyages of Discovery,* ed. James P. Ronda, 327–28 (Helena: Montana Historical Society Press, 1998).

5. On this historiographical trajectory see Gary E. Moulton, "On Reading Lewis and Clark: The Last Twenty Years," 281–98, and James P. Ronda, "'The Writingest Explorers': The Lewis and Clark Expedition in American Historical Literature," 299–326, both in *Voyages of Discovery.*

6. Ronda, "'The Writingest Explorers,'" 304.

7. Paul Russell Cutright, *Lewis and Clark: Pioneering Naturalists* (Urbana: University of Illinois Press, 1969), 379–80.

8. Thomas Jefferson, "Instructions to Meriwether Lewis, June 20, 1803," ed. Donald Jackson, *Letters of the Lewis and Clark Expedition with Related Documents, 1783–1854,* 2d ed., vol. 1 (Urbana: University of Illinois Press, 1962), 66–67.

9. Paul Cutright, *Lewis and Clark,* 1–29, explores the similarities between *Notes on the State of Virginia* and the instructions to Lewis.

10. Thomas Jefferson, *Notes on the State of Virginia,* ed. William Peden (Chapel Hill: University of North Carolina Press, 1953).

11. A catalog of all extant questions would be impossible. However, the Benjamin Smith Barton Papers housed at the American Philosophical Society contain numerous examples. See, for example, B. S. Barton to John Heckewelder, August 13, 1808, APS, Barton Papers, Correspondence; or Thomas Gray to Henry M. Gray, April 2, 1805, APS, Barton Papers, Correspondence.

12. Jeremy Belknap, *The History of New-Hampshire Comprehending the Events of One Complete Century from the Discovery of the River Pascataqua* (Boston, 1799), and Samuel Williams, *The Natural and Civil History of Vermont* (Walpole, 1799).

13. Coues, *History of the Expedition,* I:111.

14. Thomas Pennant, *Arctic Zoology,* 2 vols. (London, 1784); Alexander Wilson, *American Ornithology; or, the Natural History of the Birds of the United States,* 9 vols. (Philadelphia, 1808).

15. Thaddues Mason Harris, *The Journal of a Tour into the Territory Northwest of the Alleghany Mountains; Made in the Spring of the Year 1803, with a Geographical and Historical Account of the State of Ohio. Illustrated with Original Maps and Views* (Boston, 1805); Henry Marie Brackenridge, *Views of Louisiana; Together with a Journal of a Voyage up the Missouri River, in 1811,* (Pittsburgh, 1814); Constantin François Chasseboeuf, Count de Volnay, *A View of the Soil and Climate of the United States of America,* trans. Charles Brockden Brown (Philadelphia, 1804).

16. Zebulon Pike, *An Account of Expeditions to the Sources of the Mississippi,* 3 vols. (Philadelphia, 1810); Brackenridge, *Views of Louisiana.*

17. For an elaborated discussion of truth claims in early national America, see Andrew J. Lewis, *The Curious and the Learned: Natural History in the Early American Republic* (PhD diss., Yale University, 2001).

18. William Paul Crillon Barton, *Vegetable Materia Medica of the United States; or Medical Botany: Containing a Botanical, General, and Medical History, of Medicinal Plants Indigenous to the United States*, 2 vols. (Philadelphia, 1817), 2:xiii–x.

19. Ibid., 1:xi–xii.

20. Charles Willson Peale, *Introduction to a Course of Lectures on Natural History, Delivered in the University of Pennsylvania, Nov. 16, 1799* (Philadelphia: Zachariah Poulson, Junior, 1800), 10–12.

21. John Mack Faragher, ed., *Rereading Frederick Jackson Turner: The Significance of the Frontier in American History, and Other Essays* (New York: Henry Holt, 1994), 60.

Contributors

Robert S. Cox currently is Head of Special Collections at the W. E. B. DuBois Library, University of Massachusetts Amherst. His book, *Body and Soul: A Sympathetic History of American Spiritualism*, appeared with the University of Virginia Press in 2003.

John W. Jengo has advanced degrees in geology and paleontology, is a licensed Professional Geologist in several states, and currently works as a Principal Hydrogeologist in an environmental consulting firm cleaning up polluted sites in the Philadelphia–Delaware Valley region. He has written many peer-reviewed technical articles for scientific journals about his geological and environmental investigation work. Mr. Jengo is now focusing on writing about the geological accomplishments, mineralogical collection, and scientific context of the Lewis and Clark Expedition and has had several articles on these topics published in the Lewis and Clark Trail Heritage Foundation's quarterly journal, *We Proceeded On*.

S. D. Kimmel is currently a Research Associate of the History of Medicine at the University of Michigan. He has a dual MA in history and philanthropic studies from Indiana University and a PhD in Program in American Culture from the University of Michigan. His doctoral dissertation is titled "Freedom's Panopticon: The Rise of the Liberal Police State Out of the Theater of Civil Society in Nineteenth-Century Pennsylvania." His article "Sentimental Police: Struggles for 'Sound Policy and Economy' amidst the Torpor of Philanthropy in Mathew Carey's Philadelphia" is being published in *Early American Studies* (Spring 2005).

Andrew J. Lewis is Assistant Professor of History at American University in Washington, D.C., where he is completing a book on natural history in early republic America. His article "Swallow Submersion and Natural History in the Early Republic" will be published in the *William and Mary Quarterly* (October 2005).

Brett Mizelle is Assistant Professor of History and director of the American Studies Program at California State University Long Beach. He currently is completing a book on the cultural work of exhibitions of exotic and performing animals in early national and antebellum America.

Domenic Vitiello is an urban planner and historian with broad interests in institutions' roles in shaping cities and regions. In addition to his consulting practice, he teaches urban studies at the University of Pennsylvania. His book *Philadelphia Capital: America's First Stock Exchange and the City It Made* is forthcoming from Penn Press.

INDEX

Academy of Natural Sciences of Philadelphia, 30, 38
Agriculture, 23, 34, 61, 65, 70–78, 105–106
American Gardener's Calendar, 60, 114–118, 127, 133
American Philosophical Society, 6, 13, 16–19, 23–26, 30, 38–39, 41, 59–60, 103–104, 110, 140–141, 248
Apprentice's Library of Philadelphia, 39
Astor, John Jacob, 29

Bache, Benjamin Franklin, 74, 111
Baillet, François, 26
Balmis, Francisco Xavier, 7, 58, 94
Barton, Benjamin Smith, 6, 24–26, 59–60, 77, 107–108, 113, 120–124, 126, 185–189, 197, 200, 202, 213, 238, 243, 246
Barton, William Paul Crillon, 111, 246
Bartram, William, 104, 110, 231
Bentley, William, 226
Biddle, Nicholas, 31–32, 40–41, 43, 60, 78, 89–90, 238
Biddle, Owen, 18–19
Birch, William, 17, 27
Bison, 226–227
Blackstone, William, 56
Bordley, John, 65–66, 70–72, 73, 96

Canals, 19, 21–22, 31–32
Carey, Mathew, 31–32, 41, 43, 78–86, 88, 90
Clark, George Rogers, 5, 24, 137
Clark, William, 31, 125, 144–147, 154, 166, 189
Clark's nutcracker (*Nucifraga columbiana*), 30

Coal, 155–158
Collins, Zaccheus, 125–126
Cook, James, 7
Corps of Discovery, passim
  Botany, 8–9, 106–129
  Geology, 137–203
  Natural history, 9, 219–232, 236–248
  Reception, 236–248
  Supplies, 26–28, 142–143
Coues, Elliot, 236–238, 248
Coxe, Tench, 21
Cronon, William, 12–13

Dallas, Alexander, 74–75
Darlington, William, 109, 111
Dean, Samuel, 226–227
Denckla, Christian, 26
Dickerson, Mahlon, 86–87, 90
Duane, William, 75–77, 87, 110–111, 114–115
Dunbar, William, 6

Ebeling, Christoph Daniel, 140
Ellicott, Andrew, 25–26, 28, 189–190, 200
Elliott, Stephen, 124
Empire, 52–54, 60–64, 102–106
Evans, Oliver, 29–30, 35
Exhibitions, see Museums

Federalist Party, 72–75
Franklin Institute, 40–43
Franklin, Benjamin, 16, 21
Frazer, Robert, 80, 84

Gallatin, Albert, 28–29
Gass, Patrick, 8, 31, 54–55, 78–87, 88, 90, 99–101, 199

Geology, see Mineralogy and Geology
Gillaspy & Strong, 26
Green, Jacob, 126
Grizzly bear (*Ursus horribilis*), 224–226

Hamilton, Alexander, 73–74
Hamilton, William, 8, 31, 60, 107–109, 119–120, 126–127
"Happy family" exhibitions, 230–232
Harbenson, Benjamin, 27
Harris, Thaddeus Mason, 244–245
Harvey & Worth, 26
Hosack, David, 124–125
Hutton, James, 196–197, 212

Improvement societies, 16–18, 21, 38–39, 54–78
Indians, 105–106, 182–183, 220, 232
Internal improvement, 19, 21–22, 32–33, 57
Irish—Philadelphia, 109–110, 114–119

Jackson, David, 26
Jefferson, Thomas, 5–6, 13–14, 24, 26, 30, 59–64, 74, 79–80, 87–88, 95, 102–106, 114, 117, 119, 124, 137–142, 191–192, 196, 200, 215–216, 220–224, 240, 242–244
Notes on the State of Virginia, 5, 183–185, 242–243

Keating, William H., 40–41
Kirwan, Richard, 190–196, 212

Lancaster County Society for the Promotion of Agriculture, 74–75
Latrobe, Benjamin Henry, 23
Leiper, Thomas, 27, 41
Lewis, Meriwether, 5, 13–14, 24–28, 30–31, 59–60, 76, 78–88, 91–92, 105, 107–109, 119–123, 142–183, 192–194, 196–197, 200, 220, 239–240, 242–243
Lewis' woodpecker (*Melanerpes lewisii*), 30
Library Company of Philadelphia, 17, 38–39, 90, 101

Limestone, 151–154
Logan, George, 63–64, 71–78, 92, 97
Ludlam, George, 26
Lukens, Isaiah, 27, 38, 41
Lukens, John, 18–20

Mackenzie, Alexander, 6, 84
Magpie, 222–223
Marbois, François Barbé, 5, 242
Marshall, Humphry, 6, 103–104
Martin, Robert, 27
Massachusetts State Agricultural Society, 70–71
Mastodon, 224
McKean, Thomas, 76–77, 87
McKeehan, David, 78–86, 89–90, 99–101
McMahon, Ann, 111, 128
McMahon, Bernard, 8–9, 60, 95, 109–129
McMahon, Thomas P., 110, 127–128, 131
Mease, James, 33–35, 38, 63
Michaux, André, 5–6, 24, 59, 104, 114, 139–140, 242
Michaux, François André, 114
Mineralogy and Geology, 137–203
  Economic geology, 150–165
  Ethnogeology, 182–183
  Geomorphology, 166–172
  Glaciology, 168–170
  Hydrology, 165–166, 170–182
  Lithology, 148–165
  Sedimentology, 170–174
  Stratigraphy, 145–148
Mogeme, Henri, 37–38
Morris, Robert, 21–22, 28–29, 72
Mountain lions, 229
Muhlenberg, Henry, 74, 124–126, 128–129
Museums, 215–232

Nationalism and nation, 219–232
Natural history, 219–232, 236–248
Nuttall, Thomas, 111, 128

Ordway, John, 80, 84
Orukter amphibolos, 29–30
Osage orange (*Maclura pomifera*), 107

Index

Paleontology, 189
Parker, Thomas, 26
Patterson, Robert, 24–25, 29, 38, 41
Peale, Charles Willson, 9, 24, 30, 37, 60, 219–226, 231–232, 240, 247
Peale, Titian Ramsey, 221–222, 225
Peale's Philadelphia Museum, 24, 26, 30, 38, 219–226, 231–232, 240
Pennant, Thomas, 244
Pennsylvania Society for Encouragement of Manufactures and the Useful Arts, 22
Pennsylvania Society for the Improvement of Roads and Inland Navigation, 22
Perkins, Jacob, 35, 36, 40
Peters, Richard, 65–66, 69–71, 76–77, 98
Philadelphia (Pa.), 13–45
    Commerce, 14–16, 21, 32–34
    Education, 39–40
    Manufactures, 33–35
    Politics, 70–78, 90–92, 109–115
Philadelphia County Society for Promoting Agriculture, 73
Philadelphia Society for Promoting Agriculture, 8, 22, 33, 54, 57–78, 91, 113
Philadelphia Waterworks, 23
Philanthropy, 54–70
Pickering, Timothy, 65, 70–71
Pictet, Marc Auguste, 140
Police, 56, 65
Political economy, 53–58, 60–64, 73–74, 79–80, 85, 89–94, 96
Prairie dog (*Cynomys ludovicianus*), 222–223, 244
Pursh, Frederick, 60, 107, 121–127, 133

Republicanism, 8, 60–77, 89–92
Republicans, Constitutional ("Quids"), 76, 87, 90–91, 110

Republicans, radical, 75–76, 85–86, 90–91, 109–110, 114–119
Rittenhouse, David, 18–19, 21–22, 74
Rush, Benjamin, 24–26, 28, 59, 66

Salt, 158–160
Schuylkill Bridge, 66–68
Scull, William, 20
Sellers, George Escol, 35–38
Sellers, John, 18–22, 66
Sellers, John, Jr., 23
Sellers, Nathan, 21, 23, 32. 35–38
Sesse y Lacasta, Martin, 7
Seybert, Adam, 188–189
Shoemaker, Edward, 27
Smith, Adam, 56–57, 94
Snakes, 227–229
Steam power, 23, 29–30

Thompson, Charles, 138–139, 204
Thwaites, Ruben Gold, 238
Transportation, 19, 21–22, 29–37
Travel narratives, 244–248
Turner, Frederick Jackson, 12–13

University of Pennsylvania, 17–18, 23, 25, 39
Upsal (Estate), 112–113, 128, 132

Vaughan, John, 114

Whelen, Israel, 26–28, 32
Whitehurst, John, 138–139
Whitney, Thomas, 26
Williams, Samuel, 243–244
Williamson, Samuel, 26
Wilson, Alexander, 30–31, 124, 244
Wistar, Caspar, 24–25, 59, 189, 200
Wister, John and Charles, 27
Woodhouse, James, 188–189
Woodlands (Estate), 31, 60, 107–108, 126

www.ingramcontent.com/pod-product-compliance
Lightning Source LLC
Chambersburg PA
CBHW081113160426
42814CB00035B/302